# Imaginary Homelands of Writers in Exile

# IMAGINARY HOMELANDS OF WRITERS IN EXILE

## Salman Rushdie, Bharati Mukherjee, and V. S. Naipaul

*Cristina Emanuela Dascălu*

CAMBRIA PRESS

YOUNGSTOWN, NEW YORK

Copyright 2007 Cristina Emanuela Dascălu

All rights reserved
Printed in the United States of America

No part of this publication may be reproduced, stored in or introduced into a retrieval system, or transmitted, in any form, or by any means (electronic, mechanical, photocopying, recording, or otherwise), without the prior permission of the publisher. Requests for permission should be directed to permissions@cambriapress.com, or mailed to Permissions, Cambria Press, PO Box 350, Youngstown, New York 14174-0350.

Library of Congress Cataloging-in-Publication Data

Dascălu, Cristina Emanuela.
 Imaginary homelands of writers in exile : Salman Rushdie, Bharati Mukherjee, and V. S. Naipaul / Cristina Emanuela Dascălu
  p. cm.
 Includes bibliographical references (p.   ) and index.
 ISBN 978-1-934043-73-8 (alk. paper)
 1. Commonwealth fiction (English)—History and criticism. 2. Exiles in literature. 3. Exiles' writings—History and criticism. 4. Rushdie, Salman—Criticism and interpretation. 5. Mukherjee, Bharati—Criticism and interpretation. 6. Naipaul, V. S. (Vidiadhar Surajprasad), 1932—Criticism and interpretation. 7. Expatriation in literature. 8. Exile (Punishment) in literature. 9. Emigration and immigration in literature. I. Title.

PR9084.D37 2007
820.9'9206914—dc22

2007020764

*In Loving Memory of My Father,
Alecu Alexandru Dascălu,
and
in Remembrance of My Grandparents
Natalia and Petrea Mihăilă
and Profira and Neculai Dascălu*

# Table of Contents

| | |
|---|---|
| **Foreword** | ix |
| **Acknowledgments** | xi |
| **Chapter 1: Introduction** | 1 |
| **Chapter 2: Salman Rushdie and the Revolutionary Play of Differences** | 37 |
| **Chapter 3: Bharati Mukherjee and the Exile's Constant Shuttling** | 65 |
| **Chapter 4: V. S. Naipaul and the Search for the Writer's Homeland** | 93 |
| **Chapter 5: Conclusion** Tracing the Politics of Exile in Salman Rushdie, Bharati Mukherjee, and V. S. Naipaul | 121 |
| **Bibliography** | 155 |
|     Primary Works | 155 |
|     Secondary Works | 156 |
|     Selected Works Consulted | 163 |
|     Selected Extensive Critical Bibliography | 166 |
| **Index** | 199 |

# Foreword

In her treatise, Cristina Dascălu writes that "the exile lives in a foreign country, a culture that is not his or her own, one that is alien, 'other.' The exile's existence, therefore, is underpinned constantly by a sense of his or her geographical displacement. To fit in with the dominant culture, the exile most often appropriates expectations that are alien; the exile assimilates the roles and expectations of 'the Other(s)' among whom they find themselves. In t[his] process, the exiled displace who they are."

Dascălu is not only a writer of distinction who demonstrates a clear, uncluttered style and a rare lucidity, but she has thoroughly and meticulously drawn on the work and theories of consummate minds in the field of literary theory, including Frantz Fanon, Homi Bhaba, and Jacques Derrida.

*Imaginary Homelands* explores, as the talented young poet-scholar Grant Matthew Jenkins notes, "the important theoretical and practical implications of exile across national, generic, and ethnic boundaries" and fills and fulfills a significant niche and need in post-colonial literary studies and narrative. Jenkins observes further that this significant study in contemporary post-colonial and decolonial displacement "is one of the most lucid and concise examinations of exile" yet to appear.

Exploring in her study the disparate works of Salman Rushdie, Bharati Mukherjee, and V. S. Naipaul—three writers whose works are nearly never presented or discussed in a contextualized and communitized context, Cristina Dascălu is able to fully, even wholly, explore the displacement and acculturative experience of exile, which thousands, if not millions, of fellow world citizens confront in our planetary community today. With considerable aplomb she, in the pages of *Imaginary Homelands*, explores and demonstrates the relevance of this experience and the full context of its implications.

This important work is sure to prove to be perhaps one of the most vital and energetic studies of its kind produced in the forepart of the 21st century and will without question contribute to numerous dissertations and be referenced in scholarly articles yet to be written. Her work, presented here, is sure to become a must-read for serious students as well as scholars of post-colonial literary and decolonialization theory for years to come.

Lyle W. Morgan II, PhD, FCollP<br>
Professor of English<br>
Director of English Education<br>
Pittsburg State University

# ACKNOWLEDGMENTS

My family has always been very important to me. For their love and support during the years, I first and foremost thank my parents, Maria Mariana Dascălu and Alecu Alexandru Dascălu, and my sister, Mariana Gabriela "Gabi" Dascălu.

I thank Cambria Press for discovering my work and contacting me with the offer to publish it. Special thanks go to Ms. Toni Tan, the director at Cambria Press, for her professionalism and very prompt help whenever needed.

I am grateful to my PhD dissertation chair, Dr. James G. Watson, Frances W. O'Hornett professor of literature, for his timely responses, faith in me, and very positive reception and promotion of my poetry and fiction and this book. I am especially appreciative of the feedback received from the anonymous outside readers for Cambria Press and from the many reviewers of the manuscript, writers, scholars, and university professors from all over the world who provided forewords and book cover comments: Prof. Dr. Rodica Albu; Farhad Mirwais Azizi; Prof. Dr. Odette Irenne Blumenfeld, head of the English Department; Prof. Dr. Codrin Liviu Cuțitaru, consul general of Romania at Vancouver, Canada; Dr. Justin Everett, assistant professor and director of the Writing Center; Paul Grabianowski; Prof. Dr. John Greene, chair of the Theatre Department; Dr. Grant M. Jenkins, assistant professor of English and director of the Writing Program; Dr. Lyle W. Morgan II, director of English education; V. Rev. Father Dumitru Păun; Dr. Aytül Özüm, assistant professor and specialist, postmodern English literature, cultural studies and literary theory; Av. Nelu Prodan, Esq., honorary consul general of Romania, USA; Dr. Fran Ringold, editor-in-chief of *Nimrod* and Poet Laureate of Oklahoma; Professor Natalija Sulciene; James Vroom, Humanities and Multicultural Studies Librarian, Carnegie Mellon University; Dr. Sufei Wei; and Prof. Dr. Yevgeny Yevtushenko, Poet Laureate of Russia.

I imagined that at the completion of this project, I would have a group of professors and administration and a group of friends to thank. I consider myself extremely fortunate that in many cases, I now find it difficult to form two separate lines. Special thanks to Mary P. Walker, associate dean, and Ms. Joyce Goodrum, administrative assistant at Tulsa Community College; Prof. Stephen E. Meats, chairperson of the English Department at Pittsburg State University and poetry editor for *The Midwest Quarterly*; Dr. Allen R. Soltow, vice president for research and Mr. Robert "Bob" Heath, assistant director and advisor of Association of International Students (AIS) at The University of Tulsa.

My gratitude also goes to professors, administration, colleagues, friends, and students at Al. I. Cuza University, University of Tulsa, Central European University, and Pittsburg State University and to my friends and family in the United States, Romania, and everywhere else in the world. You are too many to mention here, but you will always be in my heart.

# IMAGINARY HOMELANDS OF WRITERS IN EXILE

## Chapter 1

# Introduction

The effects of the displacement of peoples—their forced migration, their deportation, their voluntary emigration, their movement to new lands where they made themselves masters over others or became subjects of the masters of their new homes—reverberate down the years and are still felt today. The historical violence of the era of empire and colonies echoes in the literature of the descendants of those forcibly moved and the exiles that those processes have made. The voices of its victims are insistent in the literature that has come to be called "post-colonial." Although the term "post-colonial" is insufficient to capture fully the depth and breadth of those writers that have been labeled by it (for it is itself something of a colonial instrument, ghettoizing writers in English who are still considered to be "foreign"), there is a common bond among the works of those novelists who understand the process of exile and see themselves as exiles—both from their homes and from themselves.

Salman Rushdie, Bharati Mukherjee, and V. S. Naipaul can all, in different ways, be considered writers in exile. They have all traveled across the sea, all have come to a new, "foreign" land, and each one interacts with the English language as both "a home" for their words and an alien tongue. In addition, within these three writers' works, we can see the operations of exile, how the biographical and linguistic exile of these writers comes to be processed and represented, reflected and distorted, and the effect that the concept of exile (that resounds throughout their works) has on the literary and historical contexts that are their new "homes." These novelists treat exile not simply as a condition of the post-colonial world, but as a central means to understand the self. Rather than labeling them proponents of any post-colonial literature, therefore, we should perhaps call these three novelists the most important artists of a new genre: a literature of exile.

Salman Rushdie is an Anglo-Indian writing in English, often on the subject of the home he left when he was still a schoolboy. He was born in Bombay (which has since been renamed Mumbai) on June 19, 1947—the year of Indian independence and the year that acquires so much importance in his most critically acclaimed novel, *Midnight's Children* (1981). However, when still a child, he moved to England and was schooled at two of the pillars of the British establishment: Rugby and Cambridge. Consequently, his homeland was necessarily doubled between the Indian subcontinent (he was later also to live in Pakistan, with his family) and the British Isles, to where he returned a second time to work in an advertising agency before beginning his career as a novelist.

It is precisely this double identity that informs a great deal of Rushdie's literature—from his first novel, *Grimus* (1975), to his most recent novel, *Shalimar the Clown* (2005), and to his most recent nonfiction and travel writing works such as *Step Across the Line: Collected Nonfiction 1992–2002* (2002) and the article, "The East is Blue" (2004). He is able to write about both the culture of his parents and his newly adopted culture from the position of a partial outsider to both and is able to understand both sides of a sometimes (often violently) opposed set of cultural constructions. This is not to say that Rushdie's writing career has been one in which he feigns a transcendental stance, a distanced style, that sets him above both cultures, as an objective and unbiased third party. The case is quite the reverse. His writing is very much at ground level; it locates itself within the heady back and forth of cultural interchange. Like a geneticist, Rushdie splices and inextricably interweaves a double helix from the quite separate societies of which he has been a part. Salman Rushdie crosses English literary references with Quranic exegesis and mixes Indian folklore with modern American slang. The interweaving of mesmerizing performance has secured him a place, along with Gabríel García Márquez, as one of the foremost writers of magical realism. It is within the conjunction and disjunction of these different strands of cultural reference that the density and the richness of Rushdie's prose create the "imaginary home."

However, as the events that surrounded the publication of *The Satanic Verses* showed, the resonances of this cultural mix of Rushdie's novels (an admixture caused by Rushdie's role as the exile) were felt not only in literary circles. Shortly after its publication in 1998, *The Satanic Verses*, Rushdie's fourth novel—in which the figure of Mahound presented a thinly disguised representation of the prophet Mohammed—led to the fatwa issued by Ayatollah Ruhollah Khomeini. In the clash between East and West that was created by the controversy, one can see the importance of the form of writing that Rushdie, as exile, creates in his novel. For by interweaving both Western and Islamic cultures, Rushdie goes beyond the facile accusation that he is a traitor to his roots or has given in to the heathen land he now calls "home." Rather, he issues a challenge to both the fundamentalists of the Western ideal and of Islam to consider the possibility that history and truth are not the static edifices their dogmas would wish them to be. The magic of Rushdie's particular brand of magical realism is that it can force the single and unified worlds that are the sole objects of fundamental belief to face up to the changeability and shifting nature of the world.

Bharati Mukherjee is an American citizen (as she sees herself) of Indian heritage who writes of emigration as a question of negotiating the gender and ethnic implications of subjectivity. After moving from her native Calcutta (for the second time) to the United States to earn an MFA in creative writing and a PhD in comparative literature, she then moved to Canada and forged a career in writing short stories and novels as well as in teaching as a professor of literature. Explicitly added to the mix of her Indian heritage and her new adopted identities as citizen of both Canada and the United States is an important questioning of the place of gender in the post-colonial situation and at the core of identity politics. In much of her writing, Mukherjee filters her relationship to her identity (an identity that is dislocated and disrupted by her exile) through the further prism of gender—a prism that both further disrupts static notions of identity and can also be seen as a means of bridging the different ethnic poles of that identity, bringing into close contact cultures previously considered completely separated.

In her earlier works, particularly *Wife* (1975) and the short stories in *Darkness* (1985), Mukherjee's central theme was an investigation of the damaging effects that ethnic and gender violence can have on those who express an identity of difference in a society that will accept no such individuality. To some extent, this certainly must have grown from her experience of living in Canada when, even as a professor, she felt an overt racist and sexist prejudice working against her. The outlook of *Wife* and *Darkness* is markedly different from that of her two later novels, *Jasmine* (1989) and *The Holder of the World* (1993). While in no way mitigating the violence that is so often directed at female immigrants (such as that depicted in *Jasmine,* where the narrator, who has recently arrived in the United States, is brutally raped), these later novels no longer embody the immigrant figure as primarily the victimized character. They instead present a version of the exile's ability to intervene, create agency, and take positive action. In *Jasmine* and *The Holder of the World,* the difference that the characters represent is not only the reason why the world is violent toward them; it is also the very thing that allows those characters to change their situations and the worlds they live in. Mukherjee shows the ability of the exiles to shape the worlds they encounter in a positive and nonviolent manner, seizing and using the very tools of their oppression.

# Introduction

In large part, the cause of this change in the direction of Mukherjee's prose and political position can be found in the author's willingness to accept her new homeland (she had moved to the United States before either novel was written). Mukherjee now considers herself very much an American citizen, "not because I'm ashamed of my past, not because I'm betraying or distorting my past,"[1] but because the American context puts in place the preconditions necessary to examine the intermingling of cultures that forms the bedrock of her novels. In the same way as Salman Rushdie, Bharati Mukherjee has been considered a traitor to her history, having been accused of becoming Americanized by the Western neo-colonial machine. But Mukherjee's devotion to America is not that of one who has given up an old nation to embrace a new one. For Mukherjee, America is the land of opportunity and, most important of all, a nation based entirely on immigration. Mukherjee is not interested in a new American nationalism; rather, she views America as the representation of her own condition. She sees it as a landscape both formed upon and promoting the condition of exile.

V. S. Naipaul is a Nobel and Booker prize-winning author, and even more than either Rushdie or Mukherjee, he can be considered an excellent example of an exile—a product of the wide movements of the colonial period that echo in the novels he writes. Born in Trinidad in 1932, the child of indentured immigrants from India, Naipaul traveled—much like the narrators of both *The Mimic Men* (1967) and *The Enigma of Arrival* (1987)—to England when still a young man, desperate to become a writer. Like Rushdie, he studied at one of the pillars of the British establishment; while the young boy from India went to Cambridge University, the Trinidadian won a scholarship to Oxford. Naipaul felt that even at the moment of his birth, on an island thousands of miles away from the homes of his fathers, he was already an exile. In whatever place he came to rest, he could never consider himself to be at home. Even when, as a freelance writer, he traveled to India (in the early period of decolonization), he did not recognize that country as truly a part of him, despite the fact that it had such a large role in his history.

Like Mukherjee, Naipaul more often than not takes the biographical form as the basis of his novels; unlike Mukherjee, he does not see any positive aspect to the roles that the colonial subject is forced to play. Rather, the conventional fictional-biography form allows him to describe a metaphorical journey, a constant search for an identity that is impossible to find. Naipaul's novels seem to wind in and out of the different cultural positions that are available to a young man of his ethnicity and social position, seeing them as insufficient. The one role that Naipaul truly does recognize as worthwhile is that of the writer, the writer who makes a concerted difference to the cultures he represents and the writer who can transcend the poverty of present-day identity politics. For Naipaul, the political and artistic importance is in the work of art, not in the identity of the man who creates it.

Like Rushdie's and Mukherjee's, Naipaul's view of the postcolonial situation has caused controversy. Indeed, he appears to be the most conservative of the three when it comes to the politics of the new decolonized world. For instance, his treatment of the racial tensions in the West Indies presented in *The Middle Passage* (1962) was considered by many black West Indians to be racist. This accusation—though it certainly has roots in the volatile racial situation that Naipaul's novel attempts to diagnose—probably came about from Naipaul's utmost reluctance to engage with the notions of nationalism or anti-colonialism as political movements and ways to live. Naipaul is an individualist who places the ability to negotiate a single subject's history and personhood above more traditional political considerations. Naipaul's intervention occurs in the individual exile writing, the play of signifier and sign, rather than in an attempt to create a national movement.

What is central to all three writers is the important role they give to the structural place of the exile in affecting, intervening, and changing the discourse on identity and coloniality. Despite the differences in their pasts and the variations of their current contexts, Rushdie, Mukherjee, and Naipaul are all able to write about the notion of displacement with the power and the resonance that their backgrounds (as exiles) can produce. They all enact structures of freedom and play that—despite historical divergences—constitute a single, general narrative. Indeed, their fiction seems to play out this narrative in the weave of their novels' textuality, forming out of their texts the uncertainties and lacunae that develop because of their characters' geographical (and the resultant psychological) displacement. Their fiction imparts the questions of the subjects who are caught up in the post-colonial situation: Who is the exile? What is his or her importance? What movement does exile cause them to play out?

Who, then, is the exile? The exile lives in a foreign country, a culture that is not his or her own, one that is alien, "other." The exile's existence, therefore, is underpinned constantly by a sense of his or her geographical displacement. To fit in with the dominant culture, the exiles most often appropriate expectations that are alien; the exiles assimilate the roles and expectations of "the Other(s)" among whom they find themselves. In the process, the exiled displace who they are. This is iterated repeatedly in the novels of Rushdie, Mukherjee, and Naipaul. Each of these writers, in his or her own way, undermines his or her central character's right to be just that: a character, a stable entity, a full subject. More often than not, the characters in these three authors' novels are very much aware that they are creative products, not of the author's fiction but of the fiction of the colonial self, the discourse on the "foreign" and the "alien."

This is the central tenet of these writers' fictions. They are not simply producing an artistic product in which the characters can be considered fictional representations and the plots merely narratives that are rolled out for the entertainment and aesthetic pleasure of the readership. These writers represent the real world: their novels interact with history—particularly with the history of post-coloniality—in an attempt to reach out to the truth of the world. This is why Rushdie deals with characters against the backdrop of 20th-century Indian history (*Midnight's Children*), why Mukherjee delves into the origins of the English economic colonization of India (*The Holder of the World*), and why Naipaul writes of the decolonization process in a fictive version of his own Trinidad (*The Mimic Men*). The characters in these novels are not merely the creations of fictions, but representations (in no matter what fractured form) of real people who are made real by their interaction with history. Their actions are not merely component parts of fictional narratives; their respective progressions are not merely a means to the end of the completion of the novels' stories. The life stories that these novelists present are also metaphorical representations, allegorical passages of subjectivity in general, and depictions of the effects of exile on the man or woman who is cut adrift from any sense of a stable self.

That is why—and this is particularly true of Rushdie—the three novelists do not write in the realist mode and do not need the conventional tools that literary history has used to authorize depictions of the truth of the world. The realistic mode, with its emphasis on the centrality of the individual, the attempt to contain language to representations of static concepts (and, therefore, deny the free-play or imaginative flow of language), and the emphasis on a true reflection of a factual world are rejected because of their insufficiency for the task at hand. In Rushdie's novels, the fantastical proliferates—psychics, tears that turn to diamonds, devils, and angels in bowler hats—and yet this profligacy does not in any way retard Rushdie's claim to be representing the truth (a truth that does not kowtow to the restrictions of factuality). Likewise, in Mukherjee's and Naipaul's novels, the fictional is given precedence over the purely factual. Naipaul insists in *The Mimic Men* that "the edited version is all I have" (110).

This maneuver, the representation of the fictionality of reality, dovetails with the notion of the writing of the exile. For it is the notion of exile—the dislocation from any horizon against which to orientate a notion of the self—that augments the idea that any single and unitary notion of reality is a fictional simplification. By placing the characters into an obvious fictional narrative, the three novelists make explicit the constitutive fictions that are involved in the creation of the self. By choosing a style that relies on the free-play of language, which opens up the world to the puns, rhymes, false significations, and misinterpretations that language (necessarily by its structure) plays out, the writers are showing the discursive and linguistic components that go to construct the exile's subjectivity. Their novels present the world as a fiction, the truth of which can only be inscribed in fiction, and present the characters that make up the players in that fiction as playing out the roles inscribed by the authorial hand of colonial discourse. As Naipaul points out in a passage that explains the title of his novel *The Mimic Men*, "...we pretend to be real, to be learning, to be preparing ourselves for life, we mimic men of the new world..." (175).

In the same way, the central character in Mukherjee's *Jasmine* cannot be called simply "Jasmine." She has a number of names, each one indicating a different role that she plays in the colonial game, whether it be her young Indian self, or the hardworking Midwestern American housewife. In Rushdie's *The Satanic Verses*, the two central characters are actors who, at the start of the novel, are literally and metaphorically up in the air between two continents. One of them, Saladin Chamcha, sees that his life is in danger and begins to understand that his personality is nothing but roles that he played/plays; he thus "wanted nothing to do with his pathetic personality, that half-reconstructed affair of mimicry and voices..." (9). Likewise, Gibreel Farishta's move to England sends him into a spiral of revelatory dreams and messianic fantasies that place him between worlds—the worlds of myth, modern life, different religions, and different cultures. What these two characters show is that being between two worlds (as the exile inevitably is), being a hyphenated, hybrid being, leads to mimicry, a need to take on the outward form of the exile's new world.

These novels suggest that the exile cannot be analyzed with the same tools of simple binary oppositions that the humanist approach supplies: reality and appearance, original and simulacrum, and/or authentic and inauthentic. There is no essential being of the exile that is tied to the exile's homeland or original landscape. Also, the new self the exile has created is not simply an artificial invention that is bolted on. Rather, there are many selves contained within exile. Mukherjee demonstrates the various forms the relationship of the different selves of the exile can take in the opposition she presents between the narrator of *Jasmine* (who is an immigrant from India) and her adopted son (who is a refugee from Vietnam): "My transformation," the narrator points out, "was genetic, Du's was hyphenated" (222). The multiple selves can either be welded together—in which case the selves cannot stand as individual and separate, they are entirely caught in relationship to the individual's other selves—creating a hybrid or a "genetic" transformation, or they can be suspended in the air, cut off from each other, taken on as circumstances dictate. This can be considered a "hyphenated" transformation. In either case, there is no suggestion that either "self," either "role" is more real than the other is. The notion that selves can be blended or can be held in suspension seems to suggest that all selves are illusory, are roles to be played. Each self invalidates the other, and each self's existence brings into question the stability and the place in reality of the other persona that compete for attention within the individual.

There is a definite dialectic here, but one that does not lead to the suppression of contradictions in a synthesis or sublation (as the Hegelian model would have it). Rather this dialectic, the sideways shuttling that is set in motion by the collision of the various characters' different selves, invalidates the possibility of overcoming contradictions and creating a single self that will cohere. There is a lacuna at the center of the dialectical movement between the various roles that the exiled subject might play that means that there is no such thing as *the* exiled subject. The characters in these novels are multiple—like the thousands of voices that create the narrative thrust of *Midnight's Children* forming a polyphonic overlay of narrative sound—without distilling any notion of an essence or essential form that an exile might take on. The exiles are different from the land in which they live (and this applies to any land—they are not fully "at home" in the country in which they were born, or any country to which they might travel). More radically, this initial difference sets in motion a series of differences that allows difference into the realm of subjectivity itself. In the system of nationality and identity, the exile holds the position that Derrida has called (variously, but meaning a similar thing) *différance,* the pharmakon, the supplement, the "question of the 'yes'" and the trace.[2] In other words, exile takes the same place as the work of deconstruction itself. It is that which is on the margin of a system that is able to put that system in question.

Exile takes on a structural position of radical difference within the system of identity and nationality. That position poses a particular threat to those systems of post-coloniality that rely on the perpetuation of the notion of a singular and stable entity such as "the self" and "the nation." Robert Young, among many others, has pointed out how any system of oppression—but particularly colonial oppression—relies on the notion of a stable self and a notion of a piece of land that can be called, singularly and without the awkward imposition of difference, a *nation*.[3] It is the nation—singularly and without difference—that allows a people to take another man's land and rule over it. The oppressor's nation is made to appear "a civilizing influence," while the colonized's country is barely considered worthy of the term "nation" at all. Equally, it is the subject that considers itself a single self that allows the stereotypes of the black man (the black man as sexual barbarian, the black man as degenerate) to proliferate. If a man is black, then he must be thus, there is no possibility of him being otherwise. As such, the notion of the exile—working within the cultural frameworks of the oppressive situation—poses a distinct threat to colonial discourse. The exile (perhaps by copying Western ways) shows that the black man, the Indian man, the Chinese man (or black, Indian or Chinese women) can be something else.

Within the theory of post-colonialism, the idea of subject-place (the notion that the being of a subject is determined more by their structural position in a cultural system than through an internal and originary soul-like light) has taken on extreme importance particularly in the work of Frantz Fanon and following him, Homi Bhabha. They, along with a number of other theorists who have interested themselves in the existential side of the colonial situation, have seen the structural importance within the post-colonial schema of the "black man" or the colonial subject. What they are centrally involved with is the understanding of *who* the colonial is outside of and apart from the discourses that are set in motion by the colonial situation—a set of processes that are a means of oppression and subjection. However, as Fanon himself was well aware, it is a very difficult endeavor to access the reality of the subjectivity of the colonized because it is exactly this very question—the question of *who* the colonial is—that is part of the oppressive tools wielded by the colonialist system. As Fanon says:

> The culture that the intellectual leans towards is often no more than a stock of particularisms... . He wishes to attach himself to the people; but instead he only catches hold of their outer garments. And these outer garments are merely the reflection of a hidden life, teeming and perpetually in motion.[4]

The notion of the subjectivity of the colonial being simply outer garments is not to suggest that the colonial "wears" the stereotypes that are hung on him by colonial discourse. Rather, the important point that Fanon makes is that the *life* of the colonial cannot be simplified into a "stock of particularisms." The inside (which is masked by the external discourse of colonial oppression) is forever moving, is never static, and is "perpetually in motion."

The violence of the expression of the colonized through colonial discourse, then, is not simply that they are presented as stereotypes (though this is often the case as Rushdie, Mukherjee, and Naipaul realize when they explode the stereotypical representations they recorded in their novels) but that these stereotypes are presented as *fixed representations*. This is precisely the case in the often requoted story in which Fanon describes how a small boy pointed at him in a street and brands him a Negro and through that process, detaches Fanon from himself, separating him from any real expression of his living self.[5]

A similar understanding of stereotype is Bhabha's first and foremost contribution to the post-colonial scene. Bhabha says that stereotype is "a fixed reality which is at once an 'other' and yet entirely knowable and visible."[6] The stereotype (within its fixed form that will allow no flexibility or difference to threaten its stability) is a means to control and naturalize the dangerous difference as presented by the colonized and their culture. While making the stereotype "Other"—the

## Introduction 13

black man is not I, he is different—it is actually a means to tame alterity: The black man is what he is, he can be no "Other."

This is precisely why the black (and all the exile represents) poses such a problem to any notion of naturalized colonial discourse—and it is exactly this discomfort that we see played out again and again, particularly in *Jasmine, The Mimic Men,* and *The Satanic Verses.* For the exile stands at what Bhabha has called "the crossroads"[7] of the two cultures of which she or he has no part. The act that the exile engages in—the act of taking part in the host culture, trying to become a member of the culture of which the exile is not a "native"—is an act of mimicry. That act is seen as treacherous by nationalists (for example, Saladin's father in *The Satanic Verses*), while Bhabha considers it an act of defiance and destabilization for the host country. For it is within the act of mimicry and behind that act, the exile, that colonial discourse is forced to see the possibility of the "Other's" closeness to the "I," and is forced to recognize the difference that it attempted to stifle in the image of the foreigner as stereotype. The hybridism of the exile means that the oppressive discourse of colonialism can no longer concentrate on the difference *between* cultures and people—them and us, English and Indian, colonizer and colonized, self and "Other"—but must instead concentrate on "a hybridism, a difference 'within' a subject that inhabits the rim of an inbetween reality."[8]

The process of mimicking sets the subjectivity of the exile onto a trajectory of formation and dissolution, a making, re-making, fracturing, in a contrapuntal rhythm of deferral and difference. The subjectivity of the exile is one of motion, of becoming but never reaching the certainty of having become. That is why so many of the novels by these authors take the form of a journey or a pilgrimage. The narratives stand as allegorical representations that double as both the road the individual travels on and an image of the passage of the individual caught in the ceaseless transformation of the self. We see the young narrator of V. S. Naipaul's *The Enigma of Arrival* journey from his native country to England, and it is this movement from a homeland to a land he considers more suited to him, England, that defines and constructs his being. Yet, it is precisely this movement that brings into question his notion of who he is, the writer he wants to be, and the existence he is leaving behind. Similarly, in Bharati Mukherjee's *The Holder of the World,* the central character (a woman from early Puritan America) travels first to England and then to India and her subjectivity is broken and reconstructed by the process. She changes from the confined, puritanical spirit suited to her position in her original world into a woman who luxuriates in exoticism and sensual love. She is called throughout the novel the "Salem Bibi" (a Bibi being the Indian mistress of a white colonial), a hyphenated character, and a mirror held up to the American-Indian odyssey in which she has taken part.

Rushdie, Mukherjee, and Naipaul align the subjectivity of their central characters with the passage of their bodies through the world, demonstrating a central concern for not just the internal motion of subjectivity, but also the interrelation of the subject to the world. Not only this, but the ideas that we have seen cause the dissolution of the self—those ideas of roles, stereotypes, the process of mimicry— are all linked in the schematics of these novels with the notion of a landscape or geographical place. For example, it is notable that in *Jasmine* the narrator's journey from the rural India of her childhood to the city to America and finally into the cornfields of Ohio mimics the transformations in her social roles. She changes in turn from the country girl looking for a better life into a good Indian woman, an Americanized city girl, and finally the understanding and self-effacing Midwestern wife.

Equally, in Naipaul's *The Enigma of Arrival*, the narrator often consciously links cultural change and the acquisition of a new cultural understanding to the changing of the different landscapes through which he passes. Indeed, it seems to Naipaul's narrator (who is a thinly veiled representation of himself) that his knowledge of how to live, the very basis of his movement through the world, is somehow mystically imbibed from the landscape. When he reaches the quiet gardens of the country house in which he finds a new home in England, he walks often on the hillsides and seems to become a new person. While he does that, he says: "It was not like the almost instinctive knowledge that had come to me as a child of the plants and flowers of Trinidad; it was like learning a second language" (*The Enigma of Arrival* 32). The plants and flowers of his physical surroundings connect him with the social changes that he is going through.

In the novels of Rushdie, Mukherjee, and Naipaul, the notion of landscape is not simply a given, something that is natural and primal, outside and before culture. Rather, the landscapes that they paint—the bustling Trinidadian streets, the glory of Whitetown at its colonial peak, the hills outside of Jahilia where the prophet Mahound is greeted by Gabriel—are all shorthand for the cultural milieus within which these landscapes become inextricably linked to the minds of their characters. The notions of country, nation, homeland, and motherland—all the cultural edifices that both radical post-colonial theory and Marxism have attempted to demystify in recent political philosophy—are linked closely, in the minds of these novelists, with the very land on which their characters play out their lives. It is as important to the characters as their sense of self and contributes to it; there can be no conception of how the subjectivity of the characters in these novels is represented without equally understanding their connection with the national and geopolitical frameworks within which they move. In this way, a real concern of these three writers is not just the internal motion of subjectivity but also the interrelation of the subject to the world. Indeed, it is this interrelation that the narrator of Salman Rushdie's *Midnight's Children* suggests is at the very center of subjectivity:

> I no longer want to be anything except what who [sic] I am. Who what [sic] am I? My answer: I am the sum total of everything that went before me, of all I have been, seen done, of everything done-to-me. (383)

The relation of the individual to the world is contingent on the workings of the world on that individual. The landscapes the individual travels through in large part create who that individual is and put the notion of the individual into question, dispelling the certainty of full subjectivity. However, as the narration of *Midnight's Children* also makes clear, the individual has a large impact on the landscape around him, questioning its reality, interrogating the certainty of its wholeness.

As well as focusing on the notion of the colonial subject, the three post-colonial writers under examination also bring into question the notion of "country," "homeland," and "nation"—all of which are explicitly linked in these novels to a concept of "landscape" (whether physical or imaginary). It is not simply the case that such landscapes make the man, and that man is entirely dependent on the cultural edifice that is represented by a landscape or the notion of a "national" culture. The individual subjectivity also has a part to play in the construction of the landscape and the nation. This, of course, is one of the central tenets of literary theory, one of which main aims is the dislocation (and, therefore, demystification) of the notion of any kind of set geographical landscape and conception of the nation or national culture as a stable and given reality. As Benedict Anderson points out in his *Imagined Communities: Reflections on the Origins and Spread of Nationalism*, the nation is not a simple and incontrovertible given. Rather, "it is an imagined political community—and imagined as both inherently limited and sovereign."[9] It is simply the imagined nature of the national body—the very fact that it is a creation from a subjective community—that makes it appear as though it were a sovereign structure, free from any creative process and a static reality. Therefore, when we speak of a subjectivity that is created by the social roles that it performs and the place of these social roles in a notion of nationality, ethnicity, or culture, it must be made quite clear that not one of these constructions is, in itself a static base. What the three novelists show again and again is the ability of their characters to subjectively transform the landscapes of which they are a part.

V. S. Naipaul's narrator in *The Enigma of Arrival* looks across the country scene of his newly acquired home of England (as well as remembering the landscape of his native Trinidad) and says, "Land is not land alone, something that simply is itself. Land partakes of what we breathe into it, is touched by our mood and memories" (301). Here, the narrator accepts that landscapes are, to some extent, imaginary constructions, constructions created by the individual who looks over them. A similar point is made in *The Holder of the World*, when the author, Bharati Mukherjee, imagines a scenario from science fiction, in which the scientist boyfriend of her narrator creates a virtual-reality machine that will show the world of 17th-century India, but that presents the world filtered through what the individual "most care[s] about" (*The Holder of the World* 281). The same process occurs in Salman Rushdie's fiction: The subcontinent and important political events (e.g. the war between India and China or Islamist extremism) are filtered through the magical-realist life story of his protagonists. All the landscapes in these novels seem to have the consistency of the city described in the second book of *The Satanic Verses*, that is, shaped but not solid—"The city of Jahilia is built entirely on sand, its structures formed of the desert whence it rises." The city's sand is "the very stuff of inconsistency" (93).

This understanding—that the notions of culture, nationality, ethnicity, and race are as unstable as the subject—has an enormous impact on both our theoretical standpoint and our understanding of the possibility of post-colonial politics. In terms of a theoretical basis for some kind of epistemology of the colonial being, we can neither accept the existentialist model of being (the notion that the authenticity of the subject derives from its being in the world) nor the Lacanian psychoanalytical model (which contends that the Imaginary self—our notion of a stable self which is illusion—is constructed through the language of the "Other" in the Symbolic realm or, to put it another way, through the discursive practices inherent in the world). For despite the very different approaches of these two schools of thought, they both reach the same general conclusion. The subject is, necessarily, created at the whim of the outside world (whether it is his or her relationship with others or his or her place in the linguistic hierarchy). From a post-colonial standpoint, the subject is—with respect to the existential or psychoanalytical systems—a construction of the gaze of the colonizer or a subject formed by the discourse of colonialism.

These novels, however, provide a quite different basis for viewing the colonial subject. For while accepting that the subject is not a stable and static being (it *is* the construction of its surroundings), the subject can also deform and destabilize those very surroundings from which it emanates. Both these notions are suspended within the textual weave of the novels. The two notions chase each other round, as though engaged in a never-ending game of tag. As well as providing a richer and more complex theoretical view of the subject than much of post-colonial theory, these novels also have a very important impact on identity politics as it is practiced today. The basis that underlies the politics of race and ethnicity as they are practiced today—particularly in the North American and Western European policies of multiculturalism—is the sanctity and inviolability of identity. As Kwame Anthony Appiah points out (though he has some qualms over the matter), "the major collective identities that demand recognition in North America currently are religion, gender, ethnicity, 'race,' and sexuality."[10] This recognition, this belief (held almost by consensus) in identity as the central component of the political being of a citizen is precisely the stance that these novels question.

Rushdie, Mukherjee, and Naipaul all hold (much against the grain of the liberal consensus) the notion that a person must be confined by his "religion," "gender," "ethnicity," "race," and "sexuality" to be untrue. For the central tenet of identity politics is that the subject is created by cultures that are entirely and inviolably in the world. None of these writers believe in the full efficacy of this claim. The subject can make an intervention in the cultural milieu that has created him or her; the landscapes are as much a creation of the subject as the subject is created by identity. Perhaps this is why there is no notion of unquestioning nationalism in any of the three writers' works. Mukherjee, for one, has actively spoken out against immigrants' intransigence when it comes to assimilating the cultures of their new homes. Rushdie has gone even further in distancing himself from his old identity, a fatwa being issued by the followers of the religion of his homeland. It is quite clear that a traditional identity politics—a politics of respectful nonintervention in others' cultures while chauvinistically tied to one's own—is no longer possible according to the ideas that flow through these six novels.

These novels suggest that we must come alive to the power and the possibilities the exile can create. For the exile is not just a person made by two lands; his or her subjectivity is contructed by the fact that he or she is different from both. The exile is more active: The exile is one "who inhabits one place and remembers or projects the reality of another."[11] Seidel's notion of projection is extremely important. The exile, being by his or her structural position already cut off from any notion of a stable landscape by his or her geographical difference, is able to understand the nature of projection—particularly the projection of a landscape, a dream of home. By being between two landscapes, the exile is able to invalidate the notion of the single and stable nation. It is the fact that the exile makes the projection, which comes in the form of an intervention—both theoretical and political—that disrupts any discourse that would affirm the solidity of any landscape. By *landscape*, I mean cultural constructions of "nation," "culture," and "homeland."

So, just as we saw a dialectic occur within the process of mimicry, a dialectic arising out of playing many roles and resulting in the impossibility of all of them, so we see another dialectic in progress. This is a dialectic between the subject (as constructor and construction) and a notion of landscape (which is both projection and home to the subject's being). The landscape, its social customs, its roles, and the notion of it as home, all contribute to the construction of the subject. The exile, because he or she is between landscapes, is both part of and distant from the creative processes that landscapes perform. As such, the exile invalidates the notion of subject as stable and static. The exile is the outermost example of subjectivity that returns to invade the center of the concept. Equally, the subject through its projection onto the landscape of his or her desires, hopes, dreams of home, creates notions of nation, culture, and homeland.

The exile—being the subject that is *between* landscapes—is always aware of the projection's status *as* projection, construction, and aesthetic creation because of the distance created by his or her being. As such, the exile invalidates the landscape as something set in reality; it is a construction that is determined and reliant on the intervention of the subject who forms it. In both deformations, the exile takes the central role—it is the status of the exile that performs this destruction.

An excellent example of both these processes at work simultaneously is the central character of *Midnight's Children*, Saleem Sinai. He is integrally a part of the landscape to which he is born; he is created by his coincidence with Indian history, and he projects his own version of it through his novel. Neither subjectivity nor landscape can claim primacy over the other; rather both are joined in a twin process of creation and destruction, a coming-into-being without actually finally arriving. It is also clear from Saleem's intimate connection with Indian history that neither he, nor history (or at least his version of it) can survive the process. Throughout the novel, he constantly reminds us that he is breaking apart, that the very integrity of his body (representing here, as it does in Lacan's notion of the Mirror Stage,[12] the integrity of his subjectivity) is breaking asunder. His very being is constantly "crumbling." What is seen here as a semitragic statement of the impossibility of finality and fulfillment is also the movement of a dialectic between subject and landscape that is constantly producing, through the text, precisely the thing that Saleem most desires: to "end up meaning-yes, meaning-something" (*Midnight's Children* 3). However, the novel ends with the impossibility of completing the character's performance of being. Saleem can never be whole.

I would like to propose that the dialectic that is demonstrated within and through the character of Saleem is precisely the dynamic that is at the center of the six novels we are to analyze and represents one of the most important questions to be addressed to the post-colonial situation. However, as Saleem's slow breaking-apart demonstrates, this dialectic will never reach any kind of conclusion or sublation. However, this is not to say that the only thing that will be produced by the dialectic is despair. Far from it. As Saleem sees in *Midnight's Children* and as the hopeful possibilities for renewal that the end of Mukherjee's *Jasmine* and Naipaul's *The Enigma of Arrival* seem to suggest, there is something positive that can arise from the impossibility of fulfillment. The positive product of this dialectic is meaning.

Traditional theories of language (from Plato[13] onwards) propose that language is an arrival—a coming to rest within the static and unyielding truth of the *logos*. The arrival at meaning is the ascension from the dark shadows of the cave into the light of the world. However, more modern notions of language (from Ferdinand de Saussure[14] to Jacques Derrida[15]) see language rather as the play of differences, a play that is actually excluded by the notion of arrival. The insufficiency of language to reach a final and incontrovertible meaning is precisely the structural component that allows language to mean in the first place. When it comes to a discussion of how the characters in the novels—each of which can be seen as an allegorical representation of the exile—can create different meanings in their lives, it is precisely the openness and extended continuation of play that allows the rich and varied significance of their existences to be displayed. The notion of a stable and singular homeland and the conception of themselves as stable and static subjectivities are not regained. The *attempt* to return—with its meandering and doublings back and false turns—is precisely the positive aspect that these novelists stumble upon in their portrayal of the life of the exile.

Losing a notion of home is a painful process. Often in these novels, the geographical and painful emotional journey from the homeland relies on memory to nostalgically reconstruct the lost world—an idea that Edward Said has demonstrated in "Movements and Migration."[16] Memory as used here, however, does not do the work that is often ascribed to it—the reconstruction of events *as they really were*. Michael M. J. Fischer sees memory in "Ethnicity and the Post-Modern Arts of Memory"[17] mainly as a place to inhabit that allows for reinvention of self. In other words, memory—as these novels use it—is the arena in which the creative aspects of the characters can be played out, and in which the dialectic that we have seen at work can begin its shuttling. Certainly the remembrances of the characters in these novels—for example, the narrator of *The Mimic Men*'s remembrances of his childhood in Trinidad, or Saladin's remembrances of his life in England before the plane's explosion—can be seen as attempts to take hold once more of a simpler, more solid time and place. James Clifford has suggested that exiles' re-created visions of home are "place[s] of attachment and not something simply left behind."[18] But they also, through the very act of remembering, emphasize the detachment of the subject from home—the impossibility of either of those two notions being intertwined or achievable. The characters, through the act of remembering, become self-aware of the constructive processes that occur as part of their remembering. Saleem of *Midnight's Children* is very aware of these processes: "I'm prepared to distort everything, to rewrite the whole history of my times purely in order to place myself in a central role" (198).

As such, home and past are reconstructed "through memory, fantasy, narrative, and myth,"[19] as Stuart Hall argues in *Cultural Identity and Diaspora*. However, if there is a desire to return home in these novels, it is fleeting—a feeling passed over as characters feel the tragic loss of themselves deeply but look forward to new possibilities. Memory is not nostalgia. The difference is pointed up etymologically and significantly by Gayle Green in her *Feminist Fiction and the Uses of Memory*. For Green, nostalgia is "the desire to return home," whereas remembrance is "to think again," or "to recollect."[20] To feel nostalgic is to hope for a return home—whether it is a return to the homeland that the exile has traveled from, or the home as constituted by an earlier, more attractive self. It is nostalgia that the narrator of *Jasmine* feels in passing for her time in New York, or the narrator of *The Mimic Men* feels for the green time of Trinidad before his birth, or the cool Indian air of his ancestral home. As the last example shows, there is no necessity for the nostalgic feeling to be lodged in actual events in the past—rather, it is longing to return to a home, any home, whether it be the certainty of an imagined landscape or not.

Memory, on the other hand, works in a very different way. This is particularly true in the works of the three novelists in this study—for each one of them both foregrounds memory as an important narrative trait, and transforms our notions of how memory works. Greene glosses memory as "to think again" or to "re-collect." In both these definitions, there is a double movement—the thought and then the repetition of the thought, the letting go, and the re-collection. Memory in this sense is a motion forwards—a reshaping of the past, certainly—but not a return to what has gone before. It is a means for the characters of these novels to interact with the past but not in the hope of reaching out for it and enclosing it. Rather, the succession of unreliable narrators—Saleem of *Midnight's Children*; the asset finder Beigh, with her hidden motives; the narrator of *The Mimic Men*, who suggests that the "editing" is all he has—point to the fact that the multiple workings of memory are not the perfect recouping of the past, whether it be the past of a landscape or the certainty of a self, but the reshaping of the fragile strands of what has gone before. Memory is a playing out of all the half-notions, the incomplete thoughts, the part-remembrances-part-forgettings that collide and bounce off each other in the creation of the subject. Through memory, we are allowed to see the dialectic of landscape and self-shuttling through the narratives of these novels, never finding the hope of a return home.

What should be clear from our brief discussion concerning the movements of these novels and how they interact with the person of the exile, is that they do not point toward a modernist hopelessness, a wasteland of the soul that mourns the passing of authenticity and fullness. Rather, they delight—with a sort of postmodern Bacchic abandon—in the possibilities inherent in the open subject and an unstable landscape against which he or she is set. This is clear in the carnivalesque atmosphere of Rushdie's fiction that enjoys playing with the boundaries of language, its puns and rhymes, phonetic tricks and rococo images. Even in the more staid prose of V. S. Naipaul, there is the implication of hope rather than loss. Whereas the attempts at political involvement are dismissed as poor forfeits of authentic living, the importance of writing, of creating a literary and linguistic version of the world that goes beyond any factual representation, is where Naipaul places his hope for the future of his personal journey. However—and this is important—these novelists do not share the unengaged nihilism of some postmodern thinkers, who completely refute any notion of politics or ethical action for the apolitical free play of sign and signifier. Not only do the novelists see a positive *aesthetic* in the open subject and the imaginary landscapes that the structure of the exile reveals through their novels, they also point toward a means of ethical action, or a politics. In the post-colonial situation in which they orient their fiction, they answer one of the most important questions—*What is to be done?*[21]

Bill Ashcroft, Gareth Griffiths, and Helen Tiffin are quite right to identify in their invaluable overview of the recently constituted academic discipline of post-colonial studies, that it is "question[s] of the subject and subjectivity [that] directly affect colonized peoples' perceptions of their identities and their capacities to resist the conditions of their domination, their 'subjection.'"[22] In their pun on the word "subjection," they have neatly captured the twin problems that face the colonial subject within the situation of colonialism and after. Certainly, the colonized are subjected to their colonial masters—they are placed physically, financially, and mentally in chains by their oppressors. The true means of their oppression, a means that can outlast any process of "decolonization," is the power of description and constriction. The Negro, the Indian, the Oriental are oppressed not simply because of who they are; the oppression operates to make them who they are. The fact that they simply are *the* Negro, *the* Indian, *the* Oriental, is both the means and justification for how they are treated. Again, the possibilities of the colonized are limited and shut off.

This is also the case with colonial discourse's understanding of the world. Once more, there is a closing down of the possibility of nationhood, identity, and culture. While the Western, colonial culture is considered civilized and is placed at the end of the continuum of progress, the colonized world is considered barbaric and is placed at the beginning. Indeed, colonial discourse is able to perform a conjuring trick that plays with the very temporality of world history. What is a spatial piece of information—the location of a people or peoples, their geographical location in the West or the East—is turned into a temporal datum—and whereas the white man is present day, the black or brown man is situated at the beginning of time. Such a trick is pulled by Conrad's canonical novel, *Heart of Darkness,* in which the African is presented as a primal form of the European, an earlier savage form from which the European must distance himself. What is more important to our present discussion is that these forms are fixed. There is no possibility for difference to inhabit their inside, no opportunity that the world might be any different.

The world of colonial power is not simply patrolled by sovereign physical and military might. Such an imposition would be easy to overthrow. Rather at the heart of colonial power lies an ability to create a stable and *singular* reality that cannot be questioned. Once that reality becomes dominant (and, therefore, unquestionable), then such a discourse is almost impossible to fight. It is the equivalent of fighting the truth. As such, Madan Sarup is quite right to declare (following the thought of Michel Foucault) that "conceiving of power as repression, constraint or prohibition is inadequate: Power 'produces reality'; it 'produces domains and objects of truth.'"[23] Colonial power is naturalized, and oppression becomes the status quo; it is accepted by all.

It is into such a system that these novelists bring their notions of the exile. They will accept no reality as naturalized and by virtue of their position attack every status quo. The novels interrogate the notion of a single stability; they interfere with the dominant notions of the colonial by exposing them as mere roles to be played. What is more, by opening up the notion of subjectivity—allowing the self to be deformed and transformed—they open up the possibility of action that is critical toward authoritarian power. These novels question a single and unitary notion of the world: The world is multiple and is open to be transformed by the subject that goes through it. Any single representation of reality must be invested by power: By its nature, the singular must exclude the marginal, the unrepresented; so these novels embrace the world as multiple, as multiple even as the 1,001 voices that flow through *Midnight's Children*.

This view presents a problem to any traditional form of intervention and fight for liberation. For this reason, there is a distinct and insurmountable difference between the work of these novelists and the work of nationalist or Marxist notions of the end to oppression. Indeed, despite the fact that the aims of the movement that I am describing[24] are precisely the same as the nationalist and Marxist movements (i.e., the defeat of operations of power), there have been a number of attacks—some of them directed personally at the novelists in questions—from the Left. For example, Aijaz Ahmad has put up a concerted attempt to paint Rushdie as a bourgeois intellectual who mystifies the actual determinants of post-colonial oppression (not to mention, it seems, being a traitor to his roots). He speaks of how a certain ideology of exile

> makes it possible for that migrant to arrive in the metropolitan country to join not the working classes but the professional middle strata, hence to forge a kind of rhetoric which submerges the class question and speaks of migrancy as an ontological condition, more or less.[25]

The suggestion here is that by assuming that the ontological condition of exile is a motion that cuts across and transcends class considerations, Rushdie's fiction avoids any real consideration of the operation of power, and even masks it. In fact, there is a large section of current criticism that agrees with the contrary conclusion of Helen Tiffin that "post-structuralist philosophy remains the handmaiden of repression."[26]

The mistake that Marxist and nationalist schemas of opposition and intervention make is that they assume that for the possibility of politics there must be first the possibility of a victim (and hence, a stable subjectivity which can be *just* a victim) and a stable material world (in which those politics can be acted out). However, in their attempt to find a home (much like the attempts made by the characters of the novels in which we are interested), they are liable only to find the continuation of power. For—and this has certainly been proven by the experience of certain decolonized states—the end of colonialism does not necessarily mean the end of violence. Indeed, many national movements which the ascension to power has corrupted have merely replaced the colonizers in a system of power that looks remarkably similar to the one against which they struggled. Simply changing the signs at the palace does not change the regime. For while the ruling discourse continues to insist on the certainty and stability of subjectivity and to see the world as a single and unitary reality, power will still be in operation, and those at the margins will still be oppressed. All three of the examined writers, Rushdie, Naipaul, and Mukherjee, are writing in a time that can be considered, broadly, to be after the great reign of colonialism. Yet they still contend with the issues of the colonial subject, still attempt to make an intervention into the discourse of colonialism (which outlived the physical structures of its oppression) because power still operates within that paradigm. Without the openness and dynamism of the structures that these novels champion, without the ethics of the exile that, as a collection, they represent, the preconditions that made colonialism possible will continue to spread its violence in the world.

In this introduction, I have been taking these novels, mainly, as a whole (almost as though, together, they constituted a single text). This, in my opinion, is not an entirely bad thing, for there are certain important issues that track across the boundaries of individual texts, and resonate among the authors. However, as I hope the following chapters will demonstrate, there are a number of differences between these three authors that come from the differences inherent in their aesthetic approaches. While all three open up their subjects to free play, place into question stable notions of the world, and explode stereotypical representations of the migrant, they do so in extremely different ways. Each of the six novels gestures toward the place of the exile in an ethical system, but the minutiae of that system are not the same in each novel, nor do the novelists share the same dogma. Indeed, the freshness of these six novels is that—despite the fact that together they can be constructed into an argument for the value of openness in the post-colonial situation—they all eschew dogmatic notions of what the exile is, and what role he or she can play in the world.

Bharati Mukherjee combines an ontological investigation into the criss-crossing subjectivity of the exile, with a belief in the positive and interventionary possibilities of living a hybrid or "genetic" existence. The play of signifiers, the mimicry of the dominant discourse is in itself a positive mode of action—as long as it is mimicry that accepts within its production the notion of play. The central character in *Jasmine* takes on various personae, many of which could be considered, at times, racist, anti-feminist, and/or colonial in the manifestations they take. However—and this Mukherjee makes extremely clear—there is no subject position that one might take which is not determined by colonial discourse, by the discourse which surrounds and determines the subject. The next best course of action, therefore, is to subvert the roles it plays, simply by taking as many multiple roles as possible. The novel ends in a decision to keep on playing. By the main character's conscious playing of the roles, she has chosen, and owing to the play between them, the author deconstructs colonialism and creates powerful agency (through action) for the narrator while allowing the indecisiveness of play to wash across the narrator's existence.

*The Holder of the World* has a completely different viewpoint from *Jasmine*. It takes a far more ambitious, epic approach, attempting to chronicle the full sweep of colonial history in America, England, and India. Nevertheless, like *Jasmine* the main importance of its narrative is the intersection between notions of femininity and roles that can be played to dissolve a singular notion of the subject. Hannah Easton travels from her native America (she is member of the early Puritan society that settled there) to England and then to India where—as though in a complete transformation from her former self—she becomes the Bibi (a courtesan) of an Indian prince. Not only does *The Holder of the World* emphasize the importance of an open subjectivity that not only transgresses the bounds of any single or stable notion of the subject but also has the ability to transcend the restrictions of any political or social position, it also shows how the exile can make an important intervention in the world.

In *The Holder of the World*, there is a narrative within a narrative—one in which Beigh Masters, an asset hunter, attempts to track down a large diamond and to explain in precise detail Hannah's life. Although we are led to question the factuality of the specific events that Beigh is relating (she takes part in a questionable virtual re-creation of a part of history which, we suspect, is showing her only what she wants to see), we do come away with the feeling that Hannah's story made a real intervention into the history of colonialism as Beigh sees it. The old story of colonial finance and greed is cut across by Hannah's particularly open subjectivity, and it suggests the possibility for the cessation of colonial violence. In both her novels, Mukherjee chooses play, difference, the acceptance of certain violences so as to subvert them from within, and the whole transgressive carnival as the central components of life.

If Mukherjee chooses life, then Naipaul, conversely, chooses to withdraw from life and from the world of action. In *The Mimic Men*, he, too, shows a central character who becomes wearied by the roles he plays—whether the colonial subject (during his stay in England) or the freedom fighter for colonial freedom (for he is one of the leading politicians who brings about the passing of power from the colonial masters to a national movement). Instead of playing these roles, Naipaul's character seeks a medium in which he can understand the difference that emerges from them. That medium is contemplation and writing. His life can be considered real only in the writing of it—and this written life is contrasted sharply with the unreality of actual events. If the factuality of his life story is not correct, then, the narrator says, "the editing is clearly at fault, but the edited version is all I have" (110). Life is unreal. It is only through writing, editing, displacing, and deforming, that the truth of a fissured subjectivity can come to fruition.

Rob Nixon has suggested that Naipaul's writing is an attempt at "ventriloquising an English identity,"[27] in other words, like the migrant Saladin Chamcha of *The Satanic Verses*, he has come to identify himself entirely with the host culture. In *The Enigma of Arrival*, I believe that Naipaul provides a subtle but definitive answer to such a personal criticism and does so through a defence that, above all, emphasizes the very personal nature of the question. For *The Enigma of Arrival* takes the form of a biography—just as before, *The Mimic Men* had—however, it is a biography that touches so closely to the events of Naipaul's life that he feels the necessity to subtitle it, *A Novel in Five Sections*. In it, the narrator looks over the events of his life, and his slow passage to becoming a writer. His younger self (a young Trinidadian who dreams of going to England and becoming a writer) attempts to mimic the great writers of the canon and by doing so, betrays his roots and his sense of home. In this way, Naipaul examines the possibility that Nixon puts forth, that by writing he is "ventriloquising an English identity,"—and actively rejects it. The narrator looks back at his younger self and goes so far as to chide him for not understanding how to be a writer and for not understanding the full possibilities of his position as an exile.

In fact, the writer at the center of *The Enigma of Arrival*, decides upon writing as an arena by which he can understand who he is—without positing the notion that "who he is" can be in anyway complete or certain. He finds writing to be a means of combining the place where he has come from (and the turmoil created by the differing racial and colonial tensions that are inextricably linked to it) and the place that he has gone to—an attempt at some kind of synthesis of the man he was and the man he has become. What's more, while Mukherjee's characters saw life, living, as the ethical choice to take, the narrator of *The Enigma of Arrival* sees becoming a writer—and retiring as he does, to a country house in the English countryside—as a way to battle with and defeat life. There is a slightly elegiac tone to *The Enigma of Arrival*, and that tone gives the reader the sense that the narrator—whose illness suggests that he might well be coming to the end of his life—is coming to terms with the violence of the world and is doing so through the medium of his writing. However, this coming-to-terms need not necessarily be synonymous with any kind of resolution. For at the end of the novel it is quite clear that the medium of writing is one that is always looking forwards, and is, therefore, never complete. The most important conclusion one must come to regarding *The Enigma of Arrival* is wound up in its title: The notion of arrival is always under question, always under suspicion. The journeys (both metaphorical and physical) that the writer makes are never to be concluded. They are always open-ended, ever ready to be superseded.

This is the truth—if the word can still be used, so transformed as it is from its classical meaning—which Naipaul finds in writing: The literary product never finds its object (the world). It is always adrift and never certain. In the novels of Salman Rushdie, this belief that the truth can be encapsulated in writing is even more marked, and his novels provide the widest canvas and the greatest depth for the adventure of writing. He also, in my opinion, provides the most sophisticated understanding of the exile.

In his work, Rushdie tries to encapsulate everything that constitutes the colonial individual, each branch of his other subjectivity, and elides this overarching mission with the creation of the new state of India: "[I]s this an Indian disease, this urge to encapsulate the whole of reality? Worse: am I infected, too?" (*Midnight's Children* 75). Both individual and landscape are imaginary, and Rushdie emphasizes this by playing them both into semimythical semihistorical, semimagical tableaux, that do not allow for any stationary notion of reality. Writing, one feels, is not enough for Rushdie; his novels are, rather, a gesture toward something greater, some enormous weave of myth, history, and reality that can attempt to bring to life, even momentarily, the radical alterity of human subjectivity. At the end of *Midnight's Children*, the narrator (also assuming multiple roles and personae, like Naipaul's and Mukherjee's characters) seems to suggest that writing is not enough to encapsulate the difference within him: "I have been so—many too—many persons, life unlike syntax allows one more than three" (463).

Like Naipaul, Rushdie has been criticized, not just by the Right's religious fundamentalisms, but also by the Left for his conservatism as regards the racial struggle. He has become for many Marxists critics what Timothy Brennan slightly sneeringly refers to as the "Cosmopolitan Intellectual."[28] Of course, in terms of Salman Rushdie the man, this is undoubtedly the case: He has become very much part of the Western intellectual and financial elite; he was educated at Rugby and Cambridge. He himself is now an example of the Western canon. However, unlike the Marxist literary critic, we must not assume that the material means of production of a work of art define and ultimately determine its political and aesthetic worth.

Rushdie's writing, in its own way, can be considered more revolutionary than ordinary Marxist post-colonialist praxis and as providing a greater intervention. And it is precisely the forms that Rushdie's novels take—forms that are the main target for Marxist criticisms—that provide their ultimate potential for resistance. In *The Satanic Verses*, it is exactly Rushdie's carnivalesque mixture of Islamic scripture, modern myth, the experience of the immigrant, and Western literary traits that neutralizes the efficacy and authoritarianism of any of these strands of discourse singularly. By means of montage and pastiche, the migrant stories that are put forward as part of the textual weave of *The Satanic Verses*, place themselves between the overdetermined discourses of fundamentalist Islam, Western capitalism, racism, even Marxism, and—from that position at the crux of all these intersecting matrices—are able to suspend all from the arena of "reality." Rushdie's work takes up the position of the exile—is written out of the experience of the exile—and can, therefore, intervene in the passage of these various strands of culture.

All three novelists, then, put the experience of the exile through slightly different transformations and deformations; each one shows a slightly different formula to gain the same result—an important intervention into post-colonial discourse. In following the trajectories of formation and dissolution as they evolve in these novels, the three writers explore how discourses of the local are being interrogated and transformed by the marginal position of the exile, who does not attack from the outside of discourse but from its limbo-like position within it. In this context, the novels occupy a significant space relevant to current political and theoretical discourse, an area of double displacement that shares neither the linear narrative of nationhood nor the circular culture of imperialism, accepting and denying at the same time both the initial and the acquired homelands as places of safe belonging and happy fulfillment.

In these novels, there is no belonging, no fulfillment—because belonging and fulfillment belong to the discourses of violence. They also stand between any notions of a stable locality or globalism; each character, despite his or her very human role in the drama of post-colonialism, can also stand above it and without it, their stories resonating on a much grander scale. They present the painful dichotomous agency of the migrant self-caught between the diasporic objective and the ethnic mandate but, however painful such an interim position might be, they aver the importance and opportunities inherent in such a position. The exile's intrinsic hybridity (and the liminal space the exile inhabits) makes memory the necessary tool for attempting to build a place of stability, agency, and negotiation between the subject's initial homeland and the newly acquired one (which remains mainly an illusory endeavor). Memory as tool, as strategy, enables the exile to play amongst the strange dialectical movements that his or her existence has put in motion. The incompatibility of his or her various roles, various social situations, the impossibility of the sublation of the two poles of subjectivity and landscape, lead to a radical and important statement of alterity.

It is certainly true, then, that the exile in an effort to recapture his or her wholeness constructs a "home away from home," as María Cristina Rodríguez writes in her book *What Women Lose: Exile and the Construction of Imaginary Homelands in Novels by Caribbean Writers* (19). However, this is not simply a substitution, nostalgia for the old homeland in place of the host country, or the assimilation of the self completely to the social structures of the newly achieved shore. Rather, the "home away from home" is a liminal space. It is neither of nor outside of the two places of which the exile can no longer truly be considered a part. If we say this "home" is between the homeland and the host country, it should be made clear that we are not positing a third space, a space that is independent of the originary two, but an entirely different kind of landscape.

The shoreline of this new landscape can be made out only by the lines in the air created through the furiousness of movement of the exile—who is caught in a (in G. C. Spivak's phrase) "violent shuttling"[29] between the two poles of identity. This new landscape has no place in reality. It is an imaginary landscape, but a landscape on which numerous personal and political struggles can be played out. In Mukherjee's case, this new "home," this liminal space is created through the passage of life; for Naipaul, through his writing; and for Rushdie, it is the mountain peak that arises out of the clashing of a thousand images, discourses, and philosophies. This new homeland is not a regained Jerusalem for the exile (or the colonial subject) in which the exile can feel as if he or she has returned home. Rather, it is a ground that is unsure, a shifting place, on which to remain surefooted; the exile must leap from place to place and never feel he or she can come to rest for too long.

Bharati Mukherjee, V. S. Naipaul, and Salman Rushdie contribute to a notion of the colonial subject as the site for the exploration of difference and alterity; the exile opens up the notion of a reified subject and a reified culture. The condition of exile as reified and hybrid subject opens up closely held notions of never exhausted continuity of play. Within the colonial context, play is both a force for the confrontation with power and that which will assure that identity can never be found. These novels have a double purpose: to document the impossibility of completeness, the inevitability that the exile must continue his or her wandering, and to make explicit the opportunity that this provides. These novels document both the pain of loss and loss's place in the struggle for liberation.

# Introduction 35

## ENDNOTES

1. "Mukherjee," *English Databanks Fu Jen: World Literature*, 20 Feb. 2006 <http://www.eng.fju.edu.tw/worldlit/india/mukherjee.html>.
2. Jacques Derrida, *Writing and Difference*, trans. Alan Bass (Chicago: University of Chicago Press, 1978); *Of Grammatology*, trans. Gayatri Chakravorty Spivak (Baltimore: John Hopkins University Press, 1976); and Derrida, Jacques, "Ulysses' Gramophone: *Hear say yes in Joyce*." trans. Tina Kendall, *James Joyce: The Augmented Ninth*, ed. Bernard Benstock. (Syracuse: Syracuse University Press, 1988) 27–75.
3. Robert Young, *Colonial Desire: Hybridity in Theory, Culture, and Race* (New York: Routledge, 1995).
4. Frantz Fanon, *The Wretched of the Earth*, trans. Constance Farrington (New York: Grove, 1968).
5. Frantz Fanon, *Black Skin, White Masks*, trans. Charles Lam Markmann (London: Pluto, 1986) 112.
6. Homi Bhabha, "The Other Question ...," *Screen* 24.6 (1983): 18–36.
7. Homi Bhabha, "Of Mimicry and Man: The Ambivalence of Colonial Discourse," *October* 28 (Spring 1984): 130.
8. Homi Bhabha, *The Location of Culture* (London: Routledge, 1994) 13.
9. Benedict Anderson, "Imagined Communities: Reflections on the Origin and Spread of Nationalism," *Shaping Discourses: Reading for University Writers*, ed. April Lidinsky, vol. 11 (Boston: Pearson, 2002) 7–20.
10. Kwame Anthony Appiah, "Identity, Authenticity, Survival: Multicultural Societies and Social Reproduction," *Multiculturalism: Examining the Politics of Recognition*, ed. Amy Gutmann (Princeton, NJ: Princeton University Press, 1994) 151.
11. Michael Seidel, *Exile and the Narrative Imagination* (New Haven CT: Yale University Press, 1986) 10.
12. Jacques Lacan, *Écrits* (New York: Norton, 1977).
13. Plato, "Allegory of the Cave," *The Norton Reader*, ed. Linda H. Peterson (New York: Norton, 2000) 652–655.
14. Ferdinand de Saussure, *Course in General Linguistics*, ed. Charles Balley and Albert Sechehaye, trans. Wade Baskin (New York: McGraw-Hill, 1966).
15. Jacques Derrida, *Of Grammatology*, trans. Gayatri Chakravorty Spivak (Baltimore: John Hopkins University Press, 1976).

16. Edward Said, "Movements and Migrations," *Culture and Imperialism* (New York: Vintage, 1993) 326–366.
17. Michael M. J. Fischer, "Ethnicity and the Post-Modern Arts of Memory," *Writing Culture: The Poetics and Politics of Ethnography*, ed. James Clifford and George E. Marcus (Berkeley: University of California Press, 1986) 194–233.
18. James Clifford, "Diasporas," *Routes: Travel and Translation in the Late Twentieth Century* (Cambridge, MA: Harvard University Press, 1997) 244–277.
19. Stuart Hall, "Cultural Identity and Diaspora," *Colonial Discourse and Post-Colonial Theory: A Reader*, ed. Patrick Williams and Laura Chrisman (New York: Columbia University Press, 1994) 392–403.
20. Gayle Greene, "Feminist Fiction and the Uses of Memory," *Journal of Women in Culture and Society* 16.2 (1991): 290–321.
21. The question purposefully echoes Lenin's—though the context of the interrogatory could not be more different at the beginning of the 21st century than at the beginning of the 20th. Whereas the Marxist leader was interested in praxis—the practical action that arose from theoretical considerations (art, propaganda, etc.)—the novelists we are dealing with accept no such distinction between the two fields. Their writing is their action; the form of their art is precisely that of its ability to affect the world politically. Cf. Lenin, *What Is To Be Done?* (New York: International, 1969).
22. Bill Ashcroft, Gareth Griffiths, and Helen Tiffin, *Key Concepts in Post Colonial Studies* (New York: Routledge, 1998) 219.
23. Madan Sarup, *An Introductory Guide to Post-Structuralism and Post-Modernism* (Athens: University of Georgia Press, 1993) 74.
24. Let us, for the sake of simplicity, call it a "post-structuralist impulse."
25. Aijaz Ahmad, *In Theory: Classes, Nations, Literatures* (London: Verso, 2000) 13.
26. Helen Tiffin, "Transformative Imaginaries," *From Commonwealth to Post-Colonial: Critical Essays*, ed. Anna Rutherford (Sydney, N.S.W.: Kangaroo, 1992) 429.
27. Rob Nixon, *London Calling: V. S. Naipaul. Postcolonial Mandarin* (Oxford, UK: Oxford University Press, 1992) 49.
28. Timothy Brennan, *Salman Rushdie and the Third World: Myths of the Nation* (New York: St. Martins, 1989) 26.
29. Gayatri Chakravorty Spivak, *A Critique of Postcolonial Reason: Toward a History of the Vanishing Present* (Cambridge, MA: Harvard University Press, 1999) 227.

CHAPTER 2

# SALMAN RUSHDIE AND THE REVOLUTIONARY PLAY OF DIFFERENCES

If we are to trace the trajectory of the exile, if we are to understand fully the nature of his or her transformations, deformations, delineations and the radical nature of his or her alterity, if we are, in short, to come to define the exile's nature, then we must understand that it is a nature nebulous and difficult to locate. For it is precisely the notion of *location* that we must interrogate. The location of the exile can be seen as the royal road to an understanding of who the exile is. At the beginning of Salman Rushdie's *The Satanic Verses*, the two exiles who are the novel's dual protagonists can be located up in the air, suspended by nothing except their bodies' struggle against gravity. They are not, as we are, safe in the understanding that their home is singular and their identity safely anchored to the ground, that who they are is guaranteed by the land in which they live. They are—literally translating the metaphorical state of all exiles—between lands, and it is this relative inability to locate themselves that becomes the central thrust of what exile means in Rushdie's work.

Salman Rusdie, one of the lauded novelists of the present day, has come to stand for all that is exemplary in the mastering of language and literary practice. Like Gabríel García Márquez and Jorges Luis Borges, Rushdie cements magical realism as one of the important generic forms of the latter part of the 20th century. His novels are "funambulistic"[1] in character, creating a potent and exhilarating admixture of languages and dialects; they skip precariously through fantastical and closely observed landscapes crossing cultures, religions, and philosophical paradigms. Through his use of a literary genre, Salman Rushdie has found a means of expressing the precarious position of the exiles and the nature of their attempts to create for themselves a niche in the world, their grasping for some kind of meaning. Gibreel Farishta of *The Satanic Verses*, before boarding the fateful plane flight I alluded to above, remarks that exiles are *"creatures of the air, Our roots in dreams And clouds, reborn in flight"* (13).

This is the understanding, demonstrated by his use of the fantastical and the mythic, that Rushdie brings to the condition of the exile. The exile cannot rely on roots—he or she settles only as a bird might. The exile must also have an integral understanding of a notion (prominent in the Hindu religion and given a general reality by Rushdie's writing) of reincarnation. The exile, at least in Rushdie's work, is not a singular person—rather he or she is constantly having to be reborn, constantly having to move on, is constantly looking forward (while also, necessarily looking back). This two faced-ness—the hope that faces forwards, the memory that faces back—is what characterizes the exiles, is what gives them their particular position and their particular power.

The two central characters of *The Satanic Verses*, Saladin Chamcha and Gibreel Farishta, represent between them two possible lines of development, two possible trajectories that an exiled person (they are both from India and both are about to drop down on English shores) might take. In Rushdie's novel, they re-make themselves and the world around them, and we see them both search avidly for some stable and singular sense of self. The drama (and by the novel's conclusion, the tragedy) of *The Satanic Verses* does not follow the classical dramatic structure of plot events—no external reversals or revelations here—but rather an internal drama of reconstruction. These reconstructions, these tales of resurrection can take two forms, either the one demonstrated by Saladin or the path that Gibreel takes: "One seeking to be transformed into the foreignness he admires, the other preferring, contemptuously, to transform" (426).

Let us examine Saladin's path first. The narrator, who, at least within the textual world of the novel, is God, tells us: "A man who sets out to make himself up is taking on the creator's role, according to one way of seeing things; he's unnatural… .[F]rom another angle you could see pathos in him, heroism in his struggle" (49). Both the unnatural act and the heroic struggle occur within Saladin, who, ever since he traveled to England to try and forge a career as an actor, has attempted to conform himself to what is expected of him. Actor that he is, he has tried to play the role of the Englishman; he has made himself in an Englishman's image. This attempt is taken so far that, when he returns to India as part of a theatre tour, he realizes that he has become estranged from the country of his birth, and desperately tries to reject all the possible claims (including the love of his father) that the country might have on him.

The desire of Saladin Chamcha (who changed his name from Salahudin to make it sound more English, more naturalized) is the desire of the exile to leave behind his homeland and to become completely and wholly a part of the new world to which he flies. When he has a dream of the plane's forthcoming destruction while flying home, he dismisses the vision, not because he doubts its truth, but because an *Englishman* would not think it true: "This was precisely the type of superstitious flummery he was leaving behind. He was a neat man in a buttoned suit heading for London" (74). The "neat man," the "buttoned suit"—the outward trappings of Saladin's newfound Englishness—become for him the expression and the limit of his subjectivity. He comes to understand his existential situation, his identity as an expression of his outside, his outer shell. That is why, when he begins to feel the transformative effects of the history he has tried to deny (he begins to turn into a goat-like creature), he goes to a mirror for confirmation—not of the skin that would betray his Indian heritage, but the fact that he is "buttoned" and "neat:" "Looking into the mirror at his altered face, Chamcha attempted to remind himself of himself. I am a neat man, he told the mirror, with a real history and a planned-out future" (135).

The notion of Saladin's identity is completely and inextricably tied to a notion of control; it is not Englishness per se that has made the enormous change in him—it is an idea of an English regimentation, an English rationality, that his Indian heritage seems to put in doubt. He has "a real history" and a "planned-out future;" in other words, he has control of the extents of his subjectivity, and he cannot allow into that control's certainty the possibility of doubt. We soon learn that Saladin's transformation into an Englishman was a concerted effort, a process of the will, an exercise in control. As a thirteen-year-old boy, he travels to an English boarding school and faces his first kipper—never having eaten anything like it before. He spends the best part of an hour eating it, and those around him, though aware of his discomfort, do nothing to help. Through nothing more than an act of the will, he eats the whole thing, bones and all. This—the novel leads us to understand—was the first step on the road to his assimilation, and it was from that moment that he understood the necessary means by which he would become what he wanted to be: "England was a peculiar-tasting smoked fish full of spikes and bones and nobody would ever tell him how to eat it" (44).

However, like the notion of the kipper on his plate, like the notion of England as a world that was run in a rational, controlled manner, the whole construction of his English self is based on fictions, a belief in the reality of a reified view of Englishness as propagated in novels and films. It is something that his wife saw (a wife he married because of her cut-glass accent and cool English looks) and which she came to resent in him: "Him and his Royal Family, you wouldn't believe. Cricket, the Houses of Parliament, the Queen. The place never stopped being a picture postcard to him" (175). It is precisely this reified, false representation of the world, this constructed landscape that begins to erode away after the explosion that blows him from the sky. Saladin, as exile, has to face up that his attempts to become English were constructed entirely out of a montage of fictional representations of an imaginary concept of "England;" he was, in the words of Michael Gorra, "desperately trying to write into being the self that one knows one can never fully achieve."[2]

This concept of "writing the self," by drawing on the creative fictions of an imagined country's origins, dovetails with contemporary theoretical notions of the fictional subject. It is exactly this self-creation that has occupied post-colonial existentialist thinkers from Frantz Fanon onwards. Fanon himself saw the colonial's need to form himself or herself in the shape of the colonial master as part of the originary oppression.[3] The black man cannot truly be a self. In a colonial system of power and violence, he is an object to be discussed and put to work. The only way that selfhood might be achieved in such a system is an attempt to deny the colour of one's skin, to form oneself in the shape of the colonial oppressor who, with the full force of Western discourse behind him or her, is able to claim full personhood. The attempt by Saladin to write himself into his own picture of postcard perfection, to build himself as an Englishman, is very much related to the colonial situation that was (supposedly) solved by Indian independence almost fifty years earlier. For it is still the case, even today, that the dominance of Western discourse provides the white Western European as the only model for a controlled and singular self.

This is certainly the case, and yet—and this important proviso is illustrated by the progress of Saladin Chamcha through Rushdie's novel—the attempt by the colonial subject to mimic Western Europeans also produces a schism in the very controlled singularity that the exile hoped to produce. Homi Bhabha in *The Location of Culture* has delineated this particularly subversive aspect of mimicry:

> Mimicry is, thus, the sign of a double articulation; a complex strategy of reform, regulation and discipline, which 'appropriates' the Other as it visualizes power. Mimicry is also the sign of the inappropriate, however, a difference or recalcitrance that coheres the dominant strategic function of colonial power, intensifies surveillance, and poses an immanent threat to both the 'normalized' knowledge and disciplinary powers.[4]

That is, as well as being the authoritarian control of the subject in an attempt to create a self that is more amenable to the operation of power in the colonial situation, the process of mimicry also provides a "double articulation." This second movement, the second twist, holds the subject up as a means of displacing power. For in the act of mimicry, the exile is able to make marked the difference within the subjectivity of the Western European. He holds up a cracked mirror to Western man that places in doubt the certainty of his closed-off self.

This is the threat that Saladin poses, and it is specifically this threat that must be neutralized by the intervention of the official representatives of authoritarianism, the "disciplinary powers" of the British police. Saladin is taken into police custody and begins to sprout horns and grow hair—he begins to become the Eastern devil of the racist Western imagination. This transformation, we are left in no doubt, is the work of the colonial gaze, the Western power to contort and disfigure reality. The manticore, whom Saladin meets in the facility to which the police take him, says that their monstrous forms stem from the fact that the British "describe us.... That's all. They have the power of description and we succumb to the pictures they construct" (168).

The battle that is taking place, a conflict that leaves its mark on Saladin and the other exiles who are physically transformed into monsters, is one between the forces of assimilation and othering. The exile wants to be like the people of his or her host country; the exile wants to be singular and complete. Conversely, the oppressive powers of Western discourse want the exile to be completely "Other" (the stereotype of the Oriental that Edward Said saw as the central tool of colonial power), [5] and in being entirely and completely "Other,"

Western discourse desires the same end product as the exile—that his or her subjectivity be singular and complete. In this confrontation of two wills, a difference begins to emerge—a difference that is not completely "Other" (as the Western discursive imagination would like) but rather a difference that invades the binary opposition between identity and "Other" and which, as we will see, has important political as well as theoretical consequences for both the exile and colonial power.

For now, however, it is enough that we understand that the exile's structural position is primarily one that attempts to bridge the differences that are inherent in his or her twin identity. It is a bridging that never quite succeeds. Once more to return to the example of Saladin, we see that the expression of difference, the impossibility of closing the self off into an unproblematic, centered English self, works through the power of language. For Saladin's great talent is that he is a wonderful vocal mimic: "He was the Man of a Thousand Voices and a Voice" (60). Yet, even in this area of his life of which, one might imagine, he has the utmost control, one can see the slow cracking of the self that exile creates. The English Saladin has perfectly rounded vowels, speaks the Queen's English, the English of the Queen for whom—as an Englishman—he has so much respect. However, on his return to India, he finds himself starting to use the accent and dialect of his old Indian self. A flight attendant wakes him, and he addresses her with his old Indian voice: "[h]ow had the past bubbled up in transmogrified vowels and vocab? What next? Would he take to putting coconut oil in his hair?" (34).

The notion of *bubbling up*, the idea that the English self is a top layer that lies above an originary and primary Indian self is one that is very pertinent to the post-colonial question and one that Edward Said seems to suggest when he sees the Oriental as an "underground self."[6] The old language is buried under the new. Another example of an exile struggling with language in *The Satanic Verses* is Hind Sufyan, the cook at the Shaandaar Café, who bemoans "Her language: obliged, now, to emit these alien sounds that made her tongue feel tired... ." As such, the mother tongue holds a very important place in an exile's understanding of her exile. Either it must be run from, repressed, quashed, and forgotten, or it is the irretrievable homeland. The mother tongue takes on the metaphorical aspect of the motherland—whether the forgotten paradise of the exile's dreams or the infernal hell to be escaped from, language and landscape are irrepressibly present. The difference within language constantly underlines the difference within the exile's self.

Another way that the operation of difference occurs within the subjectivity of the exile is through the process of memory and nostalgia. Just as language provides a link to the old world, a bridge to an "Other" that disrupts the new ground on which the exile has come ashore, so does the operation of memory that constantly pulls the exile back to his or her old homeland and old self. Although, again, Saladin tries to repress such a feeling, the call of certain symbolically important events—for example, the tree that his father pulls out of the ground in anger at him—serves, metaphorically, to provide a root to the old land. The operation of memory and nostalgia is not simply confined to Saladin. Again, if we take the example of Hind, we see that—like the loss of her mother tongue—she desperately misses the landscape of her native India: "Where now was the city she knew? Where the village of her youth, and the green waterways of her home?" (249).

This last example illustrates the precise place of nostalgia in the experience of the exile. There is something overtly romanticized about the picture Hind paints of the India of her youth (just as, one feels, the India which Saladin remembers is overly coloured by its negative connotations). The process of memory and nostalgia (as is made very clear in Rushdie's earlier novel *Midnight's Children*) is not a neutral process, the untainted restoration of the past. It is, in actuality, a process of construction and creation—the past is filtered through the desires, the dislikes, and the attitudes of the present. "*Nostalgia*" (a word that combines the Greek words for "pain" and "returning home") has been defined in reference to a national definition of "*home*." Yet, the return home is never simplistic; it is never a simple matter of return. It has many dimensions. For example, the concept's political nature has often been obscured even if *nostalgia* plays a central role in politics and political theory (see, e.g., *Imagined Communities* and *Blackface/White Noise*). Its importance in any political struggle, or in the personal struggles as exemplified by the characters in *The Satanic Verses*, is that nostalgia is open to change, distortion—it is an operation in the present, as well as in the past. The impossible position of the exile is represented by conflicting claims: an attempt at identity with the host country against a process of Othering by Western discourse, the mother tongue against the host language, and nostalgic remembering against forgetting. If we once more emphasize that Saladin "was the Man of a Thousand Voices and a Voice" (60), then it now seems less a commendation of his vocal abilities and more a realization of the multiple strands that make up his existence. He has many voices and many different linguistic, cultural, discursive levels, all working inside of him and despite his best efforts to disappear into the seeming solid form of the English gentleman, he cannot silence the discordant noise that these voices create. His passage through the novel is one of acceptance—not, as some critics have argued, of his Indianess, but of his status as an object that is multiple and radically open to change. He is neither English nor Indian, but—the natural state of the exile—an ambivalent hybrid of those two different lands.

Such a process is painful and includes a certain and necessary operation of violence. Saladin looks back on his youth, a time at which he embraced his multiplicity and (as a condition of his multiple self) his temporariness: "When he was young, he told her, each phase of his life, each self he tried on, had seemed reassuringly temporary. Now, however, change had begun to feel painful" (63). Rather than simply "trying on" the new lives and selves, Saladin has to go through a certain amount of pain, distress, disruption. This trauma provides both the tragic aspect of Rushdie's novel and its creative force. Out of the pain of two clashing forms of life, Rushdie plucks the narrative drive of his work and the particular generic form that he uses. It is from this clash that the originality and freshness of Rushdie's narrative voice derives. He is able to translate exilic modes into diasporic idioms of post-coloniality.[7]

However, this is not to say that Rushdie's story of exile is purely useful on an aesthetic level—that it can have no contact with the outside world or make an important intervention in the actual and historical reality of the post-colonial situation. To do more than simply present the situation, it must also make an intervention into the current political and social malaise. However, while social realism attempted to change prevailing social conditions by truthfully representing the world as it is, Rushdie's fiction makes its intervention in the area of language. Such a desire is given expression (albeit slightly satirically) in the image of the amateur poet, Jumpy Joshi, who dreams of writing love poetry that has real political importance. In one of his poems (cruelly read out and exposed to mockery by Hanif the solicitor), he takes the image of the "rivers of blood" from Enoch Powell's controversial 1968 speech on immigration, and attempts to twist it to his own ends: "Reclaim the metaphor, Jumpy Joshi had told himself. Turn it; make it a thing we can use" (186).

It is clear from *The Satanic Verses* that Rushdie considers language the battleground for the important conflicts that are central to the post-colonial situation. For language is the principal instrument of power (much as Foucault realized that it was necessary to return to the "archive" if one was to understand the formations of power that occupied the past). It is the power of language that Hanif possesses and that Jumpy Joshi cannot hope to control:

> Hanif was in perfect control of the language that mattered: sociological, socialistic, black-radical, anti-anti-anti-racist, demagogic, oratorical, sermonic: the vocabularies of power. (281)

Even though the exiles might be cut off from the "vocabularies of power" (as we have seen earlier, the original, weaker language will continue to betray the exiles, reminding them that the language they speak is not their own), there is a definite and inescapable potency in their speech. This potency comes from the multiple nature of the exiles, the fact that they are neither of one place nor another. Such a power—though it can be directed to frightening ends—resides in the Imam as described in one of Gibreel's dreams. The Imam is a shadowy figure, living in exile in London but understanding the full nature of his power: "Who is he? An exile... . Exile is a dream of glorious return. Exile is a vision of revolution... . It is an endless paradox: looking forward by always looking back" (205). This double glance—back to the old country and forward to a new one that might be formed—is the structure of the intervention that Rushdie's novels can make. It is a structure of revolution reminiscent of Walter Benjamin's description of messianic revolution, brought about by the angel of history:

> This is how one pictures the angel of history. His face is turned toward the past... . But a storm is blowing from Paradise; it has got caught in his wings with such violence that the angel can no longer close them. This storm irresistibly propels him into the future to which his back is turned.[8]

Almost as though there is an unintentional link, a coincidental collusion of images and metaphor pointing the way for us toward an understanding of precisely this historical and political importance of Rushdie works, Benjamin's image leads us to the angel at the center of Rushdie's story. For it is Gibreel Farishta—the second exile who provides the second narrative thread to *The Satanic Verses*—who best envisions the importance of the exile in terms of the political change he or she can wreak. For he is the one who, while Saladin hoped to be "transformed into the foreignness he admires," seeks to "transform" the discourse which, as a stranger he has entered into. In addition, like Benjamin's angel, he does so by looking backward and sweeping forward. He enables the transformation of the discourse of the land he has come to, not by projecting a future to be gained, but by strategically arranging the multiplicity of his competing pasts. Michael Seidel has said that the exile is one "who inhabits one place and remembers or projects the reality of another."[9] In Gibreel Farishta's case, he is projecting numerous competing realities, deforming and disfiguring them, rearranging them into a dizzying montage, all in an attempt to call into question the authority of what is "real."

As the angel of his namesake, Gibreel dreams numerous dreams: of his coming to the prophet Mahound, of his appearance to a modern day Imam, of leading a young girl, Ayesha, and her followers into the sea on pilgrimage. For a while, he and his lover Allie believe these dreams to be part of a mental disturbance, a symptom of schizophrenia. However, Gibreel comes to realize that his dreams do not mean that he is mad; they are a component of the world he is living in: "The doctors had been wrong, he now perceived, to treat him for schizophrenia; the splitting was not in him but in the universe" (35). The operation his dreams perform (and what Rushdie's novel does by presenting them in its particular way) is an opening up of certain authoritative discourses (particularly those of religion and Western secularism) to the play of differences. The characters of Gibreel's dreams—even those of Jahilia in the time of the prophet—are written in present-day vernacular English in a dizzying array of styles and philosophical viewpoints. Rushdie mixes the notions of the profane with the holy (which, of course, drew the fatwa from fundamentalist Islam) and calls into question secularist viewpoints by showing the limitations of Mirza Saeed Akhtar, who would not believe that the sea would open up for Ayesha's pilgrims.

That such a story could be seen as a threat to authoritarianism need only be measured by the reaction to the book by Islamists; its efficacy as a challenge to orthodoxy can be measured in the book burnings and the fatwa that still looms over Rushdie's life to this day. Indeed, almost as though Rushdie understood the power of his book, he placed at the center of it a clash of race and religion that can be seen to prefigure some of the demonstrations that were held following the novel's publication. The trouble is in London, and the violence is centered on the powerful effect that the twin figures of Saladin and Gibreel are having on the people whose dreams they infest. Young immigrants start buying devil horns and cheap neon halos, and Saladin's horned figure becomes a rallying point for immigrant discontent: "the image of the dream devil started catching on" (286). Indeed, whereas Saladin was described in the earlier part of the book as something less than real—the falseness of his English disguise coming to infect his entire being—now, in the form of the devil, he starts to gain a new existence, this time as a symbol: "Illegal migrant, outlaw king, foul criminal or race-hero, Saladin Chamcha was getting to be true" (288).

What Rushdie is describing, and the importance of the twin mythological figures of Saladin the devil and Gibreel the angel, is that the political possibilities of the exile are linked to the fictionality of the post-colonial situation. That is, Saladin only achieves reality when his humanity is telescoped into a fictional form. The social landscape, in Rushdie's view, is not formed from the factual or the actual, the material existence of people in the world. Rather, it is formed from the fictions that people believe about themselves, the religious ideas, the discursive principles, the *myths*. In short, the post-colonial battle is to be fought in the arena of fiction, and that mythological battle occurs in a novel that purposefully turns to mythology to invalidate the cool certainties of realism. In other words, the center of battle in which the exile finds himself is a battle over "question[s] of the subject and subjectivity [that] directly affect colonized peoples' perceptions of their identities and their capacities to resist the conditions of their domination, their 'subjection.'"[10]

The power of myth, then, has a potent affect on the passage of politics and ethics in the real world. That is why, in the later part of the novel, the power of myth begins to take over *The Satanic Verses* narrative, almost against the express wish of the novel's narrator. When speaking of the necessity of a final confrontation between Saladin and Gibreel, the narrator asks himself a rhetorical question. There must be some final showdown, "For are they not conjoined opposites, these two each man the other's shadow?" (441). The landscape of the novel turns into the landscape of myth, and the balance of the competing strands of discourse within the novel's bounds are in danger of being overcome by the mythic necessity that angels and devils *must* meet in a final encounter, absolute evil and absolute good *must*, in the end, fight it out for the soul of the world.

However, the position of the exile also makes this impossible, for the exile is he or she who rejects all totalizing systems, who, looking back and yet moving forward, stands for the power of difference. As such, Rushdie cannot have his novel end in the easy certainty of good against evil (and lurking behind it, the two-sided racial conflict between black and white, colonizer and colonized). Saladin, the devil, following another representative of pure evil, Shakespeare's Iago, poisons Gibreel against his lover Allie Cone through a campaign of anonymous phone calls—wanting to destroy, simply because it is his nature as the representative of evil. Gibreel chases Saladin through a city on fire at the onset of a race riot, and finally catches up to him at the Shaandaar Café, into which Saladin plunges in an attempt to save the proprietors who are trapped inside. This simple act of selflessness places the mythical side of the novel in danger. It invades the mythical component of the story with its opposite, the human factor. "It is possible that evil is never total, that its victory, no matter how overwhelming, is never absolute" (467).

While the structural position of the exile in the novel grafts the mysticism of the homeland (and particularly of the Islamic religion) onto the modern Western world, so the Western world's understanding of the variability of humanity invades the novel's mythical scaffold. The effect is to affirm again the ultimate rejection of binaries for the free play of difference. Saladin, hearing that his father is reaching the end of his life, is able to finally come to terms with his Indianess. More, even, than this, he comes to terms with the fact that he cannot ever be wholly English, or wholly Indian. Rather, he is like a plant he sees on television, a strange and wonderful hybrid that can exist in the soil of a different country: "If such a tree was possible, then so was he; he, too, could cohere, send down roots, survive" (406). He is able to come to terms with the fact that one subjectivity—in particular the subjectivity put under the splitting pressure of exile from a homeland—can encompass many selves and that these selves cannot be considered whole or inviolable. They must all be suspended in the air and negotiated, all in a partial state of existence to which his life provides a backdrop. "Saladin felt hourly close to many old, rejected selves, many alternative Saladins—or rather Salahuddins—which had split off from himself as he made his various life choices" (523).

As this ethic of openness and multiplicity—we might call it "the ethic of the exile"—is translated into a political stance, an understanding of the actual possibilities of migration in the world, and particularly in the post-colonial world, we see that there is no world view that can be privileged over another. There is nothing that is sacred, neither mysticism nor myth, neither the Islamic religion nor Western secularism. Migration, then, is not a process that occurs between the binary opposites of two worlds but rather the destruction of the past (through the memory of the past) and the creation of a new future. This is precisely how Salman Rushdie sees his own novel, which has attracted so much anger. The people who attack it, he says, are those who are frightened "that intermingling with a different culture will inevitably weaken and ruin their own" ("In Good Faith" 394). Rushdie, if he wanted, might go further: The ruination of single stable cultures is precisely the aim of his fiction.

The work of the exile, the constant intervention and deformation, the attempt to present a wall to the violence that discourse wreaks by including what is excluded and making uncertain what is sure, must continue apace, can never be completed. As the narrator of *The Satanic Verses* says: "nothing was forever; no cure, it appeared, was complete" (540). This central rule can be applied, perhaps even more cogently, to Rushdie's most successful and critically acclaimed novel, *Midnight's Children*. For—like Laurence Sterne's *Tristram Shandy*, to which it is much indebted—it makes a great virtue out of never being complete. What is more, it brings into even closer contact the operation of exile on the individual and the operation of exile on the exile's world. Woven into its very telling is how the fictions of identity and nationality, the mythical worlds of the past and the present can be deformed and displaced and made to work against any authoritarian view of history. It refuses, explicitly and voraciously, to countenance any of the grand narratives that have governed Eastern or Western civilization, taking the stance that Jean-François Lyotard has identified as focal to the postmodern condition.[11]

*Midnight's Children* is, ostensibly, the story of Saleem Sinai's life (Saleem is both the central character of the novel and its narrator). And though the narrative ranges across a number of years either side of that date, the moment of central importance to the novel is the very second of Indian independence, midnight on August 15, 1947. Precisely at this moment Saleem is born. For the rest of his life Saleem, living contemporaneously with the new state, finds that the fate of the country and his personal fate are inextricably interlinked and that, just as the letter written to him by the prime minister on the occasion of his birth suggests, he cannot escape from the hand of history that has been laid upon him. Through this twinning of individual to his homeland, Rushdie, rather paradoxically, explores the notion of exile and the impossibility of an individual ever fully being at home in the country to which he was born.

Although Saleem goes into exile in *Midnight's Children*, it is not the physical process of exile, as it was in *The Satanic Verses*, that precipitates the self-questioning that we saw in Saladin and Gibreel. Rather, Rushdie seems to suggest that the experience of exile—being trapped between a number of homelands, never really feeling whole or solid—begins in Saleem Sinai from the moment of his birth. This is not to say that Rushdie takes an ahistorical view of subjectivity, but rather that the strange historical circumstances of the new Indian state give rise to this strange ungrounded sense of the self. To understand this we must understand the strange movements in Indian history—the long period of colonialism and unrest that culminated in independence and Saleem's birth. Even in the homeland of India, the colonized were considered to be exiles, ruled as they were by an outside hand. For example, Saleem's father was secretly pleased to be turning white, for it made him feel more at home in his businessman persona: "…he was secretly rather pleased when they failed to explain the problem or prescribe a cure, because he had long envied the Europeans their pigmentation" (*Midnight's Children* 178).

India at the time of Saleem's birth was a new country in many ways. It lacked the sense of national identity that had grown up in other lands; it even was getting used to a new shape after the partitioning of Pakistan. In many ways, it was a country that had been completely constructed, created again—being formed by an outside hand. The novel often calls the country a "dream," and it is under these conditions that the subject has to negotiate his or her identity. It seems completely understandable that the response to such a country should be to believe that "you are forever other than you were" (237).

As such, the identity that Saleem tries to form can be compared to the identity formation of the exiles in *The Satanic Verses;* he has to construct himself in relation to an imaginary edifice—the notion of "India." His life is interlinked with the history of his nation, and he must construct himself in relation to ideas regarding that nation. As Saleem says, "Even a baby is faced with the problem of defining itself. ...I was bombarded with a confusing multiplicity of views on the subject..." (130). What this confusing "multiplicity of views" points toward is a construction of the self that is negotiated against a number of linguistic and discursive factors. In one way *Midnight's Children* can be seen as a blueprint of the way a subject—particularly one who leans on history to place itself in the world—both attempts to construct, and is forced to dissolve its sense of self.

Jacques Lacan, in his psychological work, states that the ideal existence of the subject, the Ideal-I, was actually a determination and construction of the big O, "the Other," as the sum of cultural and sociological systems, what he called "the symbolic realm." This realm's structure was primarily linguistic in nature, as it rested on the process of signification. In this way, the subject is determined both literally and metaphorically by the "letter."[12] In *Midnight's Children*, this notion is emphasized and given a specifically post-colonial light with the adherence of fate to the notion of naming. For example, the soldier Shaheed—whose name is translated by Rushdie as "martyr"—is destroyed by a flying pomegranate (in actuality a grenade), just as he had foretold. He had "finally earned his name" (377). Equally, Shiva (the destroyer) is finally the one who destroys Midnight's Children and robs them of their powers. In the words of Saleem himself: "Our names contain our fate, living as we do in a place where names have not acquired the meaninglessness of the West, and are still more than mere sounds, we are also the victims of our titles" (304).

The characters in the novel seem to have their fates written into them by the symbolic realm, the cultural process of signification; they seem to be victims of their socio-cultural backgrounds. However, *Midnight's Children* does not entirely follow the Lacanian notion that the symbolic realm entirely constitutes an individual. Subjects are not entirely constructed by their circumstances. Like Saladin of *The Satanic Verses*, there is a certain amount of will involved as Saleem creates his own subjectivity, not by denying his past, but by the creative orientation of the "facts" of his history.

Memory plays a large part in this process of creating subjectivity but not as it normally might in a narration of this kind. In the classical fictional memoir, memory is utilized to create and understand the subjectivity of the person remembering—the person is as he is because certain factors have shaped his past. However, in *Midnight's Children*, memory is a more active process. It does not only simply reveal past shaping influences on Saleem's life, but it also actively shapes his present subjectivity by creating a changed past. More than once, Saleem admits that he has changed the date of Gandhi's death, to suit his own narrative purposes. In other matters, he realizes that the chronology or precise factual information of what he says cannot be true—indeed, at one point he suggests that his nemesis Shiva has died, then admits moments later that he did so through nothing more than wishful thinking.

However, the effect of these misremembering flights of fancy and inaccuracies is not to invalidate the story that Saleem is telling. Rather, they are to claim a new truth-value for myth and memory. The unreliability of Saleem as narrator is an attempt to wrestle truth from its natural factual home and to create a new validity for the kind of reconstruction in which Saleem is partaking. He says,

> Memory's truth, because memory has its own special kind. It selects, eliminates, alters, exaggerates, minimizes, glorifies, and vilifies also; but in the end it creates its own

reality, its heterogeneous but usually coherent version of events. (211)

The subject, then, through the process of memory, changes his past in an attempt to create his present—to form what he is. And this, as Stuart Hall has pointed out in "Cultural Identity and Diaspora," is precisely what the immigrant is forced to do by the distance created between himself and the lands of which he can never truly be a part. Because he is not *of dry land*, he or she must find elsewhere to create a solid basis for his or her identity—and create a self—"through memory, fantasy, narrative, and myth."[13]

History, it could be said, provides Saleem's landscape. And it is the peculiar nature of Indian history that this landscape is prone to create numerous, multiple realities, that the confusion of the exile's groundlessness can occur in a country in which Saleem has always lived. What is more, Rushdie gives his central character a peculiar gift (the most important of all the gifts given to those children who were born during the hour of midnight on the day of Indian independence). Saleem is a telepath and, therefore, can read minds—he can even hear all the thoughts of his nation. This gift places Saleem in the center of the active and passive motions of history, locating him in an uncertain place in which he is not sure whether he is creating or simply receiving history:

> [T]he feeling had come upon me that I was somehow creating a world; that the thoughts I jumped inside were mine...I was somehow *making them happen*...which is to say, I had entered into the illusion of the artist, and thought of the multitudinous realities of the land as the raw unsharpened material of my gift." (174)

Here, Saleem pours scorn on his belief that he is creating the things that he sees, that the other times, he is quite sure that he is the creator and prime mover of history.

This, I feel, sets the terms of the particular historical dialectic that is operating in the text of *Midnight's Children*. The subject both creates and is created by the world and history in which he lives. He cannot see himself as merely the object of history, his fate laid out for him, as the soldier-martyr was tied fatefully to his name. Nor should he enter into "the illusion of the artist" that he is creating history and that, at its root, the world is within his power. Rather—and again, we see the inbetweenness associated with the exile—these two poles, the world and the subject, are in a continuous interplay of construction and deformation, constantly changing and remaking the other.

This dialectic, this shuttling to and fro, means one thing in terms of the stability and certainty of both subject and the world. They must both be considered fictions because their dialectical relationship to each other means that neither can fully be considered whole. This is precisely why both India and Saleem's body start to crack under the pressure of their twin relationship—the problems of India's history mirror the slow falling apart of Saleem's body. The cracks are caused by each pole's relationship with the other: Because Saleem creates history and history creates Saleem, neither can be considered real or at least anchored in factual reality. They are, instead, self-creating fictions. Saleem presents an excellent metaphor to explain the form that these fictions take:

> Suppose yourself in a large cinema, sitting at first in the back row, and gradually moving up, row by row, until your nose is almost pressed up against the screen...illusion dissolves, or rather, it becomes clear that the illusion itself is reality. (106)

The structure that Saleem is describing is that of the gaze—the interplay between he who looks and that which he looks at. This particular gaze is the gaze of the exile, that is, the gaze of the moving subject who can see the world from far away ("in the back row") and close-up ("until your nose is almost pressed up against the screen").

Both reality and the subject are invalidated by each other, then—they are both shown to be fictions. The subject is not whole or stable. And the landscape—and by landscape I mean the cultural context, the history, the sociological outlook—of India can be changed, reordered, reconstituted. In short, it is imaginary. However, this is not to say that these notions—of subject and landscape—do not have any worth. In fact, just like *The Satanic Verses*, *Midnight's Children* suggests that there are intensely important uses to which the dialectic of twin fictions (subject and landscape) can be put. As Rushdie points out, "Reality can have metaphorical content; that does not make it less real" (200). What is more, this metaphorical content can have real and important political results. A space that invalidates and places into question authoritative forms of truth can enable a freer way of seeing, a "rebellious discourse" that challenges "God, authority, and social law."[14] It can open up a space, a location, which is not reliant on national borders or a concept of the self, "a space beyond existing political, social, and cultural binaries."[15]

It is clear from *Midnight's Children* that the dialectic created between subject and landscape is enormously important to resistance and change. To understand its importance to Rushdie, one need only look at what occurs to Saleem when he absents himself from the difficult negotiation between history and self, when he becomes certain of (or, perhaps better, apathetic to) who he is and where he has come from. When Saleem and his family move to Pakistan, they, like many migrants, try to become one with their new country. "Saleem's parents said, 'We must all become new people'; in the land of the pure, purity became our ideal" (310). They attempt—like Saladin—to wipe away their pasts, to purify themselves of their history and identify with their new home. Saleem does not achieve this aim until the night that a bombing raid kills almost all his family and his mind is wiped clean when he is struck by flying debris: "I am empty and free, because all the Saleems go pouring out of me...wiped clean as a wooden writing chest, brained (just as prophesized) by my mother's silver spittoon" (343).

This "purity," which in actuality is amnesia, not only purges Saleem of all his memories but also of the multiplicity of selves that were held in suspension by his remembering ("all the Saleems go pouring out of me..."). By cutting himself off from the dialectical interplay between himself and his historical landscape, Saleem becomes for a time the single, unitary classical ideal of the self. He is one, singular and stable. He also becomes, however, the perfect soldier—fighting without reasoning over the morality or rectitude of his actions. He becomes the Buddha (the name recollecting the Buddhist ideal of kamma-niradha, an unbecoming), who does what he is told: "emptied of history, the buddha learned the art of submission, and did only what was required of him. To sum up: I became a citizen of Pakistan." The statement is less a broadside against the state of Pakistan—though Rushdie certainly does not shy away from the horrors inflicted on the soon-to-be Bangladesh—than a statement of distaste at the necessary violence of nationalism. The subject who enters into the painful and difficult dialectic with his landscape and his past as an exile cannot become a submissive citizen of any country; he is freed of the singularity that nationalism thrives upon. To forget history, to put a stop to the constant shuttling between an open subjectivity and an imaginary history, is to allow the efficacy of power to succeed. "The struggle of man against power is the struggle of memory against forgetting."[16]

While Saleem's forays into the connections between himself and Indian history may seem ahistorical (i.e., replete with fictions and inaccuracies, determined by subjective viewpoint), they are, in fact, actually making an extremely important intervention into the authoritative account of Indian history. For by stating that he, Saleem, a historically unimportant person (at least in the classical perspective) is actually the central driving force behind history, is to free history from its materialistic bounds. For materialism, just like nationalism and religious fundamentalism, is a discourse that is singular, that will not allow a multiplicity of viewpoints and realities. Saleem's intervention states that any exile has a claim to state the truth of history, that anybody is central to the world and can claim reality for himself. Rushdie's narrator frees people to be like the magicians who "were people whose hold on reality was absolute, they gripped it so powerfully that they could bend it every which way in the service of their arts, but they never forgot what it was" (399).

Saleem's writing of history—and his acceptance of history's writing of him—overturns the usual place of the book as the means of authority and oppression. Homi Bhabha has pointed out that the book is the "measure of mimesis and mode of civil authority and order."[17] However, by making an intervention into language— through his use of puns, linguistic tricks, literary connections, and purely phonetic connections—Saleem and behind him, Salman Rushdie, claim the medium of writing for the forces of multiplicity, openness, and the freedom of play. In this way, his intervention can be considered particularly postmodern, in the sense that Lyotard used the word. But, unlike the dominant part of postmodernism, there is a politics central to *Midnight's Children*, despite the fact that it is not a politics in the usual mode, nor is its primary aim the freedom of peoples from physical tyranny. Rather, its attempt is textual, following the understanding (one that has been current in theoretical accounts ever since Foucault expounded his theory of discursive power) that the mode of the production of tyranny, the very basis that makes tyranny possibly, is an authoritarianism of the sign and not of the sword.

What, precisely, is the distinction between a politics of the sign and one of the sword? And how can we face criticisms such as those made by Aijaz Ahmad that Rushdie's prose is "occupied so entirely by Power that there is no space left for either resistance or its representation"?[18] The answer to this question can be found in the figure of Shiva, the child with whom Saleem was swapped at birth and who fulfills the role of his nemesis throughout the novel. If Saleem is interested in creating a discussion, a free interchange of ideas by setting up the conferences of Midnight's Children using his telepathic powers, then Shiva is interested only in the material "realities" as he sees them: "No, little rich boy; there is no third principle; there is only money-and-poverty, and have-and-lack, and right-and-left, there is only me-against-the-world! The world is no place for dreamers or their dreams" (255). In a way, Shiva's statement could easily be a representation of the Marxist position as critics such as Ahmad have put forward: "The world can be separated between the oppressors and the oppressed, monied and poor, colonizer and colonized; the textual answer is just a dream." Yet, by the end of the novel, Shiva has become a tool of the state and brings about the destruction of Midnight's Children, as well as the state of emergency that is tatamount to a dictatorship.

Shiva's turn to oppression, *Midnight's Children* seems to suggest, is based upon his initial system of belief, which itself was based wholly on the binaries that were present in his speech as a child. Likewise, the materialist base of Marxist criticism that relies on the separation of victimizer and victim, rich and poor, colonized and colonizer, and so on—is actually built upon the possibility of that power that it tries to defeat. Ahmad's criticism of Rushdie could well be the criticism that Shiva put forward: His novels are just dreams and "the world is no place for dreamers and their dreams." But Rushdie's "dreams" can only be opposed to a world that does not accept mutability, multiplicity, and openness. Passed through the filter of dreams, the world becomes a space in which not only oppression but also the means of oppression can be combated. Rushdie's dream worlds present a space in which history can be put to the ends of those who need it—in which it can be used strategically and where it can overflow the boundaries put on it by authoritarianism of all colours. It is a place, however, as Marlene Nourbese Philip remarks in *She Tries Her Tongue, Her Silence Softly Breaks*: "the historical realities are not erased or obliterated."[19]

The importance of Rushdie's fiction then is its openness, its multivocal quality that refrains from positing one set vision of the world and in fact, erodes all possible viewpoints. "There have always been many voices in Rushdie's novels, a multitude of spoken perspectives,"[20] Jacqueline Bardolph writes in her essay on Rushdie, "Language is Courage." The narrator of *Midnight's Children* is not one voice, but thousands of voices ("as many voices as flowed through him in his midnight meetings in which the Children of Midnight all spoke together"). Discursive singularity is impossible. Each subject is, like those meetings, "a sort of many-headed monster, speaking in the myriad tongues of Babel…the very essence of multiplicity"

(229). This is the nature of exile—whether like Saladin and Gibreel, the nature of the exile is a physical dislocation from one's country or, like Saleem, the exile can be seen as arising out of an uncertain relationship to history and the country of one's birth—to question the singularity of the subject and certainty in the world. As the cracks start to spread over Saleem's body at the end of *Midnight's Children*, he says: "I have been so—many too—many persons, life unlike syntax allows one more than three, and at last somewhere the striking of a clock, twelve chimes, release" (462). The multiplicity of Saleem's life has tired his soul and cracked his body, but is a condition that is presented as necessary, and even politically positive. As Stuart Hall has said, "Identity is at the end, not the beginning, of the paradigm."[21]

However, even at the end of *Midnight's Children*, there is not the notion that there has been reconciliation or a resolution. The ending is like a suspended cadence, closing the work but suggesting a continuation beyond it. For it is a life story that seemed as though it would never have an ending, circling back as it did, looking over known facts in a different way, changing dates and realigning happenings. And in a way, the novel suggests the story never will be done. For through the extreme power of his smell, Saleem managed to distill his story into thirty jars of pickle that he will send out to be eaten across the subcontinent. His tales will be masticated, swallowed, digested, regurgitated; they will go on changing and re-aligning in a truly visceral manner. This is very much in keeping with Saleem's notion of the openness and multiplicity of telling his story. He says late on in the novel, realizing his impending death, "The process of revision should be constant and endless; don't think I'm satisfied with what I've done!" (460). Saleem's approach to history is that it should never be allowed to settle into forms that might become reified. Following the necessary course of the exile, history should be gone over, revised, changed and reordered, freeing all the possibilities it contains.

Salman Rushdie, then, in these two novels, has attempted to chart the process of the exile, both the process that transforms and deforms a notion of self, and to understand the dialectic which the exile enters into with his history and his landscape. He writes, in the words of the literary critic Roland Barthes, "outside the sentence,"[22] from the outside, the margins, on the edge. From that position of marginality, he is able to invade the center of authoritative discourse. He juxtaposes, places in a montage, upsets, deforms, and dehabilitates modes of thought that were once thought static and stable. He also understands that his fiction can provide an intervention; for as he explains in "Imaginary Homelands," the migrant writers have a "double perspective" (19): They are both insiders and outsiders in the worlds they describe. Rushdie believes that redescribing the world is a necessary first step to changing it (14). It is from this double position—a double that does not provide a binary, but continues doubling, duplicating, displacing until the multiplicity reaches numbers that are unthinkable (in his opinion, any number over 1,001)—that he can chart the movements of the exile and utilize the exile's strange power.

## Endnotes

1. W. B. Fleischman, ed., *Encyclopaedia of World Literature in the 20th Century* (London: Ungar, 1967) 723.
2. Michael Gorra, *After Empire: Scott, Naipaul, Rushdie* (Chicago: University of Chicago Press, 1997).
3. Frantz Fanon, *Black Skin, White Masks*, trans. Charles Lam Markmann (London: Pluto, 1986).
4. Homi K. Bhabha, *The Location of Culture* (London: Routledge, 1994) 86.
5. Edward Said, *Orientalism* (New York: Vintage, 1978).
6. Said 4–5.
7. For a more extended discussion of the issue, see Nico Israel, *Outlandish: Writing between Exile and Diaspora* (Stanford, CA: Stanford University Press, 2000).
8. Walter Benjamin, *Illuminations*, trans. Harry Zohn (London: Collins, 1973) 259–260.
9. Michael Seidel, *Exile and the Narrative Imagination* (New Haven, CT: Yale University Press, 1986) x.
10. Bill Ashcroft, Gareth Griffiths, and Helen Tiffin, *Key Concepts in Post-Colonial Studies* (New York: Routledge, 1998) 219.
11. Jean-François Lyotard, *The Postmodern Condition* (Minneapolis: University of Minnesota Press, 1984).
12. Jacques Lacan, *The Four Fundamental Concepts of Psychoanalysis* (New York: Norton, 1978).
13. Stuart Hall, "Cultural Identity and Diaspora," *Colonial Discourse and Post-Colonial Theory: A Reader*, ed. Patrick Williams and Laura Chrisman (New York: Columbia University Press, 1994) 392– 403.
14. Julia Kristeva, *Strangers to Ourselves*, trans. Leon S. Roudiez (New York: Hill, 1972) 78–79.
15. Roger Bromley, *Narratives for a New Belonging: Diasporic Cultural Fictions* (Edinburgh: Edinburgh University Press, 2000) 3.
16. Milan Kundera, qtd. in Rushdie, Salman, *Imaginary Homelands: Essays and Criticisms 1981–1991.* (London: Granta, 1991) 14.
17. Homi Bhabha, "Signs Taken for Wonders," *The Post-Colonial Studies Reader*, ed. Bill Ashcroft, Gareth Griffiths, and Helen Tiffin (London: Routledge, 1995) 32.

18. Aijaz Ahmad, *In Theory: Classes, Nations, Literatures* (London: Verso, 1992) 208.
19. Marlene Nourbese Philip, *She Tries Her Tongue, Her Silence Softly Breaks* (London: Women's Press, 1993) 85.
20. Jacqueline Bardolph, "Language Is Courage," *Reading Rushdie* (Amsterdam: Rodopi, 1994) 210.
21. Stuart Hall, "The Question of Cultural Identity," *Modernity and Its Future*, ed. Stuart Hall (Cambridge, UK: Polity, 1992) 291.
22. Roland Barthes, *The Pleasure of the Text*, trans. R. Miller (New York: Cape, 1976) 47.

CHAPTER 3

# BHARATI MUKHERJEE AND THE EXILE'S CONSTANT SHUTTLING

Who is the exile? And by what process does the exile—as symbol, as metaphor—come from his or her position on the margins to inhabit, dislocate, and make uncertain a previously sure center (all the while remaining on the periphery)? The exile holds, by the word's very definition, a peripheral place, neither truly at home in his or her homeland, nor truly a native of the newly achieved shore. The exile gains acceptance in the new land while remaining inescapably "Other." The exile may play many roles, inhabit many parts, and be the sum of many different cultures. In this radical alterity and diffuseness, the exile leads us to question the notion of our own singularity and wholeness. The exile, although a part of his or her new land, remains exterior to it and never fully integrated into it. From this singular position (situated both on the outside and on the inside), the exile casts in question the very notion of the boundary.

Bharati Mukherjee's fiction captures precisely the radical nature of exile, the effects exile has on the individual, and more importantly, the effects that the notion of exile has on our beliefs about our own lives: the certainty of our identities, the functions of our memories, our convictions about our own and "the Other's," as well as others' cultures. Julia Kristeva views "writing [as] impossible without some kind of exile."[1] This is certainly the case with Mukherjee's writing, which is based on the very principle and structure of exile, its alterity, its division.

*Jasmine*, "Mukherjee's most popularly read novel,"[2] stemming from an earlier plot from the author's *The Middleman and Other Stories* (1988), entered the literary landscape in 1989, the same year as Salmon Rushdie's *Satanic Verses. Jasmine* is set mainly in the 70s and 80s (with movements back and forth on the axis of time, for better character enhancement and fluidity of plot) when the violent separatist demands of the militant Sikhs forced many Hindus to migrate from Punjab. The novel is structured around the life of its narrator (who, for reasons that will become apparent later, will for the moment remain nameless), an adolescent Hindu widow who uproots herself from the familiar and travels from Hasnapur, India, to America, in search of a new life and identity. The novel is not a conventional narration of a life (many literary works have taken autobiography as their formal model), but is told through the prism of the narrator's memory and from her present location in the American Midwest. Furthermore, though it is very much an account of the events that have happened to the main character of the novel, Mukherjee's work is also an account of the myriad cultural influences that have gone to make the heroine who she is, and through the main character, the novel becomes the embodiment of the story of exile itself:

> We are the outcasts and deportees, strange pilgrims visiting outlandish shrines, landing at the end of tarmacs. ...We ask only one thing: to be allowed to land; to pass through; to continue...I phantom my way through three continents. (101)

The narrator "phantoms" her way through the continent; that is, she can never consider herself a full, fleshly presence. The question posed is one of self-formation: What, precisely, makes the narrator who she is, and why can she not achieve wholeness? The narrator's journey takes her from the small Indian village in which she grew up, through the big city of Jullundhar after she marries an engineer called Prakash, across the seas to the United States after his death, into the home of a Punjabi academic, and then into the home of a Western couple, before she runs away to her present home with a banker in Iowa. Each setting, each stage in the narrator's journey, stands as an index to a new cultural setting, a new possible "homeland" for the exile to settle in, to try to identify with. It is against the background of these homes and these landscapes that the central character constructs a series of ambivalent subjectivities by which she can attempt to feel at home.

The novel emphasizes the cultural differences between all these homelands (no matter what country they might be in) and does not homogenize the differences between them. "India" and "the West" are not the sole binary with which the main character deals: Her Indian village is very different from Jullundhar; and Professorji's America is not the same as Bud Ripplemeyer's. Put in Lacanian terms, each "India" and each "America" has its own unique symbolic Order, and each lays its traces within the imaginary unity that the narrator seeks. This is not to say that Mukherjee's novel entirely rejects the Indian/Western dichotomy that characterizes a great deal of post-colonial literature and theory, but rather that it is aware of the complications and contradictions that remain within that dichotomy. Throughout her new life in America, the narrator is constantly perceived as "the Other," as the incarnation of the colonial stereotype of the female native. Because of this exoticism, her American husband is at first attracted to her: "Bud courts me because I am alien. I am darkness, mystery, inscrutability" (200). Similarly, she knows: "I rejuvenate him simply by being who I am" (200), and "I'm less than half his age, and very foreign" (7). It is the fascination with "the Other" that creates the constant interrogation of gender relationships in the novel:

"You were glamour, something unattainable" (199). Even when it is not a question of fulfilling the stereotype of her own ethnicity, the narrator is trapped within the darkness of her skin. The farmers of Baden "want to make me familiar" (33) precisely as a reaction to her alienness, as a defense against the danger posed by her foreignness. "Educated people" (with their liberal stake in multiculturalism) "are interested in differences" (33).

In either case, however, the truth of the narrator's being cannot be reached outside of the Indian/Western dichotomy. As Frantz Fanon points out in his study of the psychology of colonialism, "Ontology ...does not permit us to understand the being of the black man. For not only must the black man be black; he must be black in relation to the white man."[3] No matter what the differences in the cultural milieus in which the narrator comes to create herself (even while she is in India), it is always within relation to the foreign shore, the West. No matter which cultural surroundings she finds herself in, the narrator attempts to re-inscribe herself in the social order, to become one with the new homeland in which she finds herself. In the modern parlance of identity politics, she does her best to *assimilate* and in doing so, dissolve the vestiges of her old self. She learns to walk, move her hips, and mount escalators like a Westerner in order to avoid detection when she is living as an illegal alien with Lilian Gordon. Similarly, when Wylie asks her whether she has a problem with the microwave, she replies, "I don't have a thing about radiation" (169), despite the fact that she does not know what radiation is. These outward shows and mimicking of Western behavior come to have an interior, affective result on who she considers herself to be. "I couldn't tell if with the Hasnapuri sidle, I'd also abandoned my Hasnapuri modesty" (133). This is precisely how those proponents of assimilation expect the neutralization of ethnic identity to proceed in the well-behaved immigrant: first the adoption of the ways of Western living, followed by the adoption of their values.

However—and this is the double bind of the exile—as well as mimicking the host culture, the narrator also feels the need to partake in a double mimicry, that is, to mimic herself as the West would have her be seen. This is demonstrated most clearly by the interview Jasmine has with Mary Webb, who believes that in a previous life she was an Australian aboriginal. Although highly ambivalent toward the notion of reincarnation, the narrator feels the need to play the part of the committed Hindu, the mystic from the East: "I tell her that yes, I am sure that I have been reborn several times, and that yes, some lives I can recall vividly" (126). In this particular example of mimicry—in this doubling of the imago, the acting out of a stereotype within a stereotype, which creates a subjectivity for the central character much like that of a Chinese box—we also see the element of subversion that can exist in such mimicry. As can be seen in the mimicry of some of Salman Rushdie's migrant characters and as has been pointed out by Homi Bhabha, such repetition of the dominant stereotypes inscribed in a culture can become a mocking of that culture's discourse, can become a concrete position from which to attack that discourse. This is certainly the case in the trepidation caused in both Half-face and Bud, both of whom are disconcerted by the central character's ability to perform the part of the Westerner (and both of whom also find such a performance sexually stimulating). However, Mukherjee pushes this dynamic one step further than Rushdie (and also goes further than Bhabha's theoretical analysis) by illustrating the subversive power of the migrant playing a stereotype of the dominant culture. The scene involving Mary Webb is, more than anything else, a set piece of satirical writing. Mary Webb's pretensions are being laid out for ridicule, her easy acceptance of the mysticism of the Indian and its dismissal of the possibility of secular values having penetrated the religious subcontinent. The thing that crowns the satirical moment, however, is the central character's acceptance of the stereotype. For by playing the part that Mary Webb has eked out for her, she is exposing it as merely a part, a role, a lifeless stereotype with no depth.

Subversion is not the central character's central reason for utilizing mimicry and playing out the dominant discourse's stereotypes on arriving in the United States. Rather, it is a tool for survival, a means of surviving the reality of her exile. These central tenets—mimicry and acceptance of the stereotype of the "Indian woman"—are the two methods by which the narrator of *Jasmine* attempts to balance the precarious nature of her subjectivity. They are the methods by which each transformation of her identity is accomplished, how each incarnation of her as a woman, as an exile, is born unto the world. I have refrained from giving "the narrator" a more concrete denomination up to this point precisely because of the dynamic of rebirth at work throughout the novel, which gives the narrator a new name each time she is "reborn" into a new cultural incarnation. She is born and lives her early life in the village as "Jyoti," and then, when she is married to Prakash, he calls her "Jasmine" because "he wanted to break down the Jyoti I'd been in Hasnapur and make me a new kind of city woman" (77). These new names are far from arbitrarily imposed. They are names that not only inscribe the exchange of selfhood that has occurred; they also inscribe the narrator securely into the Symbolic Order of the culture she is entering. She marries Bud, who calls her "Jane," an Anglicization (and neutering) of her original Indian name.

> Bud calls me Jane. Me Bud, you Jane. I didn't get it at first. He kids. Calamity Jane. Jane as in Jane Russell, not Jane as in Plain Jane. But Jane is all I want to be. Plain Jane is a role, like any other. My genuine foreignness frightens him. I don't hold that against him. It frightens me, too. (26)

"In Baden, I am Jane. Almost" (26). The referencing of the staples of American popular culture—Tarzan and the movie actress Jane Russell and even the folksy reference to "Plain Jane"—place the narrator's new name in a symbolic chain that links and binds her subjectivity into an American cultural matrix. "Jane"—the very prosaic nature of the name makes it both desirable and detestable to *Jasmine's* central character (who has recently, of course, been the much more exotic Jasme). Its Anglicization is an attempt to make the central character safe, to inscribe her into the dominant culture, to domesticate her and render her foreignness less dangerous. Yet, at the same time, the very English name points out the ambivalence that manifests itself as an unstoppable shuttling. The outward show—Jasmine's darkness, her past—is alien and in contradiction to the safety of her name. In this opposition lies the contradiction that severs the links that might have kept her whole. She enters into the "role" and consciously takes on a new identity, but this identity is anything but secure.

Of course, there is something more to this naming compulsion, the insistence of imprisoning the subject in a name that inscribes him or her into the common cultural stock. In every instance the narrator takes on a new name, a man gives it to her—the man both names her and brings her into the world in which he is already a native. Prakash calls her "Jasmine," Bud calls her "Jane," and Taylor calls her "Jase," each one naming the woman he wants her to be. What is more, there is something particularly gender biased toward a number of the constructions that these various names create. "Jase," for example, the exotic and carefree woman that Taylor falls in love with, "was a woman who bought herself spangled heels and silk chartreuse pants" (176). It is no surprise that "Jane," after a disgruntled farmer shoots her husband, is the kind of woman who will submerge her own desires so as to look after her injured spouse. Even the one name that is not chosen by her man (her first name, "Jyoti," which is given to her by her grandmother) is bestowed on her by a representative of the old patriarchal Punjabi tradition, her grandmother, who tries to prevent her from continuing her schooling and is shocked by the fact that "Jyoti/Jasmine" wishes to move away to the city.

What seems to overarch the cultural differences that separate the different names the narrator uses and the different cultural selves that those names differentiate is a patriarchal system of control—one that is current in all cultures, a masculine colonialism that stands over and above all the other hegemonic discourses of race or color. Can we say, then, that Mukherjee's text falls into the trap that, according to postcolonial theory, many recent feminists texts have done, of producing "the 'Third World Woman' as a singular monolithic subject?"[4] That is, has Mukherjee used the female's subjection by masculinity as a transcendental signified and by doing so homogenized the cultural differences that separate "Western" and "Indian" women?

I think not and for two reasons. The first is that to see patriarchy as a single and homogeneous entity in the novel would, in itself, be a reduction of the varied ways in which masculinity exerts its influence over the narrator. We cannot consider the rapist Half-face, using all the violence and might available to a man in relation to a woman, the same as Prakesh, who produces an identity for the narrator with all the force that Half-face does but with none of the attendant violence. If anything, the similarity in the *position* of the man—as the namer and inductor of the narrator into new worlds—only underlines the difference of *function* that the man performs, how culturally different each individual man is from his counterpart in other worlds. Second, we cannot consider a patriarchal system the central means of operation in the narrator's various identity formations because of the role played by the narrator herself. Thus far, we have considered the narrator's creation of new identities—her assimilation and objectification and the new names that induct her into the social order of whichever culture—as being a question of outside agency, of an aggressive force perpetrated by a cultural imperialism on the body and soul of the exile. However, the orientation of *Jasmine's* narrator is such that she is an active force in reforming herself in the shape of the culture into which she enters (and also in interrupting and deforming that culture's discourse). She says of her relationship with Taylor that he "did want to change me. He didn't want to scour and sanitize the foreignness. My being different from Wylie or Kate didn't scare him. I changed because I wanted to" (185). Here the exile's assimilation and difference is wielded by the exile herself. Her new identity is self-born and self-created, actually in opposition to the culture she has entered into (in this case, an Academic, Western liberal culture, which purposefully *imposes* on the exile a difference and desires the exotic, "the Other").

In terms of post-colonial theory, this is an interesting move in a different direction for the notion of identity formation of "the Other" of Western discourse. In most post-colonial theorizing of the last 30 years or so, what has been stressed is the construction of "the Other" by the colonizing discourse. From Said in his *Orientalism*[5] to the more recent writings by Homi Bhabha,[6] the question concerns how the West constructs the Oriental or the colonized African. There is not much question of agency, of an ethics, that attends the theory or what the Marxists might call a *praxis*. There has been consideration of ethnicity and race, mainly by those working within ex-colonies. For example, Senghor spoke of the notion of "Negritude": "Negritude is nothing more or less than what some English-speaking Africans have called *the African personality*."[7] This "African personality" was a humanism that may be placed in opposition to the colonizing discourse of the West. Fanon, on the other hand, in a piece more practical than his theoretical work, states that "the historical necessity in which the men of African culture find themselves to racialize their claims and to speak more of African culture than of national culture will tend to lead them up a blind alley."[8] Both suggest, like Cabral,[9] that the colonized is a fighter who must use culture as a weapon. The suggestion is that the identity, whether racial or national, most suited to interrupting the dominance of Western discourse over a colonized "Other" would be static, singular, and at home. Whereas assimilation, the negating of this "at home" identity, to a myriad of identities drawn from the discourse of the Western "Other," would most probably be considered a betrayal, a collaboration. However, it is precisely this course that Mukherjee seems to be positing as a positive means of acting in the world. She puts forth assimilation, mimicry, and even collaboration as the components of an ethics of exile.

Bharati Mukerjee is a naturalized American citizen and has been in the country since 1961. She neither rejects the term "Asian-American" to describe herself, nor is she happy being called an Indian writer. She sees herself as an American writer, albeit of Bengali origin. However, despite these declarations, it would not be either correct to consider her merely someone who has assimilated uncritically a Western position (for she has been accused of "race treachery") or, which has also been claimed, to see her as mainly pitting anationalism of her new country, America, against the nationalism of the post-colonial world. America is not an identity so much as a place to re-enact transfigurations of her identity. The reason she came to the United States was that she "desired 'America,' which to [her] is the stage for the drama of self-transformation."[10] This is something different, a third term that falls between the binaries constituting cultural identity with the West and cultural identity with the Asiatic "Other." Rather, she chooses "America" as a staging post in a series of transformations that are not static (as those binary opposites are) but enacted as a drama in continual motion. As Brennan says of Salman Rushdie, Mukherjee, too, presents a "defiant challenge to traditional ways of conceiving the 'national.'"[11] The inverted commas enclosing "America" point in this direction. America is not merely a single, static edifice, but a shifting, incomplete staging post as much to be altered by the process of self-transformation as effecting it.

The emphasis on the agency of the individual in the ethics of the exile, which develops out of Mukherjee's *Jasmine,* should, at this point, be further examined. In the above quotation, the emphasis is placed firmly on the I—"*I* desired 'America,'"—suggesting that Mukherjee, her narrator, and any subject are separate from and above the identity that they create for themselves out of the detritus of culture. This was the way that Said thought of the subject in *Orientalism*. Although he followed Foucault in many of his observations on the nature of the discourse that constructed the Orient and the Oriental, he could not follow Foucault to the radical limit of the French theorist's conception of discourse and the subject. Foucault saw the subject as the product of discourses, merely another apparatus of power, discourse coming before and creating the notion of subjectivity. Said was too much of a humanist to take his theory of Orientalism to this extent: "Yet unlike Michel Foucault, to whose work I am greatly indebted, I do believe in the determining imprint of individual writers upon the otherwise anonymous collective body of texts constituting a discursive formation like Orientalism."[12]

The individual writer *can* influence discourse, can choose to intervene. There is the suspicion in Said's work (a suspicion which also can be leveled at Foucault in some of his most political works and interviews)[12] that there is a subject beneath the discursive formation of Orientalism to be saved, to be unearthed, an individual outside and above the discourse who creates his or her identity. Although this sometimes seems the model of subjectivity that *Jasmine* sets out, I would argue that Mukherjee is not actually proposing a subject capable of agency outside the discourse that forms her and that "self-transformation" is a more complex term than might be first thought.

Mukherjee's narrator puts forth two notions of subjectivity in the exile—demonstrated in the novel by the narrator and Du. "My transformation," the narrator says, "was genetic, Du's was hyphenated" (222). Both are particular strategies of identity that arise in response to the condition of exile. Du is a refugee, a Vietnamese boy whom the narrator and Bud adopted and throughout the novel, whom the narrator sees as having an experience similar to her own: He is a foreigner in a strange land; he has felt the need to fit in. However, unlike the narrator, he has been able to balance the two sides of his identification, Vietnamese-American and has been able to hold on to two different identities, two different roles. In many ways, Du seems to be the perfect American: good at school, with perfect English, and an engineer. But he can easily leave behind his American self (deciding to return to his Vietnamese sister in Los Angeles) with the same ease as an actor might have coming out of character. In this conception of identity (one similar to Said's), there seems to be a Du beneath the formation of an American identity—an original, primary Du—still existing beneath the American identity he has put on like the duffel coat the narrator buys him when he first comes to America. But this is not the case with the narrator, whose various cultural identities cannot be suspended, as Du's are, but are contributive to her very being. "Plain Jane" may be a role, but it is a role without an actor; it is as much a part of her as Jyoti was and remains to be. There is no solid identity or subject outside of the roles the narrator plays.

These two different kinds of existences, the hyphenated and the genetic, have—each in its own way—a considerable effect on the ethics of exile and on the nature of the individual's subjectivity. They both have very different conditions, and both present a different possibility for subversion of the dominant discourse. In the case of Du, the ability to resist the dominant discourse is based simply on his ability to adapt and in the end, to move on. And this is precisely what he does in the novel when he finds himself unhappy with his life with the Ripplemayers. This is also the political stance that many nationalists from ex-colonial countries take: To thy own self be true; return to your natural home. However, in the final analysis, hyphenation might be able to rid a country of its colonial masters, but it will not be able to make a meaningful intervention in the underlying authoritarian discourse that makes colonialism possible. Hyphenation, in the political sphere, will lead only to one master being replaced by another.

The central character's genetic transformation presents an entirely different possibility for resistance and subversion—despite the fact that it immediately presents itself as assimilation or collaboration. The changes within her are "genetic," meaning they are ingrained into her being. The character, thus, cannot shrug off the roles she plays because those roles constitute who she is. By playing out the stereotypes of the dominant culture, by inhabiting the matrices of their discourse, the central character of *Jasmine* is able to question them from the inside. Through her many character roles, what is put in doubt is not simply one particular cultural milieu (in the way that Du's return to his Vietnamese roots questions the American dream), but the notion of a singular identity and a singular discourse generally. Du's transformation only perpetuates the illusion of wholeness, the narrator's slipping between roles and vanishing between them, and presents an actual possibility for an ethics.

This is the reason why, throughout *Jasmine*, the narrator's different identities are figured as ghosts or spirits and why it is important that the novel takes the form of someone looking back, placing memory as its organizing principle. Very early on, before the reader is introduced to the narrator's story, Jasmine sees that "in the white lamp light, ghosts float towards me. Jane, Jasmine, Jyoti" (21). These are ghosts because they are partial beings, partly dead (the narrator having moved on), partly still alive (still active in the formation of who she is), none of which solidified into the narrator's "self." Nor do these ghosts follow each other in natural succession: The narrator is Jyoti, then she is Jasmine, then Jasme, and then Jane. Rather, each of these ghosts interacts with the others. Even the narrator's latest reincarnation (Jane) can inform the first (Jyoti): "My grandmother may have named me Jyoti, Light, but in surviving I was already Jane, a fighter and adapter" (40). In this way, the "genetic" model of identity is not linear or temporal, but spatial. It is as if, rather, all the "individuals" that the narrator has been are laid out flat on a table top, and the narrator's actual being is constituted by the movement, the *shuttling*, between these individuals: "Jyoti, Jasmine: I shuttled between identities" (77).

This notion of "shuttling" is reminiscent of one of the most important works in the post-colonial field since its inception, Gayatri Chakravorty Spivak's "Can the Subaltern Speak?" In this essay, which she later expanded and included in her *A Critique of Postcolonial Reason: Toward a History of the Vanishing Present,* Spivak attempts to find the essence of a single woman, the Rani, outside of the remits of colonial discourse. Yet, Spivak does not posit either Said's or Foucault's model of the self (because it is not a matter of choosing between the self as the humanist subject or object of discourse), but rather, a model along similar lines to these in Mukherjee's: "Between patriarchy and imperialism, subject-constitution and object-formation, the figure of the woman disappears, not into pristine nothingness, but into a violent shuttling."[14] Here, Spivak characterizes the shuttling within discourse, the movement of the self between the various identities produced by the cultural milieu, as a *violent* process. Mukherjee would not disagree: The process of identity formation she shows her narrator passing through is certainly violent and harrowing—not the least in Prakash's death, the narrator's rape, and Bud's shooting (for which she blames herself because she was not "Karin," not able to be the "perfect" American wife). However, Mukherjee also sees it as a positive and ontologically ethical means of being.

Let me return, now, to the "ethics of exile" and the place for "self-transformation" in it. A subject who is outside of and above the cultural discourse does not carry out the notion of self-transformation; no such stable subject exists in Mukherjee's notion of being-as-shuttling. However, this does not preclude the notion of agency, or rather, the notion of an applicable ethics. This is clear at the end of the novel, when the narrator decides to leave Bud for the uncertainty of life with Taylor. The ethics of exile is not a choice between identities (between Jane or Jasme) but a choice between reification and instability; it is the active choice to actively interrupt and re-create the self, to plunge the static self into the turmoil of exigency and chance.

The narrator proclaims, "Adventure, risk, transformation: The frontier is pushing indoors through uncaulked windows. Watch me reposition the stars, I whisper to the astrologer who floats cross-legged above my kitchen stove" (240). There is no certainty to this way of living but merely a promise to reposition the stars by reference to the new self. It does not suggest a destruction of the past. The astrologer who opened the novel and presented the narrator with a reified version of fate at the very beginning of her life is not dismissed, is not forgotten, but is included in the numerous positions within discourse between which she shuttles. This is the fate of the exile: to be not merely the object of discourse but of its interruption, its reconfiguration, and its reformation.

In her novel of 1994, *The Holder of the World*, Mukherjee takes up a number of the themes that she dealt with in *Jasmine* from a different perspective. Once more, the novel involves a life narrative filtered through a framing narrative that draws attention to the exigencies of memory and of history. And once more, the central figure in that life narrative is a woman and an exile, this time Hannah Easton, a 17th-century American woman from Salem who travels with her husband to India. Once more, we see the process of exile as a process of self-transformation: Hannah begins her journey as a good Puritan woman and concludes it as the "Bibi" (the name given to black mistresses of white colonialists) of a Hindu prince, a woman defined by the sensuality of the East. The nature of this self-transformation is marked because of the enormous divergence between West and East that the historical setting provides, increasing the feeling of absolute alterity, the utter "Otherness" that separates the two cultures. This self-transformation, placed as it is at the very beginning of modern colonialism, acts as an index to the (post-)colonial question that was less explicit in *Jasmine*. It explicitly enters the "postcolonial field," which "Edward Said writes about" and to which "modern anthropologists can no longer return with their erstwhile certitudes."[15]

*The Holder of the World* presents a reversal of the situation in *Jasmine*. Seventeenth-century Salem was, of course, an English colony, too. Through the novel's main character, the Western colonized subject (nevertheless a Westerner) goes East to another colony ("the Other" colonizing the other "Other"). Through Hannah, *The Holder of the World* reconstructs the primal scene of colonial discourse, the moment of the first clash of Western and Indian civilization. Nonetheless, Mukherjee does not represent this clash as a political or materialistic altercation but in terms of how the discourse of colonialism functions over the political realities of the colonial situation. Even before Hannah travels with her husband, Gabriel, to India, she is seduced by her husband's tales—by narration, by words, his obvious fabrications—and Gabriel's discourse of travel is placed firmly within the tradition of the exoticization (and, therefore, Other-ing) of the subcontinent in sailors' tales. "She thrilled to his sea-faring yarns. He had jumped pirate ships in Madagascar. He had slept in the Garden of Eden, inside an Asian mountain guarded by angels. Children enchanted the deadly cobra with a mere piped melody. ... The soil of Hindustan was ground up sapphire" (67). It is also notable that in Gabriel's tales the Orient is presented as both a sensual paradise (the "soil" that was "sapphire") and a prelapsarian one (for he "slept in the Garden of Eden"). It is more voluptuous than mundane Salem, as well as having a prior religious claim. The imaginary homeland of "India" is a contradictory construction not a single reality. Throughout this novel, Mukherjee is less interested in the actuality of Indian life than she is concerned with its status as an imaginary construct:

> The New World was hard and savage; it was soft and bountiful. It was evil, it was innocent. ...Probably every colonist and every Englishman ascribed to one or many of those views, serially or simultaneously, whatever the nature of their mutual contradiction. (72)

The fact that a view can be subscribed to "serially or simultaneously" involves a certain paradigmatic shift. Mukherjee is not trying to say that those Englishman who held these views were even changeable or hypocrites. Rather, she is pointing up the way the discourse that constructs the New World operates, its strange logic, the way that reality is reformed and deformed under the Western eye. The Western eye places the New World in a series of opposition with itself, and from this opposition, arises the ambivalence that opens up within the migrant when he or she enters a new landscape. The eye alters the landscape, just as the person who sees is also altered. That there may be a contradiction in the shifting landscape does not, for Mukherjee, alter its power to form a reality that many believe to be "true."

But it is not merely India, the colonized state, that is an imaginary construct of the colonial imagination. England, too, is presented as an imaginary homeland, "a fantasy England" (127). Nevertheless, this homeland across the sea was just as ambivalent as the new colonial land; the colonists also thought "serially or simultaneously:" "England was refined and cultured; it was soiled and sinful" (72). The situation, then, that Mukherjee presents in *The Holder of the World* is more complex than the suggestion proposed by Said, among many others, that the Orient is a construction of the West (a West, he seems to suggest, that gains stability by opposing itself to the mysteriousness of the New World.) Rather, while remaining in opposition, the two worlds can change each other, their discourse entering into a strange game of cultural tag, in which the two worlds can never hold the same position, but continuously circle each other.

It is clear that, as Chakrabarty has noted in his study of precisely this colonial moment, "'India' and 'Europe'...refer to certain figures of imagination whose geographical referents remain somewhat indeterminate."[16] Not only are the geographical referents indeterminate but so are the actual limits of their cultural and symbolic weight; there are many contradictory significations involved in the representation of "India" and of "England." However, no matter what the contradictions at the hearts of the imaginary lands, the most important (and again, imaginary) aspect of colonial discourse is the placing of the two cultures in opposition with each other: Where England is dour, India is fruitful and colorful; where India is sinful, England is a bastion of virtue; where England is corrupt and decadent, India is pure and innocent. The oppositions abound. As James Clifford points out in discussing the general operations of colonial discourse, there is a tendency to dichotomize the relationship between the "Occident" and the "Orient," binding them in an us-them contrast.[17]

It is noticeable that though the colonists themselves can, in many ways, be considered exiled from their homeland, the ethics of exile does not function in their discourse. There is no self-formation, no reinvention, and no deformation. For example, the way in which the wives of the East India Company men react to their husbands' relationships with their Bibis, is extremely telling. "Black bibis know their place, so a wife's safety lies in assigning them a place that is harmless" (133). The response of the women to the new culture—a culture that is more sexually liberal, where the marriage bonds are more fluid—is to cast the Bibi in the class structure of the land the Occidental women have left behind. The Bibi is not threatening because she has been given a place in the social hierarchy where she is "no more than a cute little pet" (131). This minimization of the threat is not purely a psychological transference of the sexual threat posed by the Bibis; it is a cultural reaction. They are pets: They are reduced to not only something harmless but also something genderless and animalistic. The connection that might have linked the English women and the Indian women (their femininity) is denied through the simple act of denying that the women are even human.

Not only are the Bibis reduced to something less than human, but they are even denied the dignity of being individuals. They are stereotypes from the store of stereotypes that make up the shared colonial portrait of the native: The Bibis are "devious temptresses, priestesses of some ancient irresistible and overpowering sensuality" (131). While the ethics of the exile is to exploit the notion of static subjectivity, to decenter it and scatter it among the competing claims of various cultural discourses, the women of Whitetown purposefully reify the selfhood of the Bibi, as Bhabha explains colonial discourse is meant to do when dealing with the colonized "Other:"

> The stereotype is not a simplification because it is a false representation of a given reality. It is a simplification because it is an arrested, fixated form of representation that, in denying the play of difference (which the negations through the Other permits), constitutes a problem for the *representation* of the subject in signification.[18]

The Bibi can be nothing other than the confining limits that colonial discourse places on her, and being nothing more than an object of sensuality, she cannot, therefore, pose a threat in any of the other areas of the white women's influence.

The importance of the imagined homelands and the Other-ing stereotypes of the colonial imagination, then, is to present a static version of the world, one in which the civilizations of West and East are diametrically opposed. As the narrator of the novel ironically notes, "How comforting a world that can be divided into halves" (270). However, as the latter parts of the novel seem to suggest, the world need not be ordered in this binary way, and once more, it is the spirit of the exile that begins to attack the certainty of that edifice. In *Jasmine*, the structure of exile, including the multiplicity of different cultures, brings into question the stability and singleness of the self. In *The Holder of the World*, the relationship of self to the world is reversed. It is the exiled self (the self that is an exile to itself and enters whole heartedly into a process of self-transformation) that can question the singularity and stability of a discourse that proposes "culture" as a monolithic and an unassailable given. In *The Holder of the World*, the self and culture enter into a dialogic relationship that interrupts the simple singularity of either, making both radically multiple. It is Hannah, "the Bibi of Salem," a woman who gives herself freely to the ethics of the exile, who can disrupt the dualism of the two separate cultures and put to play the point at which their boundaries meet.

As we saw in *Jasmine*, there is a marked ambivalence about the position of the subject on the margins who belongs to no particular landscape, who has no place to call "home." In *Jasmine* this ambivalence is seen as a cause of personal disintegration and existential difficulty. Only through the extremely personal facets of her life, is the narrator of *Jasmine* able to make some form of resistance and some subversion of the discourse that surrounds her. *The Holder of the World*, however, is drawn on a much different scale, and the ambivalence that is still present—within Hannah who is fragmented between the native Indian and the Puritanism of her homeland, between her assumed English identity and her new place as a lover of an Indian prince—works in a very different way. For on this more epic scale, this ambivalence can be seen as a political weapon of considerable strength. Although Hannah encounters the difficulties of a divided self, the main focus of the ambivalence is how it can alter the discourses within which she is involved. She is considered throughout the novel as someone who could make a difference.

An extremely important aspect of Hannah's life story is the disappearance of Rebecca Easton, Hannah's mother, who runs away with a Native American Indian leaving Hannah, who is brought up as a Puritan, with the memory of a mother who gave in to her own sensuality. Although it might appear so at the beginning of the novel, this is not merely a repetition of a common colonialist fantasy concerning the native (the cultured woman who gives into the baser side of her nature and takes a foreign mate). Rather, it is a moment of self-transformation, a transgression of the ordinary boundaries of culture that Hannah seeks to forget but understands in its fullness when she makes a similar transgression years later by becoming the Raja's Bibi. The experience of her mother opens out into a larger analogy between the colonial situation in America and in India, both in the past and in the future: "[P]erhaps piracy on the Coromandel Coast...was the seed of the frontier dream, the circus dream, the immigrant dream of two centuries later." An observant reviewer rightly commented that Mukherjee had created "a different kind of multicultural story, one that imaginatively links the 17th-century colonial New World (Puritan New England) with the Old World (England and Mughal India)," without necessarily realizing the full significance of this "different kind of multicultural story." As an American writer, Bharati Mukherjee clearly understands the power of bringing into close contact, and thus into creative fission, the notions of "the frontier dream" (which is still firmly embedded in the American national consciousness as a positive nation-building force) and the negative connotations of the colonial situation in English-controlled India.

Later in the novel, another analogy collapses the notion of a singular India into itself. On her journey, Hannah has produced Christian, Muslim, and Hindu "selves" (268). Her religious transformations, being part of various religious cultures without being of them, allow her to interrupt a single "India." There is a difference, she notes, between the colonizer's relationship with Islam and that with Hinduism: "English attitudes saw Islam as a shallow kind of sophistication; Hinduism a profound form of primitivism. Muslims might be cruel, but true obscenity attached itself to Hindus" (219). Here, the discourse of colonialism—once more using the tactics of hierarchy and stereotype—separates Islam from Hinduism, making Islam a mirror image of itself while placing Hinduism in the position (previously held by the entirety of "India") of complete and unknowable "Other." Further divisions and analogies are drawn: The desires of the Company factors and the Muslim Emperor are contrasted with the Hindu minority led by the Raja (the combined force of Western and Eastern imperial might pitted against a colonized resistance), and then, soon after, the Raja himself is compared with the colonizing force. As he calculates the possibility of victory or defeat in the field of battle, he is "as happy as some Company factor figuring a profit" (243). The effect of these comparisons and divisions is to unsettle the simplistic binaries of the colonizer/colonized, to unsettle the simplistic unitary description in a complexity of differences. It does exactly the work of deconstruction as described by Robert Young. It makes an intervention in the dominant discourse "in a way that makes the same no longer the same, the different no longer simply different," yoking "difference and sameness in an apparently impossible simultaneity."[18]

This is that which, despite the differences between and within the various cultural formations that Hannah comes into contact with, remains a ruling principle. No matter what orientation the pilgrims, the American Indians, the Company men, the pirates, the Muslim traders, and the Hindu resistance are placed in, no matter on what side of the dichotomy of colonizer/colonized Hannah places them as she disrupts the discourse of binarism, there seems to be one single unifying factor that links them all. Each individual group (not merely the colonizers, but every group) is intent on keeping its cultural and personal identity static, and that is the reason for the continuation of violence and oppression in the colonial situation. Hannah realizes this when she tries to convince the Raja, whom she loves, to give up his duty and run away with her. He refuses:

> She saw that her native New World forgetfulness would be forever in conflict with Old World blood-memory. There was no great unutterable crime, no great analog to a life time's single-minded dedication that had set Aurangzeb and Jadav Singh on their course...He was a king. They were kings. It was their duty to fight. (253)

What Hannah cannot do is to convince Jadev Singh to do as she has done and open himself up to the self-transformative power of being in exile. He is too firmly wedded to his "imaginary homeland" and his position within it. He is king; that is his position; therefore, he must fight. That is the socially constructed thing for a man in his position to do. What is more, the repetition of the notion of kingship seems to suggest, as to some extent *Jasmine* does, that the structure of holding onto a static cultural identity is in some way patriarchal. Just as the men in *Jasmine* are always the ones who safeguard a static cultural identity, so masculine systems—kingship, hierarchy, and colonial trade—keep watch so that the boundaries of static cultural systems may not be disturbed.

In contrast to the masculine need to dismiss the play of difference, Mukherjee seems to posit the power of femininity to transgress those boundaries. This is not to say that Mukherjee believes it is the nature of womanhood itself that allows these transgressive tendencies. After all, the women of Whitetown are as guilty as the Raja of attempting to hold the boundaries of their cultural system. Rather, there is something about the structural possibilities of femininity—perhaps femininity's marginality within cultural systems—that make it particularly suited to being open to the play of differences and to being part of the ethics of exile. It is Hannah and Bhagmati (Hannah's Hindu servant and friend) who make the most forceful attempts to restructure and reconstruct their identities and by doing so, to restructure the cultural formations in which they find themselves. Their distinctly feminine friendship blurs the cultural boundaries that separate them: "She wasn't Hannah anymore; she was Mukta, Bhagmati's word for 'pearl.' And she gave Bhagmati a new name: Hester, after the friend she had lost" (271). This swapping of signifiers functions in the same way as naming did in *Jasmine*: It both inscribes each woman in the other's culture and by doing so, disturbs the separation between the Western and the Indian. At the end of the novel, it is Hannah/Mukta and Bhagmati/Hester who travel to the Emperor in an attempt to stop the war, a war that stands as a symbol and ultimate expression of the violence of cultural intransigence. And according to Mukherjee, it is only Hannah who could make such an attempt, precisely because of her structural position as an exile: "Only a person outside the pale of the two civilizations could do it." Only the exile who is beyond the cultural frameworks that have made her, precisely because she is caught in an unstoppable shuttling between them, can attempt a disruption of their force and their violence.

This is the message of *The Holder of the World*. Yet this message—the one that can be gleaned from the life of Hannah Easton as an allegory or representation that explains the structural position of the exile and the construction and deconstruction of imaginary homelands in the colonial scene—is not in itself secure. The novel's framing device, its narration by Beigh Masters, the "asset-hunter" who pieces together the narrative of Hannah's life from the 20th century, adds another layer of indeterminacy to our reading and a further complexity and richness to Mukherjee's novel. Beigh's presence as the narrator striving to narrate does not stand in relation to her subject with any certainty; her retelling of the life of Hannah Easton is a *re*telling, one that is conditional and incomplete. She has gathered evidence for eleven years so that she might make a "reconstruction not just of a time and a place, but also of a person" (138). If we were to compare Beigh's reconstruction to the works of post-colonial theoretical discourse, she would be the academic trying to reconstruct the meaning of the colonial subject. Hers would be the same attempt made by Spivak in "Can the Subaltern Speak?"—an attempt to excavate from the ruins of history the meaning of the subject within her cultural context. However, as Spivak also found, this kind of reconstruction is filled with difficulty, that to reach out might also constitute an "ungrasping":

> The palace was a legend of deferment and difference... I was halted by the discourse of the European sublime and percolated through it, Kalidasa, the fifth-century Sanskrit court-poet beloved of Goethe, both out of Rani's reach... There were no papers, the ostensible reason for my visit, and of course, no trace of the Rani. Again, a reaching and an un-grasping.[20]

That Beigh's reconstruction is in question, that it might constitute a "reaching and an un-grasping," is emphasized by the contrast of her methodological approach with that of her boyfriend, Venn. Venn is inventing a machine that can reconstruct the past in all its specificity, a machine that is able to read all the discursive information of a time and a place and, therefore, reconstruct that time and place in "real-time." His aim is for veracity and for completeness: "The past presents itself to us, always, somehow simplified. He wants to avoid that fatal unclutteredness." He wants to be able to reconstruct the past in a neutral way that does not place it in any kind of hierarchy, that does not credit any single aspect of a place or time above another. In some ways, he makes the same attempt to step outside of discourse that many post-colonial critics do, attempting to stand above the colonial question and describe its operations as they really are. Venn's first attempt at creating the past involves a reconstruction of a Boston street on October 29, 1989. Beigh tests the reconstruction and walks on the street, reaches out, and touches a faucet. The experience is disappointing because it has no value, has no object. She asks, "Why did I intercept a lady in her yellow jacket demonstrating faucets in a Kansas City bathroom?" (279).

Venn's second reconstruction is of the day on which Hannah saw the battle begin on the battlements and is created using Beigh's preceding narrative. This time the moment is full of visceral excitement: Beigh dodges bullets and cannon balls, watches Bhagmati die, and touches the Emperor's Tear (an enormous diamond, the search for which began Beigh's interest in Hannah). However, the difference between the two reconstructions is that the second is based on Beigh's own personal viewpoint: "[T]he program will give you what you most care about" (281). Compared to Venn's reconstruction, Beigh's presents itself as less anchored in the real world. Beigh presents the personal aspect as a positive force, implying that the personal valuation should be placed above a neutral iteration of facts: "I talk about asset hunting, the fact that data are not neutral...There are hot leads and dead ends. To treat all information as data...is to guarantee an endless parade of faucets in Kansas City" (279). This is the danger of a postmodernist approach to the post-colonial question. There is no means for intervention if every datum has the same weight as the next, if every subjectivity is dissolved into a simple combination of electronic signatures. However, this does not mean that we must turn away from a postmodernist perspective and try to return to a halcyonic time when all was certain because the means of our analysis were truth. The criterion for placing value on a particular datum is not its truth but its *value*.

These are the necessary tactics of the asset hunter. It is not a question of truth, but one of value. As such, Beigh also bypasses Spivak's dilemma of how one can reach the truth of a subject beyond its own "deferment and difference," how one can peel aside the discourse and know the truth of a person or a land. Rather, Beigh's methodology is not interested in the truth, but it offers the value of a tactical intervention. Her Hannah, her India, her story are more valuable because of the intervention that Hannah (as Beigh has rendered her) makes in deconstructing the discourse of static certainty. All data may be equally true (or false) in this conception of the world; but to speak of truth or falsehood means that we are still in the domain of the question of factuality, of the actuality of being. But the intervention necessary in the logic of the asset hunter is one that is made on a more pragmatic basis: What can change the world, or even, as Beigh's intervention does, what can change the past?

Once more then, we are returned to the notion of ethics, of intervention. Like the narrator in *Jasmine* and like Hannah's intervention to disrupt the discourses of the colonial situation, Beigh's reconstruction of Hannah's history also acts as an intervention. She is not creating truth, but something that makes a tactical incursion into the dominant discourse. In all three examples, Mukherjee's prose injects hope into an area of literature and theory that is usually overtly pessimistic. She suggests that an intervention can be made into the stability and singularity of all deterministic discourses, including the discourses of post-colonialism. It is from this basis that, in her political pronouncements, she has criticized the "bitter, exiled discourse" of immigrants with "their tight defensiveness, their aggressiveness, and their blinkered vision."[21] She is defiant of a post-colonial literary establishment that believes "if you're India-born, you must write about India and you must write about an Indian woman or peasants being victimized."[22] Bharati Mukherjee does not attack colonialism because she is of Indian descent. She attacks all stable monolithic discourses. She deconstructs the colonial discourse, but does not shy away from equally striking against the post-colonial establishment. She does this from the position of the exile: within neither culture, despite being produced by both of them. Her writing, in this way, is infused with the ethics of the exile.

## Endnotes

1. Julia Kristeva, *The Kristeva Reader*, trans. Toril Moi (London: Blackwell, 1986) 246.
2. Bharati Mukherjee, University of Minnesota, 3 Jan. 2006 <http://voices.cla.umn.edu/vg/Bios/entries/mukherjeebharati.htm>.
3. Frantz Fanon, *Black Skin, White Mask*, trans. Charles Lam Markmann (London: Pluto, 1986) 101.
4. Chandra Talpade Mohanty, "Under Western Eyes: Feminist Scholarship and Colonial Discourses," *Feminist Review* 30 (Autumn 1988): 65.
5. Edward Said, *Orientalism* (London: Routeledge, 1978).
6. Homi Bhabha, *The Location of Culture* (London: Routledge, 1994).
7. Léopold Sédor Senghor, *The Africa Reader: Independent Africa* (London: Vintage, 1970).
8. Frantz Fanon, *The Wretched of the Earth*, trans. Constance Farrington. (Harmondsworth, UK: Penguin, 1967) 168.
9. Amilcar Cabral, *Return to the Source: Selected Speeches of Amilcar Cabral* (New York: Monthly Review, 1973) 35.
10. Bharati Mukherjee, "American Dreamer." *Mother Jones* Jan./Feb. 1997, Dec. 2005 <http://www.motherjones.com/commentary/columns/1997/01/mukherjee.htm>.
11. Timothy Brennan, *Salman Rushdie and the Third World: Myths of the Nation* (London: Macmillan, 1989) 34.
12. Said 23.
13. See, for example, *Foucault Live: Collected Interviews, 1961–1984*, ed. Sylvére Lotringer (New York: Semotext(e)) 1996.
14. Gayatri Chakravorty Spivak, *A Critique of Postcolonial Reason: Toward a History of the Vanishing Present* (Cambridge, MA: Harvard University Press, 1999) 227.
15. Vijay Mishra and Robert Ian Vere Hodge, "What is Post (-) Colonialism?" *Textual Practice* 5 (1991): 400.
16. Dipesh Chakrabarty, *Provincializing Europe: Postcolonial Thought and Historical Difference* (Princeton, NJ: Princeton University Press, 2000) 29.
17. James Clifford, *The Predicament of Culture: Twentieth-Century Ethnography, Literature, and Art* (Cambridge, MA: Harvard University Press, 1988) 258.

18. Bhabha 75.
19. Robert Young, *Colonial Desire: Hybridity in Theory, Culture and Race* (London: Routledge, 1995) 36.
20. Spivak 242.
21. Bharati Mukherjee, "Imagining Homelands," *Letters of Transit: Reflections on Exile, Identity, Language, and Loss* (London: The New Press, 2000) 69.
22. Tina Chen and Sean X. Goudie, "Holders of the Word: An Interview with Bharati Mukherjee (1997)," Dec. 2005 <http://social.chass.ncsu.edu/jouvert/vlil/bharat.htm>.

CHAPTER 4

# V. S. NAIPAUL AND THE SEARCH FOR THE WRITER'S HOMELAND

V. S. Naipaul is one of the most famous and respected writers of what has come to be called post-colonial literature. His fame and the regard in which he is held by the literary community have led to his being awarded the Nobel Prize for literature in 2001. In this way, Naipaul appears to be very much a figure of the establishment. Yet, his works do not materialize from the certainty of a position within the echelons of the canon. Instead, they deal with the uncertainty and doubt of the outsider and the exile. His colonial upbringing (which is more mixed than many of the other writers who have been described with the generic term post-colonial) spans his native Trinidad and his assumed British home, while his roots are also in the country of his parents, India, and in their Hindu religion. Thus, even in his homeland, Trinidad, Naipaul is an exile, an exile from India. In England, he is an exile from Trinidad. In India, he is not "at home" because it is a country he has never known. Naipaul's writing is imbued with this spirit of the constant exile. What is more, he is self-reflexively aware that it is precisely in writing that the contradictions of his identity (an identity that can never be purely a single thing) play themselves out and reach an uneasy synthesis. His subject, more than colonial history, is writing itself, or rather how the post-colonial situation is played out in writing. It is only in writing, his works seem to suggest, that we can reach any idea of "what it means to be a colonial subject in a postcolonial society."[1]

One of the most pressing concerns of *The Mimic Men*'s narrator, Ralph Singh, is with the nature of his writing. Repeatedly, the novel's protagonist returns to a metaliterary consideration of the process of writing, what he is writing, and perhaps more importantly, what he is *not* writing. Early in the novel, he makes the following statement, summing up for himself and the reader what is at stake in the story he tells for himself, for the land that he has helped to rule, and for the state of society that has come through the era of empire and colonial power:

> It was my hope to give expression to the restlessness, the deep disorder, which the great explorations, the overthrow in three continents of established social organizations, the unnatural bringing together of peoples who could achieve fulfillment only within the security of their own societies and the landscape hymned by their ancestors, it was my hope to give partial expression to the restlessness which this great upheaval has brought about... . But this work will not now by written by me. I am too much a victim of that restlessness which was to have been my subject. (*The Mimic Men* 38)

It should be clear from the passage that no matter how great a novel like *The Mimic Men* undoubtedly is, it is also—in the eyes of its fictional narrator—a failure. It is an exercise in incompleteness. Rather than mastering its subject, the "restlessness," the "disorder," and the "great upheaval," such an aim is made futile through the very thing that it sought to describe. Instead, all the author can hope to write about is himself, his life, and his dreams. Unable to engage fully with the project of writing about the motions and fragilities of history, he turns instead to the task of biography: to know the self, to write the self. Nonetheless, he finds even this much more humble ambition is also difficult to achieve. For like the book he would have written, *The Mimic Men's* narrator is somewhat incomplete. Ralph Singh as a writing subject, as well as the great history he would have written, is a victim of the inability to explain the postcolonial situation.

The writings of Frantz Fanon deal with the effects of colonialism on the identity of the colonized. They show how colonialism splits the colonized asunder and coerces them into taking on a double identity, disbarring them from the authentic unity of self and social role. Fanon, in *Black Skin, White Masks*, says, "I took myself far away from my own presence, far indeed, and made myself an object."[2] In the passage, Fanon describes how a circle of white people surrounds him; one of them, a child, shouts, "Look a Negro." In this act of naming, Fanon's sense of his self begins to crumble, and he questions himself as an authentic subject. This event, narrated biographically, shows the means by which the colonial can only place himself or herself in a narration as an object. Even in Fanon's own story, the author is not viewed as the first person narrator. He is the construction of the Western gaze rather than the teller of his own story.

Such self-objectification is at the core of Naipaul's narrator and his inability to consider himself whole. Ralph Singh plays roles: the nervous child in class, the dandified colonial in London, the bourgeois landowner when he returns to the Island of Isabella, and the socialist politico in his career as the leader of the mob. These roles depend on his being seen by people who will, consequently, consider him something he is not. The narrator admits this when he compares himself to a needy fellow student who constantly requires affirmation. In many ways, they are similar: "He was like me: he needed the guidance of other men's eyes" (23). Equally, we are left in no doubt that this assumption of a role, the mimicry and outward show of thoughts and feelings, not authentic, is tied up entirely with the narrator's status as an exile—not just an exile from his home, Isabella, while he is in England but also as an exile from his "native" Asiatic home, an exile from his father, and an exile from his social class: "We pretended to be real, to be learning, to be preparing for life, we mimic men of the new world" (175).

This notion of "mimic men" has been seen by many as a criticism on Naipaul's part of colonialism and colonial methods, and in part, it is also a self-critical gesture. It has been seen as the natural response to a purposeful and aggressive colonial technique of assimilation, along the lines set out by Thomas Macaulay in his "Minute on Indian Education:" "…we must at present do our best to form a class who may be interpreters between us and the millions whom we govern, a class of persons, Indian in blood and colour, but English in taste, in opinions, in morals and in intellect."[3] This may well be the case, but Naipaul does not put forward the position with any of the vehemence of the colonial freedom fighter. Naipaul is seriously skeptical of such a position. Rather, the malaise of the "mimic men" is detailed as a problem in the present and a problem brought about by the subject himself or herself. It is the subject's desire to be a whole subjectivity, to be "real," to have "life," which is the cause of the "restlessness" that afflicts Naipaul's narrator and the times of which he writes.

Critics of Naipaul's work have noticed that *The Mimic Men*'s structure and form (the movements from past to present, the shifts in time and location, the fluidity of narration) are indicative of the protagonist's turmoil. John Thieme goes so far as to suggest that it mirrors the novel's "social and psychological disturbances."[4] This, it seems to me, it stretches the point a little too far and shows insensitivity to the tenor and pace of Naipaul's work. The shifts are not violent or sudden; nor does the narrator show signs of "psychological disturbance." Instead, I think it is closer to the mark to read nonlinear plot and the author's inability to find wholeness not as a state of affairs that is sudden, violent, and a disturbance, but as conveying the constant forward motion the narrator's life takes. Naipaul represents the taking on of roles and the creation of "mimic men" as a way of life—not as the result of colonial violence, or the narrator's mental imbalance. This playing of roles (sometimes Naipaul calls it "drama") is seen as something not imposed but purposefully taken on and used. It is seen as a necessity of human existence; the narrator comments on the uprisings in his village that they were less to do with the authenticity of the mob's political views and more to do with their need to play a part: "Disorder was drama, and drama was discovered to be a necessary human nutrient" (153).

Naipaul and Fanon differ in this much, then. While Fanon believes that the objectification of the colonial is an aggressive means of subjugation, Naipaul sees it as an active choice by the role player, a choice that derives from something that is central to our notion of humanity. That is why, in England, the narrator can play a part that is more outré, racier than the boy he was in Isabella: "It was up to me to choose my character, and I chose the character that was easiest and most attractive. I was the dandy, the extravagant colonial" (24). We see again that agency and choice determine what role the narrator assumes. However, the nature of the choice the narrator makes opens up our understanding of the way that Naipaul sees colonial subjectivity—and it is more nuanced than a simple matter of choice. Why was the character of "the extravagant colonial" the "easiest"? It was the easiest because it fits in with the image that the people he meets in London expect of him; it is the easiest because it does not shake anyone's preconceptions. After making the claim that his character was his choice, the narrator seems to change that stance. Speaking of his landlady, Leni, he says, "I thought she accepted the character as a character and sought merely to heighten it. But she it was—it is so obvious now—who, by suggestion and flattery, created the character of the rich colonial" (25). Although the individual is free to choose his or her character, there are other considerations. An adherence to colonial stereotypes and the draw of exotic otherness are not the least of them.

Subjectivity is free, and according to Naipaul's novel, one plays parts and one chooses the parts one plays. This is not, however, the same as affirming the constant free play of identities, a belief that who one is can be decided on a whim and then dismissed with equal casualness. Limits and other factors press down on the individual, shape his decision, and push him into certain furrows of identity. The roles we play cannot be considered just roles that are presented to an audience and then discarded as an actor wipes off his greasepaint. The narrator has flings with foreign women he can barely understand, keeps a sex diary, and frequents London prostitutes. All this happens despite the fact that, in actuality, his sex drive is low. These acts cannot be considered to be playing out his role (at least not in any ordinary sense), because such acts have no audience. They are not the acts of a character that can be thrown on and off as the whim takes: "As though we ever play. As though the personality, for all its byways and willful deviations, all its seeming inconsistencies, does not hang together" (31). Not only is the subject not free to choose, neither is he entirely free of the desire to hold his character together (and for Naipaul's narrator, to try to identify a wholeness that is authentically *there*) and cannot be dismissed as simply a "role" or a "part."

The choice of the nature of one's subjectivity, although a real choice, is not entirely free of a consideration of what the world expects. It is clear in the novel that the world is central to the narrator's feeling that he is not whole, that there is something missing. Naipaul is not just interested in the openness of subjectivity in general but specifically in the nature of the subjectivity of the exile. The subjectivity of the exile is brought into question because of the "distance from any clear-cut national identity or notion of home."[5] That "identity" and "home" are interlinked in this quotation from Rob Nixon is particularly apt because these twin poles of subjectivity and the world Naipaul suggests are in a dialectical relationship with each other, each both validating and invalidating the other.

The narrator looks on the city of London and comments: "In a city as nowhere else we are reminded that we are individuals, units. Yet the idea of a city remains; it is the god of the city that we pursue, in vain" (22). The full stop that separates these two sentences is the hinge on which the two concepts of "identity" and "home" swing. First, the city reminds us that we are separate from one another and the world. The novel does this by insisting on the busying back and forth, the alienation of metropolitan life, and the lack of community or family. Yet, it is exactly in the nature of man—again, Naipaul seems to grant this trait to all of humanity by using the inclusive "we"—to look for a notion of completeness, of oneness with the world that the city most obviously denies. That we chase after this notion "in vain," suggests that Naipaul, just as when he is dealing with the notion of a solid subjectivity, also finds difficulty in admitting the possibility of a landscape, a world in relation to which the individual unit can orient himself or herself. Just as his characters are people who play imaginary roles, also his cities and his towns and countryside provide those characters with imaginary landscapes.

Once more, it is not a simple case of saying that Naipaul considers "the city" which is an index in *The Mimic Men* to the notion of surroundings. The notion of a "home" is merely a string of signifiers, an imaginary place that is created by the individual only to fulfill his or her own needs. The city, while presented as a nebulous and difficult to grasp entity, is also figured as something solid, something "real." The narrator lives "In the great city, so three-dimensional, so rooted in its soil, drawing colour from such depths, only the city was real" (32). These two notions of the city—as an imaginary landscape that is impossible to grasp and a "solid," "three dimensional" edifice with "roots"—are not necessarily contradictory. Just as the individual is both a construction and a fixed entity, so the city is an imaginary place that also takes a solid place in the structure of identity. These two imaginary and solid constructions are locked into dialectic, a furious to-and-froing. The subject requires the solidity of the city to provide it with roots, a place to belong, while the city needs the individual to give it form, to make it real. The two concepts are mutually dependent, and each frustrates the other's ability to fully be.

This is particularly true of the exile and the colonial simply because the structure of colonialism—with its "unnatural bringing together of peoples" and forced deportations—is more likely to create subjects who have contradictory attitudes toward their roots. The narrator of *The Mimic Men* is a case in point. He is brought up on the island of Isabella (a Caribbean island not unlike the Trinidad on which Naipaul himself was born), a thriving multicultural state that contains the descendants of white colonials, black slaves and in the narrator's case, "Asiatics." As a child, he imagines the life he would lead were he to be in the land of his ancestors. The imagined life of the character and the psychology of memory, as well as the constructed landscape, the "imaginary homeland," are presented in the novel in a self-consciously idealized manner, drawing attention to the illusionary nature of its idealism, its imaginative aspects:

> I lived a secret life in a world of endless plains, tall bare mountains, white with snow at their peaks, among nomads on horseback, daily pitching my tent beside cold green mountain torrents that raged over gray rock, waking in the mornings to mist and rain and dangerous weather. I was a Singh. (118)

Most important, this idealized (even falsified heritage) is constitutive of the narrator's subjectivity. "I was a Singh" (118), he exclaims, cementing his racial heritage, the imaginary landscape he has created to stand in its place, and his subjectivity.

However, it is not merely a landscape which is far away that can be considered illusionary. Even the land in which Naipaul's characters live becomes a poor reality as compared to the imaginary landscapes that they construct in an attempt to find a sense of home. In the case of the narrator's father, his imaginary landscape is the landscape of Isabella, though at an earlier time, a time of missionaries and strength of religious feeling:

> When I read this book I used to get the feeling that my father was a man who had been cut off from his real country, which in my imagination was as glorious as the Isabella described in the diary of the missionary's lady: nowhere else would people see magic in a white turban, a hibiscus hedge, a bicycle and the Sunday-morning sun. (107)

The story that the narrator relates from his reading of *The Missionary Martyr of Isabella* is put in terms similar to his imagining of his ancestor's lands. The white turban, the hibiscus hedge, the bicycle, all take on higher, more symbolic meaning, and the green fertility of the land seems to be an age away from the dank sterility that the narrator finds in the island in his own time. Nevertheless, like his imagination of snow-topped peaks, the history contained in the religious volume does not show a world that was better and has now passed. There was never a time when the narrator's father was at home in his "real country," the reason being that the "real country" does not have any firm foundations in reality. "Real" here means the country that would confirm the identity of the narrator's father to himself and to his son, a country where his father would fit. This "real" country does not actually exist, which causes their "restlessness" and sends the father into the woods as a religious leader and the son overseas.

The narrator's overseas journey to London performs a much more important function in the novel than simply changing the scenery or the setting. The journey overseas is an attempt to find the "real country"—the country that will confirm the narrator's being, a place where he can be in control of his world and himself. It is precisely for this reason that the novel's protagonist determines to leave Isabella to go to school in London. It is also the reason why he will later leave London to return to Isabella and then, when his political career leaves him in ruins, take the opportunity to return to London under the pretence of leading the bauxite delegation: "[I]t was now that I resolved to abandon the ship-wrecked island and all on it and to seal my chieftainship in that real world from which, like my father, I had been cut off.... I was consciously holding myself back for the reality which lay elsewhere" (141). Again, the notions of placing a "seal" on himself, certifying his worth and his certainty, and gaining control of his world through a "chieftainship" are to the fore. However, as in the rest of the novel, this hope is not fulfilled: indeed, it cannot be fulfilled. "Reality" does not simply lie "elsewhere" geographically, and one cannot take a plane or a boat to it. "Reality" is *structurally* foreign; it is necessarily "elsewhere" because of the systematic nature of identity. A subject's identity is not fixed. It is not a concept that admits to it the possibility of arrival. As Michel Foucault points out, we can no longer arrive at the answer to the question of what the self is, we must instead ask, "Departing from what ground shall I find my identity?"[6]

The notions of "self" (which are "imaginary roles") and the notion of "home" (which is made up of "imaginary landscapes") are in a dialectical relationship with each other; but it is a dialectic that does not and cannot reach the point of sublation. For when Naipaul's narrator attempts to confirm the veracity of his Asiatic past by the certainty of his subjectivity ("I am a Singh"), it is clearly an illusion. Equally, when he tries to confirm his identity by means of its adherence to a landscape (e.g., in London when he plays the "rich colonial," a role suited to someone from his part of the world), it is nothing more than a role that is plucked from the stereotypes of imperialist discourse. Neither reaches the point of consummating the other; neither reaches fulfillment.

Although the existential "restlessness" that we have seen Naipaul dramatize is not confined to the structure of the post-colonial situation, it is the post-colonial situation that confirms and exacerbates the difficulties in the interplay between subjectivity and landscape. As Alan Lawson has remarked, in his discussion of the movements of Westerners to colonial outposts, the changes caused by the movements of people have very large and wide reaching effects on social and subjective structures: "...[T]he sense of distance, both within and without, was so great that a new definition of self—metaphysical, historical, cultural, linguistic and social—was needed"[7] What is more, this new "definition of self," unsure and fragile as it is, must necessarily be guaranteed by the colonial power; the new language, new culture, new metaphysics, are all held in place by the social systems of the invading power. This can be quite clearly seen by the cross-section of Isabella society provided by the narrator's school class at Isabella Imperial (the very name of the school belying its roots in colonial enterprise). The ascendancy of the white aristocracy is represented in the figure of Deschampneuf, black poverty in the shape of Browne. They, and all the strata of society in between, are held together by the school and its mimicry of empire—the teaching of the classical languages, the nicknames, and the master's behaviour.

This fragile concord, this new sense of self in the colonies, is shaken once more with the advent of post-colonialism and the freeing of former colonies. Naipaul's protagonist is centrally involved with the process on Isabella. He leads the political struggle against the oppression of the old colonial masters. But rather than seeing the nationalistic struggle as an opportunity to forge a new identity, or to unite those who have been oppressed around a common ethical identity—this was certainly so in the cases of political activists and post-colonial thinkers like Fanon and Léopold Sédar Senghor—Naipaul is viewing the loss of colonial power as yet another blow to the possibility of forming any kind of cultural identity. He paints the post-colonial Isabella as a place with no direction or certainty. Just as in colonial times the country had no "…internal source of power, and no power was real that did not come from outside" (246). Equally, the narrator has a certain fear of the mob whose belief in political ideals is "imaginary" and who, like the group that surrounded his father, only takes up the call to arms because they are searching for "drama" (153).

V. S. Naipaul can, thus, be categorized as a post-colonial writer—he deals with the post-colonial situation with focus, verve, and great skill—yet his politics are not those of post-colonial, revolutionary nationalism. He himself has emphasized his lack of political feeling: "I think that one reason why my journalism can last is because I never had any such ideas about Left or Right. One just looked at what had happened. There are no principles involved in one's vision."[8] The vision at the center of *The Mimic Men* is not political; rather, it diagnoses politics as another symptom of the malaise that the novel has been describing. When Ralph Singh becomes a politician at the center of the freedom movement, he does so with little conviction. Indeed, the narrator believes that he and the people around him are once more playing parts in a drama. The things he does and says are mere mimicry. Where once the boys of imperial college mimicked the manners and beliefs of their colonizers, now they go through the mechanical motions of political process: "Borrowing phrases! Left-wing, right-wing: did it matter? ...[W]e used to borrow phrases which were part of the escape from thought" (237). Overall, politics is presented as precisely this, "the escape from thought," one more symptom of the "restlessness" that is created by man's loss of certainty in himself and in his landscape; it is another part he plays, another imaginary landscape he creates.

As such, the narrator leaves his political life and goes to stay in an English hotel, where he begins to write, creating the book that we have before us. By this metatextual trick of foregrounding the act of reading and placing the artefact the text, into the story of the life he has created, Naipaul is foregrounding the act of writing, giving it special prominence and demanding we pay attention to it. As mentioned earlier in this chapter, the book that the narrator proposed to write never got written. His hope was to give some expression to the complex and multitudinous nature of the times he has lived through and to analyze their effects. In short, he wanted to write a history, "his story." The story or narration is not purely for his reader's information and entertainment; he wishes to satisfy an "urge" in himself, and he hopes by doing so, that he will find some kind of peace. He feels "the shock of the first historian's vision, a religious moment if you will, humbling, a vision of a disorder that was beyond any one man to control yet which, I felt, if I could pin down, might bring me calm" (97). Ralph Singh hopes that by elucidating, and thus by taking control of the events of his history, he could quell the malaise, the dissatisfaction that he feels at his inability to be whole or find his "real homeland," that is ultimately to construct the real, authentic self.

However, the seeds of the impossibility and inevitable failure of his undertaking lie within his very statement. The thing he is trying to "pin down" is "beyond any one man to control." This is not merely because the extent and magnitude of the complexity that history offers to the poor historian is too great. It is because, like the self, like the homeland and like politics, history too lends itself to the play of the imaginary. If one searches for certainty and solidity from history, this search too will provide a merely illusory picture. We see it occurring in the very telling of the narrator's personal history. The narrator sees it too and shows a self-conscious distaste for the machinations of history even as he himself is writing it. For example, in the incident in which the Deschampsneuf's horse, Tomango, goes missing (and is found killed some days later, having been made part of a violent sacrifice), the narrator considers the way that the event has been passed down through history. He compares it to the 1913 Derby, at which Emily Davison's walking beneath the King's horse was a conscious act of writing history and enacting the body politics of the cause of women's suffrage. The comparison is relevant to the author's and the narrator's view of history: "They are both events, which, becoming history, lose their horror and obscenity and appear the natural, almost logical, expression of a mood; they are events which now have been oddly *expected* and dramatically right" (168). History flattens the events of which it is made (just like the roles played by exiles in the London boarding house are "two dimensional" (17) and creates a simple picture, one that works as a dramatic spectacle. Although the narrator of *The Mimic Men* looks for some kind of calm, and perhaps a way of describing his incompleteness, he finds the same incompleteness in history. This is the main reason why the great history that the narrator had planned to write (in place of the novel we are reading) never gets finished.

It should be clear by now that writing lies at the very center of the exiled subjectivity's malaise, that it is the thing that both authorizes and ultimately frustrates the attempt for fullness or completeness. It is no mistake that in describing the frustration of the narrator to find himself, his "homeland," an authentic political position, or to understand his (his)story, the readers are often couched in the terms of literary discourse. Ralph Singh plays *roles* in a *drama*, and the landscapes that create his agency are *imaginary*. He speaks in *borrowed phrases* as he tries to find a way to *express* his historical experience. It is expression, narration, writing, that is placed as a central component of the "restlessness" that besets the novel's narrator and, beyond him, the exiled subjectivity. Yet, it is writing—not the writing of history but a writing of a very different sort—that ameliorates, though perhaps does not solve, the narrator's difficulties to a point where he can proclaim at the end of the novel, "I no longer yearn for ideal landscapes and no longer wish to know the god of the city" (300).

*The Mimic Men* is certainly not a historical novel. Its narrative is nonlinear, modernist, and it relies on the narrator at its center who, while not entirely reliable, determines both the shape and direction of his story's telling. Bruce King has called the work "a Caribbean East Indian rewriting of *A Portrait of the Artist* and *Remembrance of Things Past*."[9] This probably does little service to V. S. Naipaul, both ghettoizing his work by its national origin and, implicitly, continuing the frankly racist comparison between the great Western canon and the inferior mimickers of the New World (cf. Saul Bellow's often quoted question: "Where is the Zulu Tolstoy?").[10] The comparison, however, does have a modernist slant, and like those works, Naipaul's *The Mimic Men* brings the questions of memory and writing into close proximity. The novel's protagonist is not quite sure of some of the facts of his life and explicitly states, "The editing is clearly at fault, but the edited version is all I have" (110). This, however, is not merely an acceptance of the uncertainties of memory or even of the impossibility of saying specifically what one means. The edited version of his life, his *written* life, is all he has. There is no notion of his life beyond the writing of it. Even his life—in the same way that the landscapes and history were—is imaginary. Still, in the process of writing, Naipaul's narrator accepts the illusory nature of existence, its lack of completeness. When he leaves Isabella for England, he finds a piece of paper slipped into the book, he suspects by his friend, Hok. On it, a simple message is written, an incomplete message, its incompleteness signalled by ellipses: "*Some day we shall meet, and some day... .*" It is the open ending of this message that touches Singh, and gives him some kind of hope:

> There is something, after all in the staged occasion, the formal sentiment. It came to me on the ocean, this message ending in dots, telling me that all my notions of shipwreck were false, telling me this against my will, telling me I had created my past, that patterns of happiness or unhappiness had already been more or less decided. (214)

He sees within the simplicity and formality of the message a solution to his dilemma that might save him from "shipwreck" (the word the narrator uses repeatedly to describe the feeling of being lost on the voyage toward his identity). "I had created my past," it tells him. There is something in the textual nature of the message, perhaps in its incompleteness, that allows him, rather than looking for his identity and his history as complete and solid structures, to see identity as something that he has created himself, as an imaginary object. Happiness or unhappiness is determined within that imaginary object.

The text of the novel itself is like the tiny scrap of text on Hok's piece of paper and that it functions in the same way. In creating the imaginary artefact of the novel and thereby textualizing his life (for it is "the edited version"), the novel's protagonist, who is in many ways an alter ego of Naipaul himself, has enabled himself to break free from his dependence on a notion of completeness. He no longer fears shipwreck because he no longer hopes to achieve the dry land on which he once thought he stood—identity, a homeland, a history. Rather, he is happy to be awash in the sea of becoming. The narrator says he has found the book difficult to write, much more difficult than the articles he wrote during his political career. Those were written quickly and without effort because he was writing within the role that he had made for himself. He even says that the article about his father "wrote itself." While the article was "deeply dishonest," however, the book is—in a way that his great history could not have been—honest—because it accepts its own limitations: "The writing of this book has been more than a release from those articles; it has been an attempt to rediscover that truth" (226).

By the end of the novel, the writing process has done its work. The narrator no longer feels the restlessness he did before. Rather, in his almost locationless position at his desk in the country hotel (a residence for transients) that he has made his uneasy home, he believes that he has worked out to some extent the contradictions of his being, the *truth* of his state. He thinks that he might now do something of worth: write a history of the Empire or go into business again. If he does so, he says, "…it will be the action of a free man." Writing has enabled Naipaul's protagonist in *The Mimic Men* to understand that he is neither singular nor an image of wholeness.

It is writing—rather than marriage, politics, travel, education—that has allowed him to come to terms with his freedom. As such, there is some trepidation, as well as hope, at the end of that writing. "Yet some fear of action remains" (300), Singh says. Is there the possibility of action in the world (as opposed to writing, which is presented here as an innocence, an absence of action), action that does not rely on a return to the restlessness or role-playing from which writing has freed the narrator? The novel seems to suggest so. The final image of the novel finds the narrator hiding behind a column, observing, but not interacting with a woman who was once his lover. Michael Gorra has suggested that the nature of post-colonialism is that there is "no way to become the sole author of the self. Texts are made of other texts. And so the frenzy and the fear, the raw nerves, the long line of books, the body of work built up as a stay against the pain of one's own dependency, desperately trying to write into being the self that one knows one can never fully achieve."[11] *The Mimic Man* appears to propose the precise opposite: that writing is the acceptance that the self can never be achieved. It is action, living in the world, that creates a dependency on the world, the "frenzy," the "fear."

V. S. Naipaul's *The Enigma of Arrival* (1987) is written in an even stronger biographical form. Despite its subtitle, *A Novel in Five Sections,* this work has many parallels with Naipaul's own life and experience. What is more, and in a much more explicit way than *The Mimic Men,* the novel deals with the effect of writing and the experience of being a writer on a man's life. It shows how writing, through the same power as we saw manifested in *The Mimic Men,* can be both a calming influence and an effective means of coming to terms with dislocation, as well as being an ethical means of living. It is writing, far more than the surroundings in the English countryside in which most of the novel is set, that provides the narrator of the novel with "my second childhood of seeing and learning, my second life..." (*The Enigma of Arrival* 82). Nevertheless, *The Enigma of Arrival* is neither biography nor the type of fiction that falls into the generic line of fictional-biographical prose novels, beginning with the first novel worthy of the title in English, Defoe's *Robinson Crusoe.*

While the novel seems to be centered on the realistic portrayal of the people whom the narrator meets while he is living in the ancient countryside around Salisbury, this is merely the story's façade. The true subject and the story's main source of development is rather the internal nature of the writer coming to maturity, the way he sees. In this way, Naipaul's narrator does not give a realistic picture of the world held in stasis; rather, he attempts to express the mediation that has occurred between him and the world. Peter Hulme, in his *Colonial Encounters*, explicitly links imperialism and the realist register,[12] its creation of an objective and solid "truth" that is not to be questioned. Naipaul does not fall into the imperialistic trap; his "realism" (if it can be called this) is shot through with the power of the subjective imagination.

The process of coming to understand how to be a writer and how to write is the central story of the novel. The narrator travels from his native Trinidad to England, where he hopes to fulfill his fantasy of becoming a writer. He has what Naipaul elsewhere has called the "drive and restlessness of immigrants."[13] However, when the novel's protagonist reaches England, the fiction that he does write—a few descriptive pieces that are worked over again and again in frustration because they do not say anything—is dismissed by his former self as not only poor writing, but somehow dishonest. He had been searching for a certain writing persona; he wanted to mimic the voice of an urbane sophisticate who is shocked by nothing and knows everything. In other words, he was taking on the voice he had read in the British books he had poured over as a student; he wanted to be like the writer's of Britain's "golden" imperial age. "To be that kind of writer (as I interpreted it) I had to be false; I had to pretend to be other than I was, other than what a man of my background could be" (134). There is a strong sense that in writing his early stories there was an implicit denial of the narrator's earlier self, that he had become a "mimic man" of British literary tradition and, therefore, had committed a betrayal of his roots, his authentic "background." The very reason that he denied this background, however, is that it was a background he had wished to escape by becoming a writer. In an early story, the novel's narrator leaves out certain parts, one of which is an unpleasant incident in which he is given a separate room on a passenger ship as a form of makeshift segregation: "But that topic of race...formed no part of 'Gala Night.' It was too close to my disturbance, my vulnerability" (115).

As Diana Fuss points out, "identification...is an imperial process, a form of violent appropriation in which the "Other" is deposed and assimilated into the lordly domain of Self,"[14] and this is precisely what was happening to the narrator as a young writer. He wanted to depose himself as "Other" and identify with the British tradition that somehow made up his picture of what it was to be a writer. This is similar to the narrator-as-politician in *The Mimic Men*. Without any explicit attempt at deceit, the narrator of *The Enigma of Arrival* is playing the role of what he thought a writer should be, and by doing so started to feel the same "restlessness" that was such an important motif in the earlier novel. He felt that "between the man writing the diary and the traveller there was already a gap, already a gap between the man and the writer" (102). The gap was also specifically post-colonial in nature, for it was the colonial self, the Indian/Trinidadian who, far from being the urban Western socialist, is an outsider in a world he did not understand. Just as Homi Bhabha analyzes the native under the pressures that colonial discourse places on him or her, Naipaul's narrator begins to detect a "hybridity," a difference "within" a subject that inhabits the rim of an "in-between reality."[15] The narrator, as he learns to write, understands that great literature can only arise out of a closure of that gap. That happens when man and writer become one, and when actual, real experiences become the subject of writing, rather than the rehearsing of hackneyed characters and motifs of earlier works of the canon.

One might imagine from this discussion of authenticity that the closure of the gap between the man and the writer and the root of this alienation is the denial of his earlier Indian/Trinidadian self. If he were to return to that more "real" inner being, then he would become what he always dreamed of being: a writer. However, this is not quite the case. For though these aspects of the narrator's self had to be confronted (and the narrator did start to write about his homeland again, particularly in the travel book that was later rejected by his publisher but which he thought was tremendously important), this does not constitute a return to the *reality* of his past life or his past country. He wrote of his past from England, and when he returned to his native Trinidad some years later, he found that the island was very much different from how he remembered it and how he had written of it: "Trinidad had since become almost an imaginary place for me" (311). Certainly, we can say that he had thrown off the role of the English imperial writer, but we cannot say such a gesture has revealed the true Trinidadian, who writes of the true Trinidad. Rather, the Trinidad he writes of is an "imaginary place," an imaginary landscape, and an "imaginary homeland," created through memory because he is distanced from it: "Far away, in England, I had re-created this landscape in my books...but now I cherished the original because of that act of creation" (139). This is central to V. S. Naipaul's vision of what it is to be a writer: not to write the truth of a *reality* but to understand the truth that is found in distance and re-creation.

In the writing of his past, Naipaul's narrator comes to a fresh understanding of who he is,[16] an understanding based on the fragmentary nature of his character. The "truth" he subsequently writes, utilizing the distance gained because of his exile from his home, is a truth that is based not in the reality of places but in the disjunction that his experience of them brings. This is illustrated very much in his own novel. The narrator manages to bring the otherness of his life in a cottage in Salisbury and his life as a young man in Trinidad into suspension, a synthesis of varying aspects. He looks out at snow, and it reminds him of "a climate quite different" (45). Strangely enough, it actually reminds him of a beach in Trinidad. This is a reminder of a repeated motif in *The Mimic Man* whose narrator, despite coming from a country in which it never snowed, had always thought of snow as being his element. Snow is not stable, it melts, it changes shape, and, eventually, it dissolves to nothing. In *The Enigma of Arrival*, this is what happens to snow under the writer's eye: It shifts, it transforms, and it becomes a bridge between two very different worlds.

We see the same technique again after Brenda's murder when her sister comes to pick up her belongings. Brenda's dairyman husband has murdered her for her unfaithfulness. The narrator notes, "Collecting the dead person's things—it was like something from the old world, an aspect of the idea of sanctity, an aspect of decent burial, the honouring of the dead; and it seemed to call for some ritual. But there was none" (72). Here we see writing's ability to bridge difference without eradicating it, to hold the twin worlds of Naipaul's experience in a synthesis without transcending the differences, which remain very real.

It also touches upon the ambivalence felt by the migrant writer—the writer who writes in exile—over the country or countries of his past—the country he has left and the country he has now come to live in. Yet—and this seems central to Naipaul's point about what is required to become a writer—this ambivalence is not a feeling to be mistrusted or a problem to be transcended and put behind one. As the power of the image of the snow that melts and forms into sand demonstrates, the importance of a writer of Naipaul's stature is that he can express the ambivalence at the heart of his fractured identity. The fact that he is neither fully in the world of his past, nor can he be a familiar to his new country with its completely different landscape (one, in this case, which is covered with snow), means that he can juggle these two backgrounds and these two landscapes while never truly being a part of either. He can exist within different landscapes (real or of memory) and can become an actor upon them rather than merely an object against the landscape(s) of his background. It is this ability that Naipaul weaves into his writing, giving it its power to stand above the cultures that created it.

In its very prose, *The Enigma of Arrival* seems to play out the truth expressed by its narrator late in the novel that "Land is not land alone, something that simply is itself. Land partakes of what we breathe into it, is touched by our moods and memories" (301). The landscape of Salisbury is changed irrevocably under the eye of the writer who can suspend the real and by doing so, find truth. "Land is not land alone," recalls the dichotomy expressed in *The Mimic Men* between land and landscape ("All landscapes eventually turn to land..." [13]), and, similarly, writing is the process that creates landscapes, "imaginary homelands," landscapes of memory that express the hopes and wishes of the writer protagonist as much as the character of the land from which they are formed. Nevertheless, it is only through the writer's ability to transcend any individual piece of land that these landscapes can be constructed, can exist. Just as the young writer who tried to create urbane pieces of social commentary had to remember his roots, his past, and the landscapes of his history, the older writer had to have also the fresh contact of that other world, the world of cows and trees and ancient racehorses put out to pasture. Singularity of experience breeds familiarity and contempt. Both require a freshness of perspective, an ability to suspend notions of being "at home" with the self to write. In the countryside near Salisbury, Naipaul's narrator discovers a new world of flora and fauna: "It was not like the almost instinctive knowledge that had come to me as a child of the plants and flowers of Trinidad; it was like learning a second language" (32). The comparison to language is very important, not only because it emphasizes the difficulty involved on the part of the narrator to come to terms with and understand the new world he is living in. It is also striking because it gives an impression of the new and more evolved consciousness of the world around him that the new landscape has brought. Where once he looked at plants and flowers in Trinidad "instinctively (and, therefore, one must assume, without thinking much), he now looks at this new world with the advantages of being alien to it. Just as those who learn a new language become highly aware of its resonances, its sounds, the depth and richness of a system that appears mundane and unremarkable to native speakers, so it takes a certain alienation to understand a new world, and to write its story. V. S. Naipaul, through his novels' protagonists, invests all his senses to very carefully point out the relevance of any minimal detail to the big picture.

*The Enigma of Arrival* has been placed into the category, along with many others of the so-called novels of "post-colonial literature," of works that deal with the colonist's "return home." Paul White notes that the trope of return is specifically prevalent in literature from ex-colonies: "it must be noted that amongst all the literature of migration the highest proportion deals in some way with ideas of return, whether actualized or remaining imaginary."[17] On a reading that touches the very surface, this could be considered so with *The Enigma of Arrival*. The final of the novel's five sections is entitled "The Ceremony of Farewell" and it deals with the death and cremation of the narrator's sister. Perhaps reflecting events in Naipaul's own life, the novel is dedicated to the memory of Naipaul's brother, Shiva, who died a couple of years before it was published. This actualized (as well as metaphorical) return is, however, neither how the novel ends nor is it the main point of the story. The symbolic death, rather than initiating a concerted attempt to return, pushes the narrator further out into his writing. The feeling of the closeness of death that it awakens in the author urges him into making an even more concerted effort to finish the book he wants to write about the process of writing itself, the book that is to become *The Enigma of Arrival.*

The irony of the notion of the "return" is that, like the notion of "arrival," such an arrival is always suspended. For how can the exile return home? As we saw in the journeys of *The Mimic Men,* the exiled writer (in both novels the central character is a writer) is never happy with the place he is; he is always moving forward, onwards. And just as the only place where the narrator of the *Mimic Men* felt comfortable was in a neutral hotel, one in which none of his various personas competed for attention, and where he was able to sit down and write, the only place that the narrator of *The Enigma of Arrival* is happy is on the precipice of beginning to write. If there is a "return," it cannot be considered an arrival but always as a return to setting forth, a constant step into the unknown.

Instead of seeing the metaphor of "return" as the central premise of this *The Enigma of Arrival*, Elleke Boehmer points out that cultural expatriation is the central motivation and intrinsic component of post-colonial literary experience (particularly in this novel's case), and that expatriation is also one of the most important driving impulses behind literature worldwide.[18] For in the novel's very title lies its most pressing concern. The novel, the writer, never arrives. In fact, the act of writing is always the act of the exile, of the person who can never return. Like the impossibility of finding the far shore of identity in *The Mimic Men*, so we see the impossibility of reaching the "world" as seen by the young novelist at the center of *The Enigma of Arrival*. It is not mere pettiness or homesickness that makes the narrator uncertain on his arrival in England: "just as once at home I had dreamed of being in England, so for years in England I had dreamed of leaving England" (95). Rather, it is an early sense of what is to become a central tenet of the narrator's writing, that is, the understanding of the ultimate deferral of writing about the world, the need for a rhythm of *contretemps* in any brushes with the reality of landscapes. He no longer sees his desire for the place where he is not as a longing, something that leaves him unfulfilled, but rather the structure of what it is to write: "As a child in Trinidad I had put this world at a far distance, in London perhaps. In London now I was able to put this perfect world at another time, an earlier time" (121). The creation of the perfect world, unreachable in geographical actuality but imaginable because of exile, is at the very center of Naipaul's writing. It is this "Otherness" that allows the narrator of the novel to claim some success in his hope "to arrive" (despite the fact that there it would never really be an arrival) "in a book, at a synthesis of the worlds and cultures that had made me. The other way of writing, the separation of one world from the other, was easier, but I felt it false to the nature of my experience" (141).

V. S. Naipaul's writing then, like the aesthetic claims of his narrator, is based upon the structure of exile—and this accounts both for his ability to synthesize the worlds and the cultures that make him and the slightly elegiac tone of the novel. For the novel is elegiac. It constantly reminds the reader of the uncertainty and ephemeral nature of the world, while offering the consolation that there is wonder to be found in precisely that uncertainty. Like the novel's aesthetics, this elegiac mood resides in the structure of the post-colonial's hybrid being and the fissures in his subjectivity. The narrator of the novel looks at the ruins and "superseded things" that seem to go hand in hand with the nature of the countryside in which he lives, and he seems to see some aspect of their certain decay within himself: "That idea of ruin and dereliction, of out-of-placeness, was something I felt about myself...a man from another hemisphere, another background" (19). The passing of nature in the countryside seems to emphasize the very lack of solidity of that place, as it reminds the narrator of the disorder and chaos of his own home, and more poignantly, of the disorder and chaos that the many landscapes of his history have wreaked inside of him. This factor, which unites both the cottage and his home in Trinidad, is placed in contrast to New York and London, which are solid, secure, nothing like the "ridiculous and disorderly existence of the 'half-made places in the world.'"[19] Yet, it is the narrator's past, his own inability to cohere inwardly, that allows him the sensitivity to understand the turbulence and changeability of the world of the countryside: "I had thought that because of my insecure past—peasant India, colonial Trinidad I had been given an especially tender or raw sense of an unaccommodating world" (87).

Once more, we see in the sensibility of the writer (the true sensibility, not the one that Naipaul's narrator sought as a young man), the ability to bridge a gap and to see within the landscape of the Salisbury countryside the worlds of peasant India and colonial Trinidad, and more importantly, within himself, the same nature of incompleteness and ruin. Ruin is welcomed rather than fled from. It is openly accepted, and it is seen as something almost positive. Perfection has its attractions, and the notion of the utter beauty of nature, which filled the narrator when he first moved into his little cottage, was, in its way, perfect. However, quite naturally, the narrator accepts that this perfection cannot last: "I had lived, very soon after coming to the valley, with the idea of change, of the imminent dissolution of the perfection I had found" (87). Perfection requires, by its very nature, the repression and denial of those things that might render it imperfect or create fissures in its perfection. Looking at the once beautiful, now decaying gardens of the manor's recent imperial past, the narrator seems as though he might have liked to see them in a perfect state, but then he strongly rejects the suggestion, preferring the incompleteness of the imperfect: "But in the perfection, occurring at a time of empire, there would have been no room for me" (52). The narrator himself, with his fissured, incomplete history, is a son of imperfection, for perfection requires the whole, the spotless. He would prefer the passing away, the continuation of disruption, to this certainty that could have neither created him nor allowed him to write.

This could well bring into question V. S. Naipaul's political position concerning the colonial system and imperialism in general. Such questions have been posed and accordingly, Naipaul has often been written off as a conservative who has turned his back on his people and the political struggle at the heart of the post-colonial world. Perhaps there is something true in that statement; as we have seen, Naipaul is anything but traditionally political, as substanced in his treatment of the politics in *The Mimic Men* speaks for itself. However, in a quieter and subtler way, perhaps, *The Enigma of Arrival* provides a greater challenge to the orthodoxy of the colonial's attitude toward his earlier repression. A neighbour of his brings his old mother to the cottage and tells the narrator that she had lived there many years before. The old woman is disorientated and saddened by the changes that the narrator has made over the years. By altering the cottage, the narrator says, "He had destroyed or spoilt the past for the old lady, as the past had been destroyed for me in other places, in my old island, and even here, in the valley of my second life" (286).

In the first place, there should undoubtedly be some reaction to the comparison of the past being destroyed "in my old island," (one assumes the narrator is referring to the destructive hand of the colonial powers) with simple renovations to a cottage on a country estate in Wiltshire. Secondly, and in the wider context of the novel's acceptance of the disruption of change—the way, in fact, that it welcomes it—it does seem as if the colonial change, the change that was put in motion by the imperial conquest, is to be suffered with magnanimity. Certainly, there is regret on the part of the narrator at the passing of perfection. And could not the perfect garden of the manor be another garden, the garden of supposed innocence, disturbed by the violence of colonial settlement? However, he neither fights it nor puts up any real opposition.

He learns to live with it and welcomes it. I would not argue with the fact that this willing acceptance certainly could represent a view toward the colonial situation that disparages open political action, yet there is a more subtle reaction to the oppressive "Other" and investment in true agency through the power of discourse. The possible acceptance would certainly be consistent with the ethic of inaction that concluded *The Mimic Men*. There is an argument, one to be taken seriously, that would suggest that this is purposeful ignorance, "philistinism,"[20] an attempt by Naipaul to block off the world around him (that would necessitate political action) and cocoon himself in his exile. However, I do not believe this is the case. Naipaul is not merely putting his head in the sand when it comes to the politics of post-colonialism; rather, he is making a definite choice and takes an ethical stance. Just as in his earlier novel, Naipaul's protagonist chooses the world of writing over the world of action; the protagonist of *The Enigma of Arrival* does precisely the same. The novel concludes with the narrator running back to England to begin the very novel we are reading.

*The Mimic Men* and *The Enigma of Arrival* are both, in many connected and diverging ways, the fulfillment of a particular worldview that is not stereotypically "post-colonial." Both novels represent the colonial as exile, as dreamer of imaginary landscapes, and as insolubly divided and multiple. However, more than anything, they represent the colonial as writer, and writing as the natural ethical means of action for the colonial in a world that has entered the era of post-colonialism. These are, in one way, very personal books. As the narrator points out in the last section of *The Enigma of Arrival*, "The story had become more personal: my journey, the writer's journey, the writer defined by his writing discoveries" (309). They are also wide-open edifices, which taken in the width and breadth of all human action and history, allow through the personal, the attempt to reach a provisional formation of the nature of the colonial in the post-colonial world. More than anything, they attest to incompleteness, openness, and instability of the subject, of the world, and of life—and they attempt not to capture this ineffable impression but to allow it to play out within them.

## ENDNOTES

1. Selwyn Cudjoe, *V. S. Naipaul: A Materialist Reading* (Amherst: University of Massachusetts Press, 1988) 99.
2. Frantz Fanon, *Black Skin, White Masks*, trans. Charles Lam Markmann (London: Pluto, 1986) 112.
3. Thomas Macaulay, "Minute on Indian Education," *Post-Colonial Studies Reader*, ed. Bill Ashcroft, Gareth Griffiths, and Helen Tiffin (London: Routledge, 1995) 430.
4. John Thieme, *The Web of Tradition: Uses of Allusion in V. S. Naipaul's Fiction* (Hertford, UK: Hansib, 1987) 114.
5. Rob Nixon, "London Calling: V. S. Naipaul and the License of Exile," *South Atlantic Quarterly* 87.1 (1988): 3.
6. Michel Foucault, *Essential Works of Foucault Vol. I: Ethics*, ed. Paul Rainbow (New York: The New Press, 1997) 230.
7. Alan Lawson, "The Discovery of Nationality in Australian and Canadian Literatures," *The Post-Colonial Studies Reader*, ed. Bill Ashcroft, Gareth Griffiths, and Helen Tiffin (London: Routledge, 1995) 169.
8. Ronald Bryden, "The Novelist V. S. Naipaul Talks about His Work to Ronald Bryden," *The Listener* 22 Mar. 1973: 367.
9. Bruce King, *V. S. Naipaul* (New York: St. Martin's, 1993) 70–71.
10. Qtd. in Gary Shapiro, "On the Post-Nationalist Writer," 11 Feb. 2006 <http://www.nysun.com/article/12795>.
11. Michael Gorra, *After Empire: Scott, Naipaul, Rushdie* (Chicago: University of Chicago Press, 1997) 7.
12. Peter Hulme, *Colonial Encounters: Europe and the Native Caribbean, 1492–1797* (London: Methuen, 1986).
13. "V. S. Naipaul 'East Indian,'" *Literary Occasions: Essays*, ed. P. Mishra (London: Picador, 2003) 41.
14. Diana Fuss, "Interior Colonies: Frantz Fanon and the Politics of Identification," *Diacritics* 24 (1994): 23.
15. Homi Bhabha, *The Location of Culture* (London: Routledge, 1994) 13.
16. Fawzia Mustafa, "V. S. Naipaul," *Cambridge Studies in African and Caribbean Literature* (Cambridge, UK: Cambridge University Press, 1995) 168.

17. Paul White, "Geography, Literature and Migration," *Writing across Worlds: Literature and Migration* (London: Routledge, 1995) 14.
18. Elleke Boehmer, *Colonial and Postcolonial Literature: Migrant Metaphors* (Oxford, UK: Oxford University Press, 1995) 232–233.
19. Abdulrazak Gurnah, "Displacement and Transformation in *The Enigma of Arrival* and *The Satanic Verses*," *Other Britain, Other British: Contemporary Multicultural Fiction*, ed. R. A. Lee (London: Pluto, 1995) 7.
20. Wilson Harris, *The Womb of Space: The Cross-Cultural Imagination*. (Westport, CT: Greenwood, 1983) 120–121.

CHAPTER 5

# CONCLUSION

## TRACING THE POLITICS OF EXILE IN SALMAN RUSHDIE, BHARATI MUKHERJEE, AND V. S. NAIPAUL

Who, then, is the exile? This question, which resonates throughout this study, has become, to a certain extent, redundant. The identity of the exile is precisely the thing which the exile avoids, defers, displaces, and twists away from. The question of "*Who?*" is the question that the exile simultaneously poses and suspends. Exile proliferates the very notion of identity—not just the individual exile's identity but also the possibility of identity in general—into a conspiratorial matrix of difference. It pushes questions of identity out of the reach of those who would attempt to grasp hold of identity's primal unity. The exile *is* not (he cannot *be*, he cannot exist)—at least in the common Western conception of being. He is rather the sum of competing and contradictory forces that play out over the surface of the exile's being, without ever constituting a stable and single edifice.

If the exile can be said to have a "being" at all, then, it can only be understood as one based on the formation of certain circumstances, of history, of discourse, of culture—what Walter Benjamin might have called a "constellation."[1] However, these very structures—history, discourse, and culture—can no longer be considered looming edifices of constitutive control and hegemonic power. For the strange logic of the exile invades these structures too works within them, and they, like the exile, cannot be considered single, unitary, or stable. The exile steals from them their authority by the power of his or her interruption. They, too, follow this logic and the structure that both pervades the exiled individual and gives the exile the power for resistance.

In the preceding analyses of the writings of Salman Rushdie, Bharati Mukherjee, and V. S. Naipaul, I have attempted to chart the trajectory of the logic of the exile as it passes through the authors' writing. I have aimed to render (however problematically) the flow of constitution and dissolution that occurs on the boundary of both language and self and which forms the particular literary power of these writers and determines their placement as writers of the post-colonial situation.

Now, in this conclusion, I would like to situate these various writers back into a dialogue with both the theory and practice of post-colonial scholarship in an attempt to see how the various movements within and between the six texts play themselves out against the wider background of the post-colonial situation. Perhaps more importantly, I wish to cement the argument I speculatively began in the preceding chapters that these three writers, though extremely different in matters of style, material, and/or execution, all present a seriously radical answer to the malaise that the post-colonial situation presents. They are certainly not, as some critics have presented them, writers who have benefited from the comforts of exile and have been unproblematically accepted into the mainstream of their chosen land (for Naipaul, England; for Mukherjee, the United States; for Rushdie, England and the United States). They are neither conservative nor apolitical. However, they do come to the notion of a post-colonial politics with an innovative mode of functioning and from a new place of departure. Their politics is not of the old kind but of a markedly new aspect: The target of their revolutionary destruction cannot be put in such simple terms as party, nation, or racial group.

Let us consider the various kinds of exile that make up the cast of characters within *Midnight's Children*, *The Satanic Verses*, *Jasmine*, *The Holder of the World*, *The Mimic Men*, and *The Enigma of Arrival*. All these novels concentrate on the personal nature of the central character's exile. In a number of cases, the novels are narrated from a first-person perspective, taking on the literary genre of the traditional faux-biography. They inhabit the biographical form all the better to examine the nature of subjectivity and exile's effect upon it. Some—and I am thinking particularly of Saleem of *Midnight's Children* and the narrator of *The Mimic Men*—have very definite and important links with the history of the country from which they come. In the former case, Saleem is born on the first day of Indian independence; in the latter, the central character is one of the leaders of a movement for independence in the British-dependent Caribbean island of Isabella. However, these connections with history occur only tangentially; they are always events that seem to slide past the characters in the stories, creating a spark of creative light but then disappearing once more.

Nonetheless, this is not because history is unimportant to the novelists. The specter of history always seems close to appearing over the largely unhistorical surface of the prose. The novelists involved are not trying to write "histories." In fact, it is explicitly stated in *The Mimic Men* that a history of "the restlessness, the deep disorder...the great explorations, the overthrow in three continents of established social organizations, the unnatural bringing together of peoples" is not possible (*The Mimic Men* 38). What these novels emphasize is the strange codependence of the individual and the movements on a larger scale: the clash of nations, the cleavage of religions, and the desperate battle between and within cultural difference(s). Like the central character of Bharati Mukherjee's *Jasmine*, these novels are trying to portray individuals who connect to the worlds in which they live in a way that is far from concrete and is more spectral. They attempt to "phantom [their] way through the continent" (*Jasmine* 101).

This idea of movement and of tangential connection with their surroundings (both literal—the people they speak to, the lives they lead—and metaphorical—the history played out around them) is also expressed in the notion of journeying. For instance, Ralph Singh, the central character of Naipaul's *The Mimic Men*, journeys across continents traveling to England to seek himself, Beigh Masters of Mukherjee's *The Holder of the World* attempts to travel through time using a sophisticated reality re-creator invented by her boyfriend, and Gibreel Farishta in Rushdie's *The Satanic Verses* journeys interiorly by passing through dreams that paint a strange and distorted religious-scape. Motion and a feeling of movement are central to each novel.

However, these variations on the theme of journeying cannot be conceived as normal journeys. For one thing, there is a feeling within each individual journey that there is no conclusion, that "arrival" is not a central tenet of setting off. Just as it is for the ancestors of the people of Jahilia, so it is for the characters in these novels: "[J]ourneying itself was home" (*The Satanic Verses* 94). This is why so many of the novels refuse to arrive at any kind of categorical conclusion. The main character in *Jasmine*, who has spent a large part of her time standing still, trapped in a marriage that is stifling her, decides in the final stages of the marriage (and final pages of the novel) to go forward and continue the journey. This is not simply an attempt to eschew the little arrival of settling down and building a home. Rather, it is a refusal to accept the "arrival" of herself to herself, the settling down in a single character—that of a browbeaten wife. Jasmine is continuing her travels not merely to change her geographical location but to change herself to accept all the possible characters that she can become. Likewise, at the end of *The Enigma of Arrival*, the narrator seems to "have arrived home," back where he started, in his native Trinidad. Nevertheless, in the last paragraph, this arrival is seen as less as "a return home" and more as a second starting out. The journey he is about to start out on is, once more, a personal one, and is, once more, an attempt to change himself. He is about to return to England, in order to write the book that we are reading, a book that presents his life, alters and edits it, and re-creates him as an individual.

## Conclusion

In such ways, the novels of Rushdie, Mukherjee, and Naipaul diverge from the main currents of post-colonial theorizing and writing in that they are written in what we can call a first-person imperative. These authors write *through* the individual and about the individual, whereas traditional post-colonial theory deals mainly in a third-person perspective, written sometimes as though from the clouds, looking down at the post-colonial situation and subject. To demonstrate the difference, I would like to turn to the literary theorist who really coined the notion of post-colonial studies (despite the fact that, of course, people were involved in post-colonial writing before him), Edward Said.

Edward Said's *Orientalism* is very much in the mould of the theorizing that came before and after it. It deals with the post-colonial situation as it might be if it were viewed from above, in the form of a transcendentalist analysis. Its basic thesis is that the notion of "the Orient" is not in itself a factual entity, an actuality, or a solid reality. Rather, it is a construction of various discourses and textual traces, a creation that formed through the processing of certain materials and the sum of the mass of overlapping epochs of thoughts and epistemical systems. In very much the same way that Michel Foucault attempted to display the unreality of the solid constructions of the West through discourse analysis, a Nietzschean archaeology of what makes the Western enlightened world what it is,[2] so Edward Said— through the understanding of the multiple constructions that go to make up "the Orient"—is able to dismiss the ideology that sees "the Orient" as stable, reified, existent.

However, Said's analysis of the discourse that has formed "the Orient" goes one step further than Foucault's analysis of the Occident. For Foucault, the Western Age of Enlightenment was constructed from within. For Said, "the Orient" is created by its opposite; Orienta*lism* is the creation of "the Orient" by the West; "The Orient is an idea that has a history and a tradition of thought, imagery, and vocabulary that have given it reality and presence in and for the West."[3] "The Orient" is "given" its reality; its reality is constructed by the Western iteration of the traces that constitute its being. Thought, imagery, vocabulary, the whole linguistic and textual matrix of the West's textual powers go into giving "the Orient" its character and its reality.

This is not all that Said's archaeology unearths. The construction of "the Orient" is not only the product of Western discourse and Western language; it is also an integral part of that Western discourse. It is, therefore, important, even vital, to the West to create "the Orient," its textual and linguistic reality, because "the Orient" provides an unknown "Other" in relation to which the West's boundary can confirm to itself that it, on its own account, is whole, stable, and complete.

> European culture...set[s] itself off against the "Orient" as a sort of surrogate and even underground self; an ongoing discourse perpetuated by the basic assumption of the Orient as mysterious, unchanging, unable to represent itself, and ultimately inferior.[4]

As the whole thrust of post-colonialism that has issued from this point of genesis has confirmed, the construction of "the Orient" by the West is not neutral. The main purpose of his construction is to place the actual geographical place—"the Orient"—as a dark figure that haunts the West; it, thus, becomes or is made to be seen as the underside, the place of sin and as Said quite rightly points out, a place that is "inferior." The creation of discourse is political because such a construction is both the reason and the justification for the subjugation of the people of "the Orient," the subcontinent, and of all the places of the world that colonial power brought to subjugation.

As this short analysis of Said's thinking should show, he works within a framework that is necessarily, almost purposefully, in the theoretical realm. There is nothing principally human about the standpoint that Said takes; it is a point of view above and outside of the discourse, assumed from a transcendental position; it can look down on the discursive practices just as one might look down at the weave of a piece of cloth. Yet, this is not to say that the concerns of the individual do not enter into Said's analysis. He also speaks from an underlying humanist position. For example, he says that despite the fact that "the Orient" is a creation of discursive practices, there is still a place for individuality to make its mark on that discourse: "I do believe in the determining imprint of individual writers upon the otherwise anonymous collective body of texts constituting a discursive formation like Orientalism."[5] He also considers the colonialist discursive practices that form "the Orient" as a means of violence—violence perpetrated on human individuals who, without the oppressive force of this discourse, would be able to live their lives as "free beings." It is specifically this distancing from a complete notion of discourse—one that suggests that an authentic subjectivity can exist outside of discourse—which Robert Young criticizes as being, in itself, ethnocentric. For the "idea of the human which Said opposes to the Western representation of the Orient is itself derived from the Western humanist tradition."[6]

Edward Said then makes provision in his theory for the human, for the individual; conversely, this still cannot be said to be mining the same vein as the three novelists. Said's discourse analysis, whatever else might be said of it, does not deal primarily with human action, with a principle of ethics. The human factor in his cultural theory can take up only the position of the victim; the individual does not act. Nonetheless, as we have seen, the logic of the exile as it has been traced through Rushdie, Mukherjee, and Naipaul has to do with an ethics (first and foremost, the ethics of exile) or at least the way the progress and deformations of subjectivity can create a means of resistance to the dominant discourse. Just as Partha Chatterjee has emphasized the need to be aware of the domestic and personal nature of the creation of discourse ("The home, I suggest, was not a complementary but rather the original site on which the hegemonic project of nationalism was launched"[7]), so the novelists realize that only from a first-person perspective can a proper analysis of the post-colonial situation be accomplished.

Simultaneously with the first-person perspective, these three novelists also create a more radical critique of Western dominance than Said, who still wedded to the notion of a simplistic humanism, was able to fully accomplish. While emphasizing the role of the individual in resistance to the dominant discourse, the novelists also deny the possibility of the stable individual that, as Young quite rightly points out, is itself a creation of a colonial Western discourse.

The main intervention in a post-colonial thought in Rushdie's, Mukherjee's, and Naipaul's novels comes about through the individual and individual journeys or the individual's close proximity to historical events. In a way that Said's transcendental viewpoint could not manage, these novelists deal with the actual way that subjectivity negotiates the contradictions of a discourse that is created by "the Other" (i.e., the West). This in turn brings into question the possibility of the characters being able to form a full subjectivity. For example, the central character in Naipaul's *The Mimic Man* sees himself taking on many roles: the exotic colonial in London, the wealthy and married man who returns to the island of his birth, and, later, the revolutionary who fights for a world free of colonial oppression. Nonetheless, he finds that each of these roles is still a construction of and by the West; even the role that has him fighting Western colonialists is a construction of Western discourse. Therefore, he comes to realize that the world of the colonized has no "internal source of power, and that no power was real that did not come from outside" (246).

By playing these varied roles and by inhabiting the parts he plays *inauthentically*, he comes to realize that is all they are: simple roles that have been written, constructed for him in the epic colonial drama. So, by analyzing Said's notion of *Orientalism* (or at least the creation of colonial discourse because he does not come directly from the Orient) on the level of human interaction and the individual subjectivity, Naipaul's work dissolves the very notion of subjectivity itself. By holding onto the notion that there was a *real* person beneath all the roles, the central character of *The Mimic Men* might have been once more pulled back into the play of discourse that would mean he still was the oppressed, the *colonized*. Naipaul, through the narrator, reveals the post-colonial man as a "mimic man:" "We pretended to be real, to be learning, to be preparing for life, we mimic men of the new world" (*The Mimic Men* 175). However, it is precisely this pretence, the "unreality," that enables Naipaul to achieve a critical position and to lay bare the fictionality of the West's colonizing discourse.

Mimicry plays a large part in all the six novels—and for good reason. As we have seen, the novelistic approach (as opposed to theorists who take a transcendental view) concentrates on the way that individuals try to negotiate their subjectivity within the discourse created by the West. Mimicry becomes a central part of that negotiation. For if colonial power is to use all the coercive force of textuality, language, ideas, and appearances, then it is exactly within these realms that the individual must attempt to form his or her subjectivity and if possible, stake out a claim to the means of resistance. This is also the central theme of one of the most important theoretical contributions to the post-colonial debate, Homi K. Bhabha's *The Location of Culture*.

Far more than Said's *Orientalism*, Bhabha's *The Location of Culture* works profoundly on the level of strategy and negotiation. Bhabha is concerned with the notion of subjectivity in the colonial situation and in that way owes a lot to the writings of Frantz Fanon. What concerns Bhabha is precisely the operations that we have seen occur within all the six novels: the work of subjectivity in a position that creates and multiplies the difficulties associated with radical difference:

> It is in the emergence of the interstices—the overlap and displacement of domains of difference—that the intersubjective and collective experiences of nationality, community interest, or cultural values are negotiated.[8]

That is, it is within the overlapping and cross-cutting threads of cultural discourse that the creation of all the solid edifices that we have seen the six novels call into question (self, the nation, community, culture) are created *as* realities and can be changed and deformed. In other words, as Bhabha also seems to imply with his suggestion, the book is the "measure of mimesis and mode of civil authority and order."[9] It is the linguistic and textual threads—imaged here by Bhabha as "the book," the good book, or the book of law—that implicitly enforce the *status quo* and that contain the possible dangers that difference or "Otherness" might present to order or to colonial power. Why then, speaking with particular reference to the colonial situation, might we hold that the exile threatens order and the *status quo*? As Said points out, albeit viewing the situation from his limited perspective, the reason why there is a creation of a static field of discourse which describes and circumvents the difference of "the Other" (the reason why the notion of "Orientalism" becomes a reified reality that gains the status of "truth") is because of a need by the West to consider itself whole, and to vanquish from itself the difficulties inherent in admitting difference. Bhabha takes up this theme but casts this particular aspect of Western culture in terms of psychoanalytical categories—the West is suffering from precisely the problem of the child who must dislocate himself or herself from the world (during "the mirror stage"—in Lacanian terms) in order to feel himself or herself whole. In other words, the reason for the creation of colonial discourses that emphasize the absolute alterity of "the Oriental," the Indian or the *foreigner*, is to better enable the West to create an Imago of the self. In the Lacanian sense, again, the production of colonial discourse is an attempt to form an *"Imaginary self."* However, where Bhabha diverges from Said's analysis (and where he is more in keeping with the three novelists we have been discussing) is that he does not believe that there is an essential self that lies beneath discourse who is a victim of oppression perpetrated by discursive practices. For example, in his treatment of the stereotype, Bhabha makes very explicit that

> The stereotype is not a simplification because it is a false representation of a given reality. It is simplification because it is an arrested, fixated representation that, in denying the play of difference (which the negations through the "Other" permits), constitute a problem for the *representation* of the subject in signification.[10]

The stereotype is not simply an act of violence because it twists and distorts the truth "on the ground;" Bhabha's argument is not one of the ideological misrepresentation of the truth. The reason a stereotype is an act of violence against the people whom the stereotype comes to represent is because it limits the possibility of their difference; it is a closed form that will not offer itself up to the deformative effects of play. A stereotype is forever, always will be, precisely the same image as it always was. Not only that, it limits the movement of individuals through the world, it reifies *them*, sets them into the shape of the mould that stereotype provides.

The narrator of Naipaul's *The Enigma of Arrival* correctly understands this point. He has come from his native Trinidad to become a writer. As such, he takes on all the mannerisms and does all the things that he believes writers should do; he, thus, fulfils the stereotype of the writer. However, he comes to see the poses that he strikes as false, something of an inauthentic nature: "I had to pretend to be other than I was, other than what a man of my background could be" (*The Enigma of Arrival* 134). It might seem as though the narrator understands that as a man of Indian ethnicity, he cannot be the white writer and, consequently, should return to the kind of life where a man of his race and color belongs. This is not the case at all. The operative word in this quotation is "could"—rather, by becoming what he thinks a writer should be, the narrator is dissolving the possibilities that he, as a writer, can perform. His background, far from being a limit to the freedom of his action, increases that freedom. By being "the writer," he is denying his background (e.g., he does not write about racial difficulties when he composes the story about his journey to England from Trinidad). The fact that he is foreign does not limit his ability to be a writer. Rather, the fact that he is neither of England nor of Trinidad, the fact that he is an exile, allows him to extend the possibilities of his backgrounds and the cultures he has passed through. It is important to note that when the narrator plays the role of "the writer," he is not on the wrong path because the character is not *who he is*. Rather, it limits what he *could be*.

This is the power that the migrant, the one in-between, the hybrid person has: the enormous opportunity for resistance. For when the migrant interacts with stereotypical postures, with reified categories of being, then he or she begins to deform these categories precisely by the fact that the migrant's varied backgrounds cannot be contained by them. What they *could be* bursts out of such simple constrictions. Migrants interacting with stereotypes are a particularly marked feature of Rushdie's *The Satanic Verses*. This novel explicitly states that the operation of stereotypes occurs through the descriptive power of the West, the "Orientalism" that is created by the Western perspective: "They describe us. That's all. They have the power of description, and we succumb to the pictures they construct" (*The Satanic Verses* 168).

In *The Satanic Verses*, Chamcha immigrates to England and wants to fit in with the dominant hierarchy of power; he wants to be considered "English." To this end, he changes his name, the new Saladin sounding much more Anglo-Saxon, and he does absolutely everything he can to fit into the new community in which he finds himself. In other words, he is attempting to live out a stereotype (just like the narrator of *The Enigma of Arrival*) that would be too constrictive to the opportunities that reside in him, what he *could be*. Due to this act of mimicking the colonial oppressor, and thus, deforming the possibilities of his own existence, Chamcha is transformed into a monster—part-goat and part-man. In one way, the transformation can be seen as an attempt by Western discourse to re-inscribe Chamcha into the stereotypes that have been propagated since the very beginning of colonial times. This "Other," who attempts to be like Us, has been punished for his pretension by appearing just as he should and thereby, succumbing to the pictures that they construct—a monster, a strange hybrid. The notion of the colonial subject as in part, animalistic, has an extremely long-standing history in Western discourse; it even goes back to the time of Shakespeare. When Othello speaks of "goats and monkeys,"[11] (in Act IV, Scene 1, Line 261), his Elizabethan audience would most certainly have recognized the implicit reference to a bestial side of Othello that would prove his undoing.

This transformation can, though, be seen in a different light. For it is important to note that Chamcha becomes part-man, part-goat—what the biogenetic field would call "a hybrid." It is this position as hybrid that constitutes Chamcha (and all exiles) and it has a particularly potent force. For by mimicking the colonial master, Chamcha has set off a kind of disjunction in the hitherto seamless discourse of oppression and objectification. By being "the Other" but claiming some kind of identity, Chamcha has—to borrow a circumlocution favored by Bhabha—turned his mimicry to mockery. The monstrous within Chamcha (at least as far as Western discourse is concerned) is not the actuality of his physical form but the opening he creates in the unbreachable solidity of the Western Imago. It is "a hybridism, a difference 'within' a subject that inhabits the rim of an inbetween reality."[12] This "rim," this hyphenated "in-between reality" mocks the seeming certainty of the West's image of itself. It is mirrored in the magical realism of Rushdie's prose, which is neither wholly fantastical nor wholly real but a kind of in-between worlds. It dislocates and interrogates the West's stability, its wholeness. This is the monstrous visage that Chamcha shows to the Western world. It is not necessarily the monster that the West believes the colonial to be but the monster that has been locked away in the recesses of the collective imagination, the notion set in play by the exile, but not residing in him or her, that the very fabric of our reality is open to flux, play, and difference.

Returning to a consideration of the function of the central characters of Rushdie's, Mukherjee's, and Naipaul's novels, we see that they have two very different roles. They are both victims of a discourse by which and against which they must always measure themselves, always facing a norm that they either must resist or assimilate themselves to, and the means of fracturing the discourse that oppresses them. Such an ambivalent role is precisely the material that the personal narratives presented in these novels are woven from. For it is the function of art not to teach but to present. While Said and Bhabha may be making an attempt to explain the motions of difference that invade and disrupt the unitary discourse of the West, Rushdie, Naipaul, and Mukherjee present it. They succeed, by the disruptions, deformations, and discontinuities in the linguistic objects, in presenting just how these deformations work both in collective history and on individual subjects or individual his-story. They try, as the narrator of *Midnight's Children* says, to give voice to "the myriad tongues of Babel; they were the very essence of multiplicity, and I see no point in dividing them now" (274).

This journey into "multiplicity" and this attempt to capture speech in "myriad tongues" is bound to lead to a certain amount of ambivalence. This ambivalence toward the country, the tongue, and the people that the exile has left and toward the new land in which the exile finds himself or herself is manifested in the personal journeys of the main characters. These characters do not have any certainty; rather, they often find it difficult to negotiate the many different worlds in which they find themselves. As the narrator of Mukherjee's *Jasmine* points out, "My genuine foreignness frightens [Bud]. ...It frightens me, too" (26). The exile is in a frightening world in which he or she must mimic the manners of the new as well as keep within himself or herself such aspect of the person the exile was. This is why the novels are what one might call "novels of self-discovery." *Midnight's Children, Jasmine, The Mimic Men,* and *The Enigma of Arrival* all fit this category. Their narrators attempt to find themselves; the progression of their narratives is less influenced by the forward motion of an outward plot than an innerscape that must be traversed to reach the goal of finding a meaningful self.

This is the goal for Saleem of *Midnight's Children*, who takes the reader through the entirety of a novel and most of Indian history in an attempt to try to find himself: He desperately desires to place his life in a context that will make it meaningful. Indeed, he finds himself altering the narrative that he is writing (and the factuality of history: e.g., the date of Gandhi's death) precisely because he wants to forge some kind of meaning out of his life: "Am I so far gone, in my desperate need for meaning, that I'm prepared to distort everything, to re-write the whole history of my times purely in order to place myself in a central role?" (*Midnight's Children* 198). He is desperate at all costs to avoid "absurdity" (4). Yet, it is exactly in this endeavour, by attempting to construct his life out of the historical situation that was laid against his background, that he becomes shaken, impotent, and by the end of his novel, ready, like his grandfather, to "crack," to let his various parts scattered to the wind.

He has the same difficulty as the central character in Naipaul's *The Mimic Men*. Like Saleem, Naipaul's narrator wants to embrace the full gamut of colonial history, to understand its movements and its meanings. This is the background to his life, the very thing that has made him who he is. Again, like Saleem, he is unable to get hold of this history, and in the process, he is unable to grasp of himself. He says, "I am too much a victim of the restlessness which was to have been my subject" (*The Mimic Men* 38). The correspondence of the individual to history in these novels almost always ends in the dissolution of the subject into his or her many constituent parts, which, like the parts of Saleem, may be scattered in the wind. Their attempts seem to be very much akin to the gestic motion suggested by Spivak concerning the attempt to find the truth of subjectivity. They are acting out a "reaching and un-grasping."[13]

These novels seem to indicate that in the search for self, there are many different voices, many different impositions, and many different cultural influences. Therefore, it is problematical for all these various components to inhabit one, singular self or one unitary presence. In fact, what these novels seem to suggest is precisely the findings of postmodernism, with its emphasis on decentered subjectivities and a self that is invaded by the disquietudes of difference. Michael Gorra neatly sums this up when he says there is

> no way to become the sole author of the self. Texts are made of other texts. And so the frenzy and the fear, the raw nerves, the long line of books, the body of work built up as a stay against the pain of one's own dependency, desperately trying to write into being the self that one knows one can never fully achieve.[14]

These particular novels, because of their artistic form, are able to interrogate this theoretical position by giving it flesh and bone. They operate in a dialogic fashion. They enable "*another's speech in another's language*...a special type of *double*-voiced discourse."[15]

Because they are often written from the point of view of a subject in the process of decentering and dissolution, these novels are able to act out the exilic condition. As Rushdie says of his novels, they manage not only to represent but also to give life to "the very experience of uprooting, disjuncture and metamorphosis (slow or rapid, painful or pleasurable) that is the migrant condition..." (Interview 2). Furthermore, these novelists are not only concerned with the performance of the ambivalence and confusion that is caused by the dissolution of the subject *per se*. They are centrally concerned with the dissolution of the subject in a particular set of conditions: in a society that can be considered post-colonial. So not only do the subjects have to negotiate the many voices and many roles, they also have to encounter the ambivalence that occurs because of their proximity to changing surroundings and cultures. They are, more than anything, slowly dissolving their subjectivities because of the many subject positions they can take with respect to the cultural milieus in which they exist and have to negotiate. The concern of these novels is not simply with opening up subjectivity but also with the relation of those subjectivities to the notions of "landscape" and "home."

In dealing with how the subjectivity of the exile reacts when placed in close proximity to these concepts, it might be worth remembering the question posed by Foucault on this point: "Departing from what ground shall I find my identity?"[16] His question is rhetorical, but it is a question that seems to resonate through the work of the three authors under consideration. This point becomes clear in Naipaul's *The Mimic Men*. The narrator has already attempted to define himself against the colonial past, which failed him—it was the "restlessness," which meant he was unable to close the gaps in his being. In a similar way, he tries to put a seal on the authenticity of the self by changing his surroundings.

> [I]t was now that I resolved to abandon the ship-wrecked island and all on it and to seal my chieftainship in that real world from which, like my father, I had been cut off[;] I was consciously holding myself back for the reality which lay elsewhere. (*The Mimic Men* 141)

This attempt fails, just as all the other characters in the five other novels fail to orient themselves against their backgrounds. Whether it is Hannah's attempt in *The Holder of the World* to become whole by taking on the roles of the Puritan society that surrounds her or the narrator's attempts in *The Enigma of Arrival* to travel to England to become an English writer like the rest of those who make up the "canon" of literature that he so admires, they all fail. The key to their failure is the idea expressed in *The Mimic Men* that "the real world" was something that "lay elsewhere." This is not a simple expression of the distance of desire; it is rather a part of a system of "imaginary homelands." Every central character sees the world in which he or she is living as unreal. Yet, the character could be whole if only he or she were in a real world. In spite of this, it soon becomes clear that such a "real world" is always and necessarily elsewhere.

Homelands are, these novels seem to suggest, necessarily "imaginary." Indeed, like the India of *Midnight's Children*, they are dream worlds in which semimagical things can occur that disrupt and distend a singular notion of history. Saleem says that the 1,001 children who were born on the day of Indian independence were "also the children of time: fathered, you understand, by history. It can happen. Especially in a country which is itself a sort of a dream" (*Midnight's Children* 137). Of course, Rushdie is commenting on the strange historical position of India, as a newly freed country, a nation that has never really been a nation because of its pre-colonial division and colonial subjugation. But he is also commenting on the inability to see India (and India's history) as a solid reality. Rather, it is a dream, and a dream that is dreamt up, like the entire novel, within the master dreamer, Saleem himself. He says, on discovering his mistake over the date of Ghandi's death, "in my India, Ghandi will continue to die at the wrong time" (*Midnight's Children* 197). The emphasis here is on *my* India, the India that *I* have created and in which the idea of a history that is factual (and singular) need not apply. Ghandi dies to suit the individual who is constructing the landscape and history for himself. As Jameson comments about the nature of the postmodern notion of history, "the past as 'referent' finds itself gradually bracketed, and then effaced altogether."[17]

In the words of the narrator of *The Enigma of Arrival*, then, "Land is not land alone, something that simply is itself. Land partakes of what we breathe into it, is touched by our moods and memories" (*The Enigma of Arrival* 301). Far from being a possibility that the drifting of an individual's subjectivity can be anchored to a stable landscape, the landscape itself is decentered and movable, and the individual subject takes a large part in that process. The landscape is dependent on the person who stands within it, but the "person" who stands within it cannot achieve full personhood without reference to a stability that does not exist. What this constitutes is a shuttling, a dialectic of incompleteness, that invades both the notion of a stable subjectivity and the notion of a singular reality. Both the subject and the landscape can be altered simultaneously, simply through the creative power of their contact. Take, for example, the return of Saleem's grandfather: "Now, returning, he saw through travelled eyes. Instead of the beauty of the tiny valley circled by giant teeth, he noticed the narrowness, the proximity of the horizon; and felt sad, to be at home and so utterly enclosed" (*Midnight's Children* 5). The landscape is altered under the eye of the subject who has himself been altered by other landscapes, and on seeing it, the subject changes once more. For that reason, Saleem's grandfather feels enclosed, despite being at home. This interplay continues throughout the trajectories of both the subject and the landscape; each alters and invades the other, and neither of them is able to reach completeness. There is always a "distance from any clear-cut identity or notion of home."[18]

This distance does not mean that there can be no positive aspect to the interplay of self and landscape. Though this mutual creation and re-creation cannot end in either achieving a single, stable identity, the creative process can do some good. For example, the interplay of landscape and subjectivity bring together the two central female characters in Bharati Mukherjee's *The Holder of the World* into a unity that does not attempt to suspend or erase difference. The characters go through a somber ceremony of renaming: "She wasn't Hannah any more; she was Mukta, Bhagmati's word for 'pearl.' And she gave Bhagmati a new name: Hester, after the friend she had lost" (*The Holder of the World* 271). This simple sentence manages to include within its structure all the paths of difference that have been plotted throughout the novel and that have gone into constructing these two different women. They include within them the landscapes of the Puritan world and of India—thus, the power of the exotic (in the use of the name "pearl"), as well as the power of memory. The landscapes that Hannah has traversed visibly engrave themselves on her in the interchanging of names, a vocal demonstration of the changes that have occurred. Of course, these two women will also make a large change on the landscape as well, being at the very center of the changing power of history.

Reality, these novels suggest, does not necessarily need the things that once validated it for the rational mind: stability and singularity. Rushdie writes in *Midnight's Children*, "Reality can have metaphorical content; that does not make it less real" (240). This is the wonder of the metaphorical method of approaching these issues. As opposed to a purely theoretical approach, the artistry of these writers makes a more important impact on both the postmodern concerns of subjectivity and discourse construction, as well as on the dominant discourses in the world of post-coloniality. These authors do not attempt to negotiate with the subject or the world as factual entities; rather, they can put in process a negotiation *within* the subject and the world. They can already begin to alter the constitution of those very notions that theoretical discourses are trying to analyze and explain.

This interplay of landscape and subjectivity and the acceptance of them both as open entities will have an enormous effect on what has come to be known as the "politics of post-coloniality." These novelists, because of their place in the Western canon—and also, one might add, due to their acts of distancing themselves from the countries they are in exile from—have come to be described as apolitical. As I have tried to argue throughout, though, their novels are far from apolitical and they provide a very potent possibility for resistance. However, we must be quite clear what this resistance entails. It is certainly a very different concept to some of the revolutionary Marxists who opened up the possibility of a post-colonial world with their resistance to oppression, and quite a different kind of politics to the nationalist party politics that loom over the countries that have freed themselves from oppression. However, this politics is *not* conservative, nor is it conciliatory. It is very much in the radical vein, perhaps more radical than many of the other proponents of the politics of post-coloniality.

To orient this discussion, I turn to some of the most important critics of what has been called the postmodern turn in the post-colonial movement. Many of them come from the Marxist tradition and certainly agree with the Marxist requirement for praxis and the tactical intervention in the "real world" by theory. Two such theorists who concentrate particularly on the corrosive effects of a postmodern post-colonialism are Aijaz Ahmad and Araf Dirlik.

Ahmad characterizes the move away from a political form of post-colonial thought (with an emphasis on tactical means, attempts at resistance, and material forms of oppression) to what could be characterized as a textual form, a retrograde step. It is a move driven, in Ahmad's opinion, by the "coming-to-awareness" of those who wrote in the post-colonial vein of their place in the discursive systems of oppression that were preconstitutive of and contributive to the colonial situation:

> [A]t least some of the intellectuals of the contemporary West learned to question their own place in the world, and hence to question the hegemonic closure of the texts upon which their epistemologies were based.[19]

To some extent, Ahmad sees this development as a positive step. He so criticizes Said and his *Orientalism* for being too ethnocentric in its approach to "the Orient," which, according to Ahmad, presented Orientalism as "unified, self-identical, transhistorical, textual."[20] Ahmad is well aware of the difficulties presented by the possibility that, reflexively, those texts that attack an essentializing approach to the Orient can be hoisted on their own petard and come to embody precisely the methodological approach which they are seeking to attack.

However, Ahmad believes that this entrance into a "textual" kind of criticism has impeded the actual act that post-colonialism sees as its ultimate aim: the freeing of peoples from oppression. The criticism of Said that he has made the Orient into something which is "transhistorical, textual" comes from a desire to orientate the notion of colonial power back into a notion of historical development, material conditions and the actuality of existence. Indeed, he sees the "turn" in post-colonialism studies away from the attempt to pose political questions, to the posing of textual ones as a result of certain ideological and material interests in Western discourse, to hold back the tide of revolutionary change. He says that since the 1960s—which can be considered the origins of the postmodern critical thought at its height in the 1980s—"dominant strands have been mobilized to domesticate, in institutional ways, the very forms of political dissent which those movements had sought to foreground, to displace an activist with a textual culture."[21] Rather than a step forward on the post-colonial question, he sees the postmodern turn as an attempt by Western discourse to shore itself up against the activist attacks that may have shaken it in a more real and powerful way.

This is the point at which Dirlik picks up the thread of thought opposed to a textual form of post-colonialism of the sort practiced by the three novelists. Rushdie, Mukherjee, and Naipaul have shown how the subject is dissolved, particularly through its contact with history. They show that because of the disruptive effects of the subject's context, it cannot be considered singular or stable. This, according to Dirlik, is the central difficulty with the postmodern approach to post-colonial thought. Such an approach necessitates a political price: "The political price paid for this achievement, however, has been to abolish the subject in history, which destroys the possibility of political action."[22] For a political act to have any meaning (e.g., saving the colonized from colonial oppression), Dirlik believes we must hold on to the idea of the subject as a victim to be saved, a political hero to do the saving.

This difficulty of not being able to imagine a means of resistance without the notion of a stable subjectivity, a human being, a victim who is oppressed, dovetails with Dirlik's other attempt to return to a more politically aware time, his desire for a neo-structuralism. Dirlik thinks it is a negative attribute of postmodern and post-colonial thought that it employs "a situational approach that valorizes contingency and difference over systemic totality."[23] For Dirlik, the colonial situation is systematic: There are people at the top (the oppressors), people at the bottom (the victims), and in between, there are various apparati of power (armies, propaganda, etc.). The colonial system can be analyzed and resisted through the tactical dismantling of those apparati of power. Both Dirlik and Ahmad range themselves against the central importance of an understanding of the play of differences as a system of oppression. For them, the problem is unambiguous: Those who are oppressed are easily identifiable and the only thing required of post-colonial thought is to find a way of dismantling the system.

This account is both a simplistic and an idealistic notion of how oppression is carried out, both in the means that are employed and in its effects in the real world. And it is precisely the exile that shows the difficulty with a post-colonial theory that does not accept difference at its center. Who, for example is Hannah Easton in *The Holder of the World*? Is she the colonial? The oppressor? Can she merely take her place in the apparatus of English rule in India? Or is she, as the Bibi, the victim of colonial pressure—not just from the English, but also from the warring tribe of her husband and the King? Moreover, where does her femininity fit into these systems of oppression? And perhaps most importantly, from what position can someone make these distinctions about the many layers and functions of Hannah Easton within the colonial system? As Rushdie's narrators often tell us, one's perspective determines the historical situation in which one is in.

This is why Dirlik's philosophy also needs to question the possibility of a position of critical truth. The three novelists deride theorists for standing outside or above the discourse by centering their own "stories" on a human level with subjects who need to negotiate the difficulties of the colonial situation. For these novelists, there is

# Conclusion

no outside from which culture can be viewed; everyone is always and already within the system. However, Dirlik envisions the possibility of an "outside" from which culture can be viewed.

> It is not that there are no outsides but that those outsides must of necessity be conceived of as post-Eurocentric, as products of contradictions generated by the dialectic between a globalizing Euro-America and places that struggle against such globalization.[24]

Dirlik sees the possibility of being outside of the discourse of postcolonialism as achievable through a Hegelian sublation: When the thesis and antithesis of the West and the rest of the world are finally formed into a synthesis, then it will be possible to view the colonial system from the outside.

Yet again, however, this notion is called into question by the exiles in the novels of Rushdie, Mukherjee, and Naipaul. For they are, in their own way, an allegorical representation of the sort of synthesis that Dirlik is suggesting; they are decidedly *post*-the clash of civilizations that he is proposing. However, these novels do not pose a resolution that is achievable from these syntheses. None of the characters achieve a transcendental position from which to fully understand the colonial situation of which he or she is a product and has been forced to act against. In this way, there is "no arrival." Rather, the system that each one of the novels seems to propose is that of the continual attempt at synthesis, the continual shuttling without the resolution that Dirlik proposes. Landscape interacts with subject, subject interacts with history, and history interacts with landscape. There is never an end. The true political significance of these writers is that there is a means of resistance in the continuation of the attempt in the possibility of such an attempt's sublation. There is, in the words of Afzal Khan, an "ideology of liberation" at work in these novels and these writers can "transform their past, their culture, and their people."[25]

Critics of the kind of fiction that the three novelists write often maintain that it is merely a hollow gesture, speaking the language of post-colonialism without any effectiveness. As Harootunian states,

> Sometimes, the mere enunciation of cultural difference and thus identity is made to appear as a political act of crowning importance, when it usually means the disappearance of politics, as such. The politics of identity based on the enunciation of cultural difference is not the same as political identity, whose formation depends less on difference than on some recognition of equivalences.[26]

Ahmad makes the specific criticism of Rushdie's novels that they are "occupied so entirely by Power, that there is no space left for either resistance or representation."[27] The question at stake, then, is to try to create a politics that does not rely on "some recognition of equivalences," a politics not of the old mould that requires the formation of parties or sects, unions or parliaments, but a politics that is based on difference and dispersal rather than on the affirmation of unity.

The first step toward such a politics is an understanding that to concentrate on the legacy of historical imperialism, to concentrate on a reified past of colonial oppression, to simply look back at colonial violence, at the expense of a concerted attempt to engage with the present will "end up in a dead end."[28] All the novels are written in and of a world that has passed through the stage of colonialism and an epoch that has seen all of the major empires of the 19th and 20th centuries disbanded. *Midnight's Children*, for example, takes the very day of Indian independence as a seminal turning point in the narrative. That is not to say that there is no political work to be done, but that the political work is very different from an attempt to free the majority of the world's people. Nor is it to say that history is unimportant to the kind of politics that is worked through by these writers. These novels (with perhaps the exception of Mukherjee's *Jasmine* and Naipaul's *The Enigma of Arrival*, which are more domestic in character) explicitly interact with both the concept and the "reality" of history.

On the other hand, they do not treat history as the rigid construct that critics such as Ahmad and Dirlik do. For them, history is the ground on which events occur and at most, is able to give an explanation for the various arrangements of power. For

# Conclusion

Rushdie, Mukherjee, and Naipaul, history is a weapon in the fight for resistance. It is not the ground on which events are played out, but it is an event in the struggle for the post-colonial world and post-colonial subjecthood. While Ahmad and Dirlik see history as the collusion of certain material forces, Rushdie is able to play with history, transform it, and rearrange it to serve his metaphorical purposes. This rearrangement is not performed idly but tactically; the changes that Saleem admits to in *Midnight's Children* are interventions in the way India is represented in the post-colonial arrangement of power. The distinction is, perhaps, best illustrated by an example from Mukherjee's *The Holder of the World* in which Beigh (using her boyfriend's reality re-creator) sees a particular version of history—a history, probably, that she would prefer to see. For her, facts are not neutral; they have value. This is how a politics of difference interacts with history.

None of these writers have any time for nationalism (neither the nationalism that underpinned the colonial project when it was wielded by Western powers nor the nationalism that has grown up to aid anticolonial movements). This stance has led them to be seen as outcasts from their homelands. Mukherjee has been called a traitor when she has openly attacked what she sees as isolationism in the immigrant communities in the United States, denigrating their "bitter, exiled discourse" ("Imagining Homelands" 69). Famously, on the publication of *The Satanic Verses*, a fatwa was issued on Rushdie's life and he had to go into hiding. However, the reason for the stance these writers take is their commitment to a politics that does not stand for any notion of unification or insularism. As Rushdie has said of *The Satanic Verses*, the problems that are addressed in the book have resonances in the outside world:

> [J]ust the sort of great problems...have arisen to surround the book, problems of hybridization and ghettoization, or reconciling the old and the new. Those who oppose the novel most vociferously today are of the opinion that intermingling with a different culture will inevitably weaken and ruin their own. ("In Good Faith" 394)

Those who are not interested in the mixture of ideas and the coming together and parting of the play of differences are those who are opposed to the mixing of cultures. While Marxist post-colonialists see the beginning of post-colonial movements as a positive step on the road to freedom, the three novelists see them as retrograde, regressive, and equally as contemptible as the nationalistic justifications given by those who perpetrated the crimes of colonialism in the first place.

This is the point made by Naipaul in *The Mimic Men* when his narrator, Ralph Singh (or Ranjit Kripalsingh, before changing his name to fit in at school) without any real desire to do so, becomes the head of the movement for freedom from colonial oppression in his fictional homeland. Ralph does not feel connected with the process and says that all this new breed of politician does is put himself in the position of "borrowing phrases" and that such action is "part of the escape from thought" (*The Mimic Men* 237). The political phrases are borrowed from the class that once ruled them. These politicians are, just as he and his classmates were at school, the "Mimic Men" of the title. This is the result of the clash between the Ethnocentric West and the rest of the world: It is a fight between a man and his reflection in the mirror. Colonialism has occurred; it is a fact of history; and there is no return (despite what some post-colonial thinkers might wish) to a state of innocence in which the subjects of colonialism can act freely outside the discourse to which they have been subjected. There is no outside to the post-colonial situation, the three novelists seem to suggest, and the future and any politics of post-coloniality that seeks to forge it must negotiate within the system. This politics must produce, at the very center of discourse, an outside of the inside, an inner rim. It must follow, like the central characters in the novels, the trajectory of the exile.

One of the most important sentences in any of these three novels is one of the simplest. It is a statement by the central character of Bharati Mukherjee's *Jasmine*. In Mukherjee's novel, the central character takes on many roles and many names; she has assimilated into the dominant discourses of whatever land she has been a part of and has met the expectations of the men who offer her protection. At the first level of interpretation, Mukherjee's *Jasmine* seems to be a simple story of victimhood in which an illegal immigrant who is also a woman (both of whom are the classic victims of the West's view of the world) has to change herself to fit in with the world. Nonetheless, at the very center of the novel, there is an affirmation of this behaviour as an ethical stance, and one that could have serious political ramifications: "I changed because I wanted to" (*Jasmine* 185).

This simple statement is anathema to much of the politics of post-coloniality that sees resistance to the discourse of colonialism as a matter of confrontation. Change, particularly the kind of change that could be considered assimilation or collaboration, is a betrayal of the central core of post-colonialism's values. However, as Mukherjee makes quite clear in the progress of the central character through the novel, her changing is neither assimilation nor collaboration. In fact, the ability to change, to open one's own subjectivity up to all the various degrees of cultural difference, is a progressive step that satirizes the dominant discourse (the discourse of the exotic Indian migrant) without positing a second discourse to take its authoritarian position. This tactic can actively change the discourse to which the subject can subscribe. It can make not only a personal but also a historical difference. As the central character says at the end of the novel (which for the progress of ever-openness is actually one more new start), "Watch me re-position the stars" (*Jasmine* 240).

This ethics is very much personal in Mukherjee—though it has definite implicit political ramifications. In Rushdie's *Midnight's Children*, the personal and the political are almost simultaneous. And because Saleem was born when he was, becoming as he did, a symbol of the newly freed India, his openness to textual deformation actually shows a way of making an intervention in the dominant discourse without creating a new authoritarian viewpoint. Gandhi dies, in Saleem's India, while he is watching an Edenic scene on the projection screen—and by this seemingly coincidental co-occurrence of events, a whole new notion of Gandhi's death as being the fall from innocence is set in motion. However, as Saleem later admits, the co-occurrence was not coincidental at all; it was, rather, motivated (albeit subconsciously), and it was a formation that relied on an intervention to change history. It is important that, after Saleem realizes his mistake, he, nevertheless, does not rectify it, but holds firm to his "fictional" view of events. What is more important than factuality is that Saleem has made an intervention in the course of history, and thus, in the dominant understanding of Gandhi's death as "an event." By starting a whole new chain of significations—between Gandhi's death, the story of the fall, and all the cultural connections that these events set off—Saleem is changing the dominant discourse that surrounds Gandhi's death while refusing (by explicitly stating its fictional status) to proffer it as a more authoritative narrative.

Naipaul, perhaps even more than the other two writers, confronts the accusation that the "retreat" into a textual post-colonial stance is somehow apolitical. For he has both the narrator of *The Mimic Men* and the narrator of *The Enigma of Arrival* (who is almost an exact biographical representation of himself) see that the end of the question is writing. In both these novels and through their narrators, Naipaul uses the narrative device of ending the stories by having the narrator writing the book that the reader has been reading. In the case of *The Mimic Men*, he actually has the narrator give up a career in politics to sit in a hotel in England and write his own "his-story."

Indeed, it could be argued that both novels, if read in a cursory way, are actually tales of disengagement in which someone avoided the political questions of the day to concentrate on his own introverted narrative. But this is not the case. Naipaul faces up to the enormity of the confusion of the post-colonial situation and rather than seeing it in the black-and-white terms of many theorists, decides to make the intervention that is not only possible but also ethical. The narrator of *The Mimic Men*, while he is performing his political role as playing a part, goes along with the discourse into which he has been written. When he chooses writing as an affirmative and powerful way to resist the oppressive power discourses, he feels more freedom. This freedom comes not simply from transcending his situation but from being able to understand and negotiate the different roles and discourses into which he has been inscribed. By concentrating on his own personal situation, the narrator is able to make a more important political stance than when he was written into the discourse of politics uncritically. By the end of the novel, he feels that he is able to confront "a vision of disorder that was beyond any one man to control yet which, I felt, if I could pin down, might bring me calm" (97).

All the characters in these novels seem to achieve a suspension of the kind described by Robert Young in his treatment of deconstruction. It is a suspension "that makes the same no longer the same, the different no longer simply different," that enables "difference and sameness" to be held in "an apparently impossible simultaneity."[29] And the necessity of this suspension is that there is no possible return to the old kind of politics, a politics based on unity and equivalence, or on the subject as victim of violence. There is no return to the old kind of politics just as there is no return for the exile to the landscape that he calls "home" because no such landscape exists. The new politics of post-coloniality can only go onwards, without nostalgia and without hope of "arrival." The only "home" these writers propose is a non-location and the only possibility is to "dwell in hybridity as home."[30]

There are certain threads that run throughout my argument, just as they run throughout the novels that I have attempted to analyze, to deconstruct, and to locate within the matrix of post-colonial thought. One thread is the necessity of mimicry and its possible power to subvert the dialogic but suspended synthesis of the open subjectivity and the imaginary landscapes that are both constructed by and contribute to the construction of the notion of the post-colonial. A second is the ambivalence of the subject toward these landscapes, a third is the importance of the ethic of the exile, an ethic that reverberates through these texts and poses a new form of politics. These various threads or themes interweave and interact, just as the texts of the novels do themselves. They are implicit in but not constitutive to the three novelists and their work. In their juxtaposition emerges a kind of metatext lines of similarity and difference that seem to arise from within and between these texts as they interact within the wider context of post-colonial thought. None of them contain the whole of my conclusion; no single novel or novelist can be demonstrated to have expounded the view of the exile and imaginary home that has emerged. Some of the insights they have provided come from explicit authorial suggestion, others from characterization, still others from treating the figures that emerge from the texts as allegorical forms that play out the drama of post-colonialism as though in a kind of dumbshow. None of these interpretative techniques would I like to present as the only legitimate interpretations, nor would I render any of them invalid. They have evolved from an open reception to the text and to the movements that occur within.

What has arisen is a blueprint, a sort of general gesture, toward a view of post-coloniality that is shared by all six texts. Together, these novels provide both a view of the post-colonial world and a politics by which individuals can live within it while, at the same time, being able to perform some sort of act of resistance. Such an act would be characterized by both playing out the roles of colonial discourse and subverting them—by creating distance between the role-players and the roles they take on. It would contain an attempt to make sense of their own subjectivity through the landscapes they come into contact with (their past, the country of exile, their new "home," the history of their people, and their own his-story) and a realization that, though the subjectivity lies between all these poles, no combination of them will fully complete a singular and stable self. It would, in a simultaneous move, consist of the alteration of the landscape by the subject in a dialogue of diverted presence, a *contretemps*, in which neither subject nor landscape could achieve resolution but would always be open to the changing motion of play. Most of all, it would contain the denial of any role, land, discourse, or ideology that would seek to limit free play, that would demand that the exile say, "This (definitively) is who I am, this (definitively) is where I come from, this (definitively) is where I am going."

# Conclusion

Although the apex of the historical colonial moment has probably passed and although much independence has been won, oppression and violence have not ceased altogether. There is an opening—an opening that Rushdie, Mukherjee, and Naipaul all exploit—that would allow the suspension of oppression and violence (for it will never truly cease), whether it manifest itself in the form of colonial power, the hegemony of discourse, or even in post-colonial thinkers who take on the mantle of the colonials to whom they are opposed. Through the literature of exile that these authors write, through their fiction (for it is only in fiction that such an opening might appear), we gain access to this opening and might use it, tactically, strategically. These writers give us the space (within violence, within oppression) to put up a resistance, a space that we might (though only provisionally) call (a) "home." It is the only home worthy of exiles. It is an "imaginary land," a landscape that exile makes possible, one that will never be closed off, completed, or fulfilled.

## ENDNOTES

1. Walter Benjamin, *Illuminations* (New York: Harcourt, 1968) 263.
2. Michel Foucault, *The Archaeology of Knowledge* (London: Routledge, 1972).
3. Edward Said, *Orientalism* (New York: Vintage, 1978) 5.
4. Said 4–5.
5. Said 23.
6. Robert Young, *Colonial Desire: Hybridity in Theory, Culture and Race* (London: Routledge, 1995) 131.
7. Partha Chatterjee, *The Nation and Its Fragments* (Princeton, NJ: Princeton University Press, 1993) 147.
8. Homi Bhabha, *The Location of Culture* (London: Routledge, 1994) 2.
9. Homi Bhabha, "Signs Taken for Wonders," *The Post-Colonial Studies Reader*, ed. Bill Ashcroft, Gareth Griffiths, and Helen Tiffin (London: Routledge, 1995) 32.
10. Bhabha 75.
11. William Shakespeare, *Othello*, *The Complete Works of William Shakespeare* (London: Wordsworth, 1998) 820.
12. Bhabha (1994) 13.
13. Gayatri Chakravorty Spivak, *A Critique of Postcolonial Reason: Toward a History of the Vanishing Present* (Cambridge, MA: Harvard University Press, 1999) 242.
14. Michael Gorra, *After Empire: Scott, Naipaul, Rushdie* (Chicago: University of Chicago Press, 1997).
15. Mikhail Bakhtin, *The Dialogic Imagination: Four Essays*, trans. Caryl Emerson and Michael Holquist, ed. Michael Holquist (Austin: University of Texas Press, 1981).
16. Michel Foucault, *Essential Works of Foucault Vol. 1: Ethics*, ed. Paul Rainbow (New York: The New Press, 1997) 230.
17. Fredric Jameson, *Postmodernism, or The Cultural Logic of Late Capitalism* (Durham, NC: Duke University Press, 1991) 18.
18. Rob Nixon, "London Calling: V. S. Naipaul and the License of Exile," *South Atlantic Quarterly* 87.1 (1988): 37.
19. Aijaz Ahmad, *In Theory: Classes, Nations, Literatures* (New York: Verso, 1992) 58.
20. Ahmad 92.
21. Ahmad 90.

22. Arif Dirlik, "Borderlands Radicalism," *After the Revolution: Waking to Global Capitalism* (Hanover: Wesleyan University Press, 1994) 89.
23. Arif Dirlik, "Rethinking Colonialism: Globalization, Postcolonialism, and the Nation." *Interventions* 4 (2002): 433.
24. Arif Dirlik, "Is There History after Eurocentrism?" *History after the Three Worlds: Post-Eurocentric Historiographies*, ed. Arif Dirlik, Vinay Bal, and Peter Gran (Lanham, MD: Rowman & Littlefield, 2000) 36.
25. Fawzia Afzal-Khan, "Cultural Imperialism and the Indo-English Novel: Genre and Ideology," *Cultural Imperialism and the Indo-English Novel: Genre and Ideology in R.K. Narayan, Anita Desai, Kamala Markandaya, and Salman Rushdie* (University Park, PA: Penn State University Press, 1993) 5.
26. H. D. Harootunian, "Postcoloniality's Unconscious/Area Studies' Desire." *Postcolonial Studies* 2.2 (1999): 140.
27. Ahmad 127.
28. Michael Hardt and Antonio Negri, *Empire* (London: Harvard University Press, 2000) 137.
29. Robert Young, *Colonial Desire: Hybridity in Theory, Culture and Race* (London: Routledge, 1995) 36.
30. Iain Chambers, *Culture after Humanism: History, Culture, Subjectivity* (London: Routledge, 2001) 170.

# Bibliography

## Primary Works

Mukherjee, Bharati. "American Dreamer." *Mother Jones* Jan./Feb. 1997. Dec. 2005 <http://www.motherjones.com/commentary/columns/1997/01/mukherjee.html>.

---. *The Holder of the World.* London: Virago, 1994.

---. *Jasmine.* St. Ives: Virago, 1991.

---. *Letters of Transit: Reflections on Exile, Identity, Language, and Loss.* London: The New Press, 2000.

Naipaul, Vidiadhar Surajprasad. "East Indian." *Literary Occasions: Essays.* Ed. Pankaj Mishra. London: Picador, 2003. 35–44.

---. *The Enigma of Arrival: A Novel in Five Sections.* London: Viking, 1987.

---. *The Mimic Men.* London: Andre Deutsch, 1967.

---. *Naipaul Nobel Prize Acceptance Speech, 2001.* Dec. 2005. <http://www.caribvoice.org/CaribbeanDocuments/naipaul.htm>.

Rushdie, Salman. *Imaginary Homelands: Essays and Criticisms 1981–1991.* London: Granta, 1991.

---. "Imaginative Maps." Interview with Una Chaudhuri. *Turnstile* 2.1 (1990): 36–47.

---. *Midnight's Children.* London: Granta, 1981.

---. *The Satanic Verses.* London: Viking Penguin, 1988.

## Secondary Works

Afzal-Khan, Fawzia. *Cultural Imperialism and the Indo-English Novel: Genre and Ideology in R. K. Narayan, Anita Desai, Kamala Markandaya, and Salman Rushdie.* University Park, PA: Penn State University Press, 1993.

Ahmad, Aijaz. "Disciplinary English: Third-Worldism and Literature." *Rethinking English: Essays in Literature, Language, History.* Ed. Svati Joshi. New Delhi: Trianka, 1991. 206–263.

---. *In Theory: Classes, Nations, Literatures.* 1992. New York: Verso, 2000.

Anderson, Benedict. "Imagined Communities: Reflections on the Origin and Spread of Nationalism." *Shaping Discourses: Reading for University Writers.* Ed. April Lidinsky. Boston: Pearson, 2002. 7–20.

Appiah, Kwame Anthony. "Identity, Authenticity, Survival: Multicultural Societies and Social Reproduction." *Multiculturalism: Examining the Politics of Recognition.* Ed. Amy Gutmann. Princeton, NJ: Princeton University Press, 1994.

Ashcroft, Bill, Gareth Griffiths, and Helen Tiffin. *Key Concepts in Post-Colonial Studies.* New York: Routledge, 1998.

Bakhtin, Mikhail. *The Dialogic Imagination: Four Essays.* Trans. Caryl Emerson and Michael Holquist. Ed. Michael Holquist. Austin: University of Texas Press, 1981.

---. *Rabelais and His World.* Trans. Hélène Iswolsky. Cambridge, MA: MIT Press, 1973.

Bardolph, Jaqueline. "Language is Courage." *Reading Rushdie.* Amsterdam: Rodopi, 1994.

Barthes, Roland. *The Pleasure of the Text.* Trans. Richard Miller. New York: Cape, 1976.

Benjamin, Walter. *The Arcades Project.* Trans. Howard Eiland and Kevin McLaughlin. Cambridge, MA: Harvard University Press, 1999.

---. *Illuminations.* Trans. Harry Zohn. London: Collins (Fontana), 1973.

Bhabha, Homi. *The Location of Culture.* London: Routledge, 1994.

---. *Nation and Narration.* London: Routledge, 1990.

---."Of Mimicry and Man: The Ambivalence of Colonial Discourse." *October* 28 (Spring 1984): 125–133.

---. "The Other Question ..." *Screen* 24.6 (1983): 18–36.

---. "Signs Taken for Wonders." *The Post-Colonial Studies Reader*. Ed. Bill Ashcroft, Gareth Griffiths, and Helen Tiffin. London: Routledge, 1995. 29–35.

Boehmer, Elleke. *Colonial and Postcolonial Literature: Migrant Metaphors*. Oxford, UK: Oxford University Press, 1995.

Boxhill, Anthony. *V. S. Naipaul's Fiction: In Quest of the Enemy*. Fredericton, N.B., Canada: York, 1983.

Brennan, Timothy. *Salman Rushdie and the Third World: Myths of the Nation*. New York: St. Martin's, 1989.

Bromley, Roger. *Narratives for a New Belonging: Diasporic Cultural Fictions*. Edinburgh: Edinburgh University Press, 2000.

Bryden, Ronald. "The Novelist V. S. Naipaul Talks about His Work to Ronald Bryden." *The Listener* 22 Mar. 1973: 367.

Cabral, Amilcar. *Return to the Source: Selected Speeches of Amilcar Cabral*. New York: Monthly Review, 1979.

Chakrabarty, Dipesh. *Provincializing Europe: Postcolonial Thought and Historical Difference*. Princeton, NJ: Princeton University Press, 2000.

Chambers, Iain. *Culture after Humanism: History, Culture, Subjectivity*. London: Routledge, 2001.

Chatterjee, Partha. *The Nation and Its Fragments*. Princeton, NJ: Princeton University Press, 1993.

Chen, Tina, and Sean X. Goudie. *Holders of the Word: An Interview with Bharati Mukherjee*. Dec. 2005 <http://social.chass.ncsu.edu/jouvert/v1i1/bharat.htm>.

Clifford, James. "Diasporas." *Routes: Travel and Translation in the Late Twentieth Century*. Cambridge, MA: Harvard University Press, 1997. 244–277.

---. *The Predicament of Culture: Twentieth-Century Ethnography, Literature, and Art*. Cambridge, MA: Harvard University Press, 1988.

Conrad, Joseph. *Heart of Darkness*. London: Penguin, 1994.

Cudjoe, Selwyn Reginald. *V. S. Naipaul: A Materialist Reading*. Amherst: University of Massachusetts Press, 1988.

Derrida, Jacques. *Of Grammatology*. Trans. Gayatri Chakravorty Spivak. Baltimore, MD: Johns Hopkins University Press, 1976.

---. *Writing and Difference*. Trans. Alan Bass. Chicago: University of Chicago Press, 1978.

---. "Ulysses' Gramophone: Hear Say Yes in Joyce." *James Joyce: The Augmented Ninth*. Trans. Tina Kendall. Ed. Bernard Benstock. Syracuse, NY: Syracuse University Press, 1988. 27–75.

Dirlik, Arif. "Borderlands Radicalism." *After the Revolution: Waking to Global Capitalism*. Hanover, NH: Wesleyan University Press, 1994.

---. "Is There History after Eurocentrism?" *History after the Three Worlds: Post-Eurocentric Historiographies*. Ed. Arif Dirlik, Vinay Bal, and Peter Gran. Lanham, MD: Rowman & Littlefield, 2000. 25–47.

---. "Rethinking Colonialism: Globalization, Postcolonialism, and the Nation." *Interventions* 4 (2002): 428–448.

During, Simon. "Postmodernism or Post-Colonialism Today." *The Post-Colonial Studies Reader*. Ed. Bill Ashcroft, Gareth Griffiths, and Helen Tiffin. London: Routledge, 1995. 125–129.

Fanon, Frantz. *Black Skin, White Masks*. Trans. Charles Lam Markmann. London: Pluto, 1986.

---. *The Wretched of the Earth*. Trans. Constance Farrington. New York: Grove, 1968.

Fischer, Michael M. J. "Ethnicity and the Post-Modern Arts of Memory." *Writing Culture: The Poetics and Politics of Ethnography*. Ed. James Clifford and George E. Marcus. Berkeley: University of California Press, 1986. 194–233.

Fleischman, W. B., ed. *Encyclopaedia of World Literature:* New York: Ungar Publishing Company, 1967.

Foucault, Michel. *The Archaeology of Knowledge*. London: Routledge, 1972.

---. *The Archaeology of Knowledge and the Discourse on Language*. Trans. A. M. Sheridan Smith. New York: Barnes and Noble, 1993.

---. *Essential Works of Foucault Vol. 1: Ethics*. Ed. Paul Rainbow. New York: The New Press, 1997.

---. *Foucault Live: Collected Interviews, 1961–1984*. Ed. Sylvére Lotringer. New York: Semotext(e), 1996.

Franco, Jean. "Beyond Ethnocentrism: Gender, Power, and the Third-World Intelligentsia." *Marxism and the Interpretation of Culture*. Ed. Cary Nelson and Lawrence Grossberg. Urbana: University of Illinois Press, 1988. 503–515.

Fuss, Diana. "Interior Colonies: Frantz Fanon and the Politics of Identification." *Diacritics* 24 (1994): 20–42.

Gorra, Michael. *After Empire: Scott, Naipaul, Rushdie*. Chicago: University of Chicago Press, 1997.

Greene, Gayle. "Feminist Fiction and the Uses of Memory." *Journal of Women in Culture and Society* 16.2 (1991): 290–321.

Gurnah, Abdulrazak. "Displacement and Transformation in *The Enigma of Arrival* and *The Satanic Verses*." *Other Britain, Other British: Contemporary Multicultural Fiction*. Ed. Robert Lee. London: Pluto, 1995. 5–20.

Hall, Stuart. "Cultural Identity and Diaspora." *Colonial Discourse and Post-Colonial Theory: A Reader*. Ed. Patrick Williams and Laura Chrisman. New York: Columbia University Press, 1994. 392–403.

---. "Culture, Community, Nation." *Cultural Studies* 7.3 (1993): 349–363.

---. "The Question of Cultural Identity." *Modernity and Its Future*. Ed. Stuart Hall et al. Cambridge, UK: Polity, 1992. 274–316.

Hardt, Michael, and Antonio Negri. *Empire*. London: Harvard University Press, 2000.

Harootunian, Harry D. "Postcoloniality's Unconscious/Area Studies, Desire." *Postcolonial Studies* 2.2 (1999): 127–147.

Harris, Wilson. *The Womb of Space: The Cross-Cultural Imagination*. Westport, CT: Greenwood, 1983.

Henderson, Mae Gwendolyn. *Speaking in Tongues: Dialogics, Dialectics and the Black Woman Writer's Literary Tradition. Reading Black, Reading Feminist: A Critical Anthology*. Ed. H. L. Gates, Jr. New York: Meridian, 1990. 116–162.

Hulme, Peter. *Colonial Encounters: Europe and the Native Caribbean, 1492–1797*. London: Methuen, 1986.

Jameson, Fredric. *Postmodernism, or the Cultural Logic of Late Capitalism*. Durham, NC: Duke University Press, 1991.

King, Bruce. *V. S. Naipaul*. New York: St. Martin's, 1993.

Kristeva, Julia. *The Kristeva Reader.* Trans. Toril Moi. London: Blackwell, 1986.

---. *Strangers to Ourselves.* Trans. Leon S. Roudiez. New York: Hill, 1972.

Lacan, Jacques. *Écrits.* New York: Norton, 1977.

---. *The Four Fundamental Concepts of Psychoanalysis.* New York: Norton, 1978.

Lawson, Alan. "The Discovery of Nationality in Australian and Canadian Literatures." *The Post-Colonial Studies Reader.* Ed. Bill Ashcroft, Gareth Griffiths, and Helen Tiffin. London: Routledge, 1995.

Lenin, Vladimir Illich Ulyanov. *What Is to Be Done?* New York: International, 1969.

Lyotard, Jean-François. *The Postmodern Condition.* Minneapolis: University of Minnesota Press, 1984.

Macaulay, Thomas. "Minute on Indian Education." *The Post-Colonial Studies Reader.* Ed. Bill Ashcroft, Gareth Griffiths, and Helen Tiffin. London: Routledge, 1995. 428–430.

McClintock, Ann. "The Angel of Progress: Pitfalls of the Term 'Post-Colonialism.'" *Social Text* (Spring 1992): 1–15.

Mishra, Vijay, and Robert Ian Vere Hodge. "What is Post-Colonialism?" *Textual Practice* 5 (1991): 399–414.

Mohanty, Chandra Talpade. "Under Western Eyes: Feminist Scholarship and Colonial Discourses." *Feminist Review* 30 (Autumn 1988): 65–88.

"Mukherjee." *English Databanks Fu Jen: World Literature.* Managed by Kate Lui. 20 Feb. 2006 <http://www.eng.fju.edu.tw/worldlit/india/mukherjee.html>.

Mukherjee, Bharati. *Darkness.* New York: Penguin Books, 1985.

---. "A Four-Hundred-Year-Old Woman." *The Writer on Her Work.* Ed. Janet Sternburg. 2 vols. New York: Norton, 1991. 33–38.

---. "Immigrant Writing: Give Us Your Maximalists!" *New York Times Book Review* 28 Aug. 1988: 28–29.

---. *Wife.* Boston: Houghton, 1975.

---, and Clark Blaise. *Days and Nights in Calcutta.* Saint Paul, MN: Hungry Mind, 1995.

---, and Robert Boyers. "A Conversation with V. S. Naipaul." *Salmagundi* 50–51 (Fall 1980–Winter 1981): 4–22.

Mustafa, Fawzia. "V. S. Naipaul." *Cambridge Studies in African and Caribbean Literature.* Cambridge, UK: Cambridge University Press, 1995.

Naipaul, Vidiadhar Surajprasad. *Half a Life*. London: Picador, 2001.

---. In *A Free State*. London: Andre Deutsch, 1971.

---. *The Middle Passage: Impressions of Five Societies - British, French, and Dutch in the West Indies and South America*. London: Andre Deutsch, 1962. Rpt. in 2002. New York: Random House.

Nixon, Rob. "London Calling: V. S. Naipaul and the License of Exile." *South Atlantic Quarterly* 87.1 (1988): 1–37.

---. *London Calling: V. S. Naipaul. Postcolonial Mandarin*. Oxford, UK: Oxford University Press, 1992.

Philip, Marlene Nourbese. *She Tries Her Tongue, Her Silence Softly Breaks*. London: Women's, 1993.

Plato. "Allegory of the Cave." *The Norton Reader*. Ed. Linda H. Peterson, John C. Brereton, and Joan E. Hartman. New York: Norton, 2000. 652–655.

Rodríguez, María Cristina. *What Women Lose: Exile and the Construction of Imaginary Homelands in Novels by Caribbean Writers. Caribbean Studies*. Ed. Tamara Alvarez-Detrell and Michael G. Paulson. Vol. 6. New York: Lang, 2005.

Rubenstein, Robert. "Review of *The Holder of the World*." *The Washington Post: Book World* 24 Oct. 1993: 1+.

Rushdie, Salman. "The East is Blue." *XXX: 30 Porn Star Photographs*. Timothy Greenfield-Sanders and Gore Vidal. London: Bulfinch, 2004. 98–106.

---. *East, West*. 1994. New York: Random House, 1995.

---. *Grimus: A Novel*. Woodstock, NY: Overlook, 1979.

---. *Haroun and the Sea of Stories*. New York: Penguin, 1990.

---. *Shalimar the Clown: A Novel*. New York: Random House, 2005.

---. *Step Across This Line: Collected Nonfiction 1992–2002*. New York: Random House, 2002.

Said, Edward. *Orientalism*. New York: Vintage, 1978.

---. "Movements and Migrations." *Culture and Imperialism*. New York: Vintage, 1993. 326–336.

---. *Representations of the Intellectual: The 1993 Reith Lectures*. New York: Pantheon, 1994.

Sarup, Madan. *An Introductory Guide to Post-Structuralism and Postmodernism*. Athens: University of Georgia Press, 1993.

Saussure, Ferdinand de. *Course in General Linguistics*. Trans. Wade Baskin. Ed. Charles Balley and Albert Sechehaye. New York: McGraw-Hill, 1966.

Seidel, Michael. *Exile and the Narrative Imagination*. New Haven, CT: Yale University Press, 1986.

Senghor, Léopold Sédor. *The Africa Reader: Independent Africa*. London: Vintage, 1970.

Shakespeare, William. *Othello. The Complete Works of William Shakespeare*. London: Wordsworth, 1998.

Shapiro, Gary. "On the Post-Nationalist Writer." 11 Feb. 2006 <http://www.nysun.com/article/12795>.

Spivak, Gayatri Chakravorty. *A Critique of Postcolonial Reason: Toward a History of the Vanishing Present*. Cambridge, MA: Harvard University Press, 1999.

Sterne, Lawrence. *The Life and Opinions of Tristram Shandy, Gentleman*. London: Penguin, 2003.

Thieme, John. *The Web of Tradition: Uses of Allusion in V. S. Naipaul's Fiction*. Hertford, England: Hansib, 1987.

Tiffin, Helen. "Transformative Imaginaries." *From Commonwealth to Post-Colonial: Critical Essays*. Ed. Anna Rutherford. Sydney, N. S. W.: Kangaroo, 1992.

White, Paul. "Geography, Literature and Migration." *Writing across Worlds: Literature and Migration*. London: Routledge, 1995.

Young, Robert. *Colonial Desire: Hybridity in Theory, Culture and Race*. London: Routledge, 1995.

# SELECTED WORKS CONSULTED

Aciman, André, ed. *Letters of Transit: Reflections on Exile, Identity, Language, and Loss*. New York: New York Public Library, 1999.

Anzaldúa, Gloria. *Borderlands/La Frontera: The New Mestiza*. San Francisco: Spinsters, 1987.

Appadurai, Arjun. "Disjuncture and Difference in the Global Cultural Economy." *Public Culture* 2.2 (1990): 1–24.

---. *Globalization*. Durham, NC: Duke University Press, 2001.

---. *Modernity at Large: Cultural Dimensions of Globalization*. Minneapolis, MN: University of Minnesota Press, 1996.

Appiah, Kwame Anthony. "Is The Post- in Postmodernism the Post- in Post-Colonial?" *Critical Inquiry* 17 (1991): 336–357.

Ashcroft, Bill, et al. *The Empire Writes Back: Theory and Practice in Post-Colonial Literatures*. London: Routledge, 1989.

Calafețeanu, Ion. *Politicăși exil: Din istoria exilului românesc, 1946–1950*. București [Bucharest]: Editura Enciclopedică, 2000.

Carb, Alison B. "An Interview with Bharati Mukherjee." *The Massachusetts Review* 29.4 (1988): 645–654.

Dashefsky, Arnold. *Ethnic Identity in Society*, 1975. Rpt. in *The Ethnic Factor: Identity in Diversity*. Ed. Leo Driedger. Toronto: McGraw, 1989. 136–137.

Dirlik, Arif. *After the Revolution: Waking to Global Capitalism*. Hanover, NH: Wesleyan University Press, 1994.

Dissanayake, Wimal, and Carmen Wickramagamage. *Self and Colonial Desire: Travel Writings of V. S. Naipaul*. New York: Lang, 1993.

Feder, Lillian. *Naipaul's Truth: The Making of a Writer*. New York: Rowman, 2001.

Gellner, Ernest. *Nations and Nationalism*. Ithaca, NY: Cornell University Press, 1983.

Glage, Lise Lotte, ed. *Being/s in Transit: Traveling, Migration, Dislo-Cation*. Amsterdam: Rodopi, 2000.

Glodeanu, Gheorghe. *Incursiuni in literatura diasporei şi a dizidenţei*. Bucureşti: [Bucharest]: Libra, 2000.

Gramsci, Antonio. *Selections from the Prison Notebooks*. Ed. and trans. Quintin Hoare and Geoffrey Nowell Smith. New York: International, 1971.

Gussow, Mel. "Writer without Roots." *The New York Times Magazine* 26 Dec. 1976: 19–22.

Hall, Stuart. "Cultural Identity and Diaspora." *Identity: Community, Culture, Difference*. Ed. Jonathan Rutherford. London: Lawrence, 1990. 222–237.

Israel, Nico. *Outlandish: Writing between Exile and Diaspora*. Stanford, CA: Stanford University Press, 2000.

Koshy, Susan. "The Geography of Female Subjectivity: Ethnicity, Gender and Diaspora in Mukherjee's Fiction." *Diaspora* 3.1 (1994): 69–84.

Lionnet, Françoise. *Autobiographical Voices: Race, Gender, Self-Portraiture*. Ithaca, NY: Cornell University Press, 1989.

Lukacs, Georg. *A Defense of History and Class Consciousness*. Stanford, CA: Stanford University Press, 2000.

---. *The Historical Novel*. Minneapolis, MN: University of Minnesota Press, 1990.

---. *Studies in European Realism*. Toronto: Toronto University Press, 2001.

---. *The Theory of the Novel*. Minneapolis, MN: University of Minnesota Press, 1974.

Lyotard, Jean-François. *Le Postmoderne expliqué aux enfants*. Paris: Galilee, 1986.

Mura, David. "A Shift in Power, a Sea Change in the Arts: Asian American Constructions." *The State of Asian America: Activism and Resistance in the 1990s*. Ed. Karin Aguilar-San Juan. Boston: South End, 1994.

Naficy, Hamid, ed. *Home, Exile, Homeland: Film, Media, and the Politics of Place*. London: Routledge, 1998.

---, and Teshome Gabriel, eds. *Otherness and the Media: The Ethnography of the Imagined and the Imaged*. New York: Harwood, 1993.

Ruppel, F. Timothy. "'Re-Inventing Ourselves a Million Times': Narrative, Desire, Identity, and Bharati Mukherjee's *Jasmine*." *College Literature* 22:1 (1995): 181–192.

Said, Edward W. *Culture and Imperialism*. London: Chatto, 1993.

---. *Reflections on Exile and Other Essays*. Cambridge, MA: Harvard University Press, 2000.

---. *The World, the Text and the Critic*. London: Faber, 1983.

Spivak, Gayatri Chakravorty. "Can the Subaltern Speak?" *Marxism and the Interpretation of Culture*. Ed. Larry Grossberg and Cary Nelson. Urbana: University of Illinois Press, 1988. 271–313.

---. "Imperialism and Sexual Difference." *Oxford Literary Review* 8 (1986): 225–240.

---. *Outside in the Teaching Machine*. New York: Routledge, 1993.

---. *Selected Subaltern Studies*. New York: Oxford University Press, 1988. 45–86.

Suleiman, Rubin Susan, ed. *Exile and Creativity. Signposts, Travelers, Outsiders, Backward Glances*. Durham, NC: Duke University Press, 1998.

Suleri, Sara. *The Rhetoric of English India*. Chicago: University of Chicago Press, 1992.

Sultana, Rebecca. *Patchwork Creations: Acculturation and Resistance in Contemporary Immigrant Fiction*. Diss. Texas Christian University, 1999. Ann Arbor, MI: UMI, 2001.

Tay, Eddie. "Unsettling Ways of Exile: The Unhomely in the Poetry of Wong Phui Nam." *QLRS* 1.1 (2001): 1–5. 28 Sept. 2002 <http://www.qlrs.com/issues/oct2001/essays/uwoe.html>.

Theroux, Paul. *The Great Railway Bazaar: By Train through Asia*. London: Penguin, 1975.

---. *V. S. Naipaul: An Introduction to His Work*. New York: Africana, 1972.

Todorov, Tzvetan. *The Conquest of America: The Question of the Other*. New York: Harper, 1982.

Ungureanu, Cornel. *La Vest de Eden: O introducere în literatura exilului*. Timişoara, Romania: Amarcord, 1995.

Walcott, Derek. "The Caribbean: Culture or Mimicry?" *Journal of Interamerican Studies and World Affairs* 16.1 (1974): 3–13.

Žižek, Slavoj. "Enjoy Your Nation as Yourself!" *Tarrying with the Negative: Kant, Hegel, and the Critique of Ideology*. Durham, NC: Duke University Press, 1993.

# SELECTED EXTENSIVE CRITICAL BIBLIOGRAPHY

Achebe, Chinua. *Hopes and Impediments: Selected Essays*. New York: Anchor Books, 1989.

Adam, Ian, and Helen Tiffin, eds. *Past the Last Post: Theorizing Post-Colonialism and Post-Modernism*. Calgary: University of Calgary Press, 1990.

Adams, Paul L. "The Social Psychiatry of Frantz Fanon." *American Journal of Psychiatry* 127.6 (1970): 809–814.

Adorno, Theodor. *Minima Moralia: Reflections from Damaged Life*. Trans. E. F. N. Jephcott. London: New Left Books, 1974.

Afaya, Noureddine. *L'Occident dans l'imaginaire Arabo-Musulman*. Casablanca: Toubkal, 1997.

Afzal-Khan, Fawzia, and Kalpana Seshadri-Crooks, eds. *The Pre-Occupation of Postcolonial Studies*. Durham, NC: Duke University Press, 2000.

---. "Jameson's Rhetoric of Otherness and the National Allegory." *Social Text* 17 (Fall 1987): 3–25.

---. "The Politics of Literary Postcoloniality." *Race & Class* 36.3 (1995): 1–20.

Allen, Sheila. *New Minorities, Old Conflicts: Asian and West Indian Migrants in Britain*. New York: Random House, 1971.

Allen, Theodore W. *The Invention of the White Race: Volume One: Racial Oppression and Social Control*. London: Verso, 1994.

Alloort, Gordon W. *The Nature of Prejudice*. New York: Anchor Books, 1958.

Alloula, Malek. "Mes enfances exotiques." *Enfances algériennes*. Ed. Leila Sebbar. Gallimard, 1999. 117–125.

Alvarez, Julia. *How the Garcia Girls Lost Their Accents*. New York: Plume, 1992.

---. *Something to Declare*. Chapel Hill, NC: Algonquin Books, 1998.

Amin, Samir. *Empire of Chaos*. Trans. W. H. Locke Anderson. New York: Monthly Review Press, 1992.

---. *Eurocentrism*. Trans. Russell Moore. New York: Monthly Review Press, 1989.

## Selected Extensive Critical Bibliography

Amuta, Chidi. *The Theory of African Literature*. London: Zed Books, 1989.

Anderson, Benedict. *Imagined Communities: Reflections on the Origin and Spread of Nationalism*. New York: Verso, 1983.

---. Interview. "The Current Crisis in Indonesia." *Z Magazine Online* Dec. 1996. 1 Mar. 2002 <http://www.zmag.org/zmag/articles/dec96seaman.htm>.

---. Interview. "When the Virtual Becomes the Real." *nettime* 14 Nov. 1997. 1 Mar. 2002 <http://www.nettime.org/nettime.w3archive/199711/msg00019.html>.

---. Introduction. *Language and Power: Exploring Political Cultures in Indonesia*. Ithaca, NY: Cornell University Press, 1990.

Anderson, Perry. *English Questions*. London: Verso, 1992.

Anderson, Warwick. "Excremental Colonialism: Public Health and the Poetics of Pollution." *Critical Inquiry* 21 (1995): 640–669.

Andryszewski, Tricia. *Immigration: Newcomers and Their Impact on the United States*. Brookfield, CT: Millbrook Press, 1995.

Aneja, Anu. "Jasmine, the Sweet Scent of Exile." *Pacific Coast Philology* 28.1 (1993): 72–80.

Ansell-Pearson, Keith, Benita Parry, and Judith Squires, eds. *Reflections on the Work of Edward Said: Cultural Identity and the Gravity of History*. London: Lawrence and Wishart, 1996.

Aparicio, Frances R. Susana Chávez-Silverman, eds. *Tropicalizations: Transcultural Representations of Latinidad*. Hanover, NH: Dartmouth College, 1997.

Appadurai, Arjun. *Globalization*. Durham, NC: Duke University Press, 2001.

Appiah, Kwame Anthony. *In My Father's House: Africa in the Philosophy of Culture*. Oxford, UK: Oxford University Press, 1992.

---. "Out of Africa: Topologies of Nativism." *The Yale Journal of Criticism* 1.2 (1998): 153–178.

Arata, Stephen D. *Fiction of Loss in the Victorian Fin-De-Siècle*. Cambridge, UK: Cambridge University Press, 1996.

---. "The Occidental Tourist: Dracula and the Anxiety of Reverse Colonization." *Victorian Studies* 33.4 (1990): 621–645.

Armitage, David. *The Ideological Origins of the British Empire*. Cambridge, UK: Cambridge University Press, 2000.

---. "Literature and Empire." *The Oxford History of the British Empire: Volume One: The Origins of Empire: British Overseas Enterprise to the Close of the Seventeenth Century.* Ed. Nicholas Canny. Oxford, UK: Oxford University Press, 1998: 99–123.

Asad, Talal, ed. *Anthropology and the Colonial Encounter.* London: Ithaca Press, 1975.

Ashcroft, Bill. "Modernity's First Born: Latin America and Postcolonial Transformation." *Ariel* 29.2 (1998): 7–29.

---. Gareth Griffiths, and Helen Tiffin, eds. *The Post-Colonial Studies Reader.* London: Routledge, 1995.

Auerbach, Erich. *Mimesis: The Representation of Reality in Western Literature.* Trans. Willard Trask. Garden City, NY: Doubleday Anchor, 1957.

August, Thomas G. *The Selling of the Empire: British and French Imperialist Propaganda.* Westport, CT: Greenwood Press, 1985.

Azim, Firdous. *The Colonial Rise of the Novel.* London and New York: Routledge, 1993.

Baepler, Paul, ed. *White Slaves, African Masters: An Anthology of American Barbary Captivity Narratives.* Chicago: Chicago University Press, 1999.

Bagchee, Shyamal. "Writing Self/Writing Colony in Situ: Expatriate British Poetry in India." *Ariel* 23.4 (1992): 7–32.

Baker, Ernest, ed. *The Politics of Aristotle.* New York: Oxford University Press, 1962.

Bakhtin, Mikhail. *The Dialogic Imagination.* Trans. Caryl Emerson and Michael Holquist. Ed. Michael Holquist. Austin: University of Texas Press, 1981.

Balibar, Étienne, and Immanuel Wallerstein. *Race, Nation, Class: Ambiguous Identities.* Trans. Chris Turner. London: Verso, 1991.

Banton, Michael. *Racial Theories.* Cambridge, UK: Cambridge University Press, 1987.

Barker, Francis, et al., eds. *Colonial Discourse/Postcolonial Theory.* Manchester, UK: Manchester University Press, 1994.

Barnes, Julian. *The History of the World in 10 1/2 Chapters.* New York: Vintage International, 1990.

Barringer, Tim, and Tom Flynn, eds. *Colonialism and the Object: Empire, Material Culture and the Museum.* London: Routledge, 1998.

## Selected Extensive Critical Bibliography

Bartra, Roger. *Wild Men in the Looking Glass: The Mythic Origins of European Otherness*. Trans. Carl T. Berrisford. Ann Arbor: University of Michigan Press, 1994.

---. *Europe and Its Others*. 2 vols. Colchester, UK: University of Essex, 1994.

Barthes, Roland. *La chambre claire: note sur la photographie*. Paris: Cahiers du Cinema: Gallimard/Seuil, 1980.

---. *Critical Essays*. Trans. Richard Howard. Evanston, IL: Northwestern University Press, 1972.

---. *The Eiffel Tower and Other Mythologies*. Trans. Richard Howard. New York: Hill and Wang, 1979.

---. *Elements of Semiology*. Trans. Annette Lavers and Colin Smith. London: Cape, 1968.

---. *L'Empire des signes*. Geneva: Albert Skira, 1970.

---. *Essais critiques*. Paris: Seuil, 1964.

---. *Fragments d'un discours amoureux*. Paris: Seuil, 1977.

---. *Image, Music, Text*. Essays Selected and Trans. Stephen Heath. New York: Hill and Wang, 1978.

---. *A Lover's Discourse: Fragments*. Trans. Richard Howard. New York: Hill and Wang, 1978.

---. *Mythologies*. New York: Hill and Wang, 1972.

---. *Le plaisir du texte*. Paris: Seuil, 1973.

---. *S/Z*. Trans. Richard Howard. Preface Richard Howard. New York: Hill and Wang, 1974.

---, Roland Martin, and André Martin. *Le Tour Effel*. New York: French and European Publishers, 1964.

---. *Writing Degree Zero*. Preface Susan Sontag. Trans. Annette Lavers and Colin Smith. New York: Hill and Wang, 1968.

Basch, Linda, Nina Glick Schiller, and Cristina Szanton Blanc. *Nations Unbound: Transnational Projects, Postcolonial Predicaments, and Deterritorialized Nation-States*. Basel: Gordon and Breach, 1994.

Bassnett, Susan, and Harish Trivedi, eds. *Post-Colonial Translation: Theory and Practice*. London: Routledge, 1999.

Baucom, Ian. *Out of Place: Englishness, Empire, and the Location of Identity*. Princeton, NJ: Princeton University Press, 1999.

Beckles, Hilary, ed. *An Area of Conquest: Popular Democracy and West Indies Cricket Supremacy*. Kingston: Ian Randle Publishers, 1994.

Beckles, Hilary, and Brian Stoddart, eds. *Liberation Cricket: West Indies Cricket Culture*. Kingston: Ian Randle Publishers, 1994.

Behdad, Ali. *Belated Travelers: Orientalism in the Age of Colonial Dissolution*. Durham, NC: Duke University Press, 1994.

Bell, Morag, Robin Butler, and Michael Heffernan, eds. *Geography and Imperialism 1820–1940*. Manchester, UK: Manchester University Press, 1995.

Belnap, Jeffrey, and Raúl Fernández, eds. *José Martí's "Our America": From National to Hemispheric Cultural Studies*. Durham, NC: Duke University Press, 1998.

Benítez-Rojo, Antonio. *The Repeating Island: The Caribbean and the Postmodern Perspective*. Trans. James Maraniss. Durham, NC: Duke University Press, 1992.

Bennett, Bruce. *A Sense of Exile: Essays in the Literature of the Asia-Pacific Region*. Nedlands, Western Australia: University of Western Australia Centre for Studies in Australian Literature, 1988.

Berdyaev, Nicolas. *The Destiny of Man*. Trans. Natalie Duddington. New York: Harper, 1960.

Bergson, Henri. *The Two Sources of Morality and Religion*. Trans. R. Ashley Audra and Cloudsley Brereton. Garden City, NY: Doubleday, 1954.

Beverley, John. *Subalterniaty and Representation: Arguments in Cultural Theory*. Durham, NC: Duke University Press, 1999.

Bienek, Horst. "Exile Is Rebellion." *Literature in Exile*. Ed. John Glad. Durham, NC and London: Duke University Press, 1990.

Bivona, Daniel. *Desire and Contradiction: Imperial Visions and Domestic Debates in Victorian Literature*. Manchester, UK: Manchester University Press, 1990.

Blake, Ann, Leela Gandhi, and Sue Thomas. *England through Colonial Eyes in Twentieth-Century Fiction*. London: Palgrave, 2001.

Blaut, James M. *The Colonizer's Model of the World: Geographical Diffusionism and Eurocentric History*. New York: Guilford Press, 1993.

---. *The National Question: Decolonizing the Theory of Nationalism*. London: Zed Books, 1987.

## Selected Extensive Critical Bibliography

Bloom, Lisa. *Gender on Ice: American Ideologies of Polar Expeditions.* Minneapolis: University of Minnesota Press, 1993.

Boelhower, William. *Through a Glass Darkly: Ethnic Semiosis in American Literature.* New York: Oxford, 1987.

Bohls, Elizabeth A. *Women Travel Writers and the Language of Aesthetics, 1716–1818.* Cambridge, UK: Cambridge University Press, 1995.

Bongie, Chris. *Exotic Memories: Literature, Colonialism, and the Fin De Siecle.* Stanford, CA: Stanford University Press, 1991.

---. *Islands and Exiles: The Creole Identities of Post/Colonial Literature.* Stanford, CA: Stanford University Press, 1998.

Booker, M. Keith. *A Practical Introduction to Literary Theory and Criticism.* New York: Longman, 1996.

Boon, James A. *Other Tribes, Other Scribes: Symbolic Anthropology in the Comparative Study of Cultures, Histories, Religions, and Texts.* Cambridge, UK: Cambridge University Press, 1982.

Booth, Howard J., and Nigel Rigby, eds. *Modernism and Empire.* Manchester, UK: Manchester University Press, 2000.

Borges, Jorge Luis. *Labyrinths: Selected Stories and Other Writings.* Ed. Donald A. Yates and James E. Irby. Harmondsworth, Middlesex, UK: Penguin Books, 1976.

Bove, Paul A., ed. *Edward Said and the Work of the Critic Speaking Truth to Power.* Durham, NC and London: Duke University Press, 2000.

Brantlinger, Patrick. "History and Empire." *Journal of Victorian Literature and Culture* 19 (1992): 317–327.

---. *Rule of Darkness: British Literature and Imperialism, 1830–1914.* Ithaca, NY: Cornell University Press, 1988.

Breckenridge, Carol A., and Peter Van Der Veer. *Orientalism and the Postcolonial Predicament.* Philadelphia: University of Philadelphia Press, 1993.

Brettell, Caroline B. "Travel Literature, Ethnography, and Ethnohistory." *Ethnohistory* 33.2 (1896): 127–138.

Bristow, Joseph. *Empire Boys: Adventures in a Man's World.* London: Harper Collins, 1991.

Brodsky, Iosef. *Less Than One: Selected Essays.* New York: Farrar, 1980.

---. *A Part of Speech.* Trans. Anthony Hecht et al. New York: Farrar, 1980.

---. *Selected Poems*. Trans. George Kline. New York: Harper, 1973.

---. *To Urania*. Trans. Joseph Brodsky et al. New York: Farrar, 1984.

Broe, Mary Lynn, and Angela Ingram, eds. *Women's Writing in Exile*. Chapel Hill and London: University of North Carolina Press, 1989.

Brydon, Diana. "The White Inuit Speaks: Contamination as Literary Strategy." *Past the Last Post: Theorizing Post-Colonialism and Post-Modernism*. London: Harvester Wheatsheaf, 1991. Rpt. in abridged form in Ashcroft, Griffiths, and Tiffin, 1995. 136–142.

Buber, Martin. *Between Man and Man*. Trans. Ronald G. Smith. New York: Macmillan, 1965.

Buell, Frederick. *National Culture and the New Global System*. Baltimore: Johns Hopkins University Press, 1994.

Burton, Antoinette. *Dwelling in the Archive: Women Writing House, Home and History in Late Colonial India*. Oxford, UK: Oxford University Press, 2003.

Butcher, Maggie, ed. *The Eye of the Beholder: Indian Writing in English*. London: Commonwealth Institute, 1983.

Buzard, James. *The Beaten Track: European Tourism, Literature, and the Ways To 'Culture,' 1800–1918*. Oxford, UK: Clarendon Press, 1993.

Cabral, Amilcar. *National Liberation and Culture*. Syracuse: Syracuse University Program of Eastern African Studies, 1970.

Calafeteanu, Ion. *Politica si exil: Din istoria exilului romanesc, 1946–1950*. Bucuresti: Editura Enciclopedica, 2000.

Camus, Albert. *L'Homme revolte*. Paris: Gallimard, 1951.

---. *Le Mythe de Sisyphe: Essai sur l'absurde*. Paris: Gallimard, 1942.

---. *La Peste*. Paris: Gallimard, 1947.

Carrier, James G., ed. *Occidentalism: Images of the West*. Oxford, UK: Clarendon, 1995.

Célestin, Roger. *From Cannibals to Radicals: Figures and Limits of Exoticism*, Minneapolis: University of Minnesota Press, 1996.

Centre for Contemporary Cultural Studies. *The Empire Strikes Back*. London: Routledge, 1983.

Césaire, Aimé. *Discourse on Colonialism*. New York: Monthly Review Press, 1972.

Chakrabarty, Dipesh. "Postcoloniality and the Artifice of History: Who Speaks For 'Indian' Pasts?" *Representations* 37 (1992): 1–26.

Chambers, Iain, and Lidia Curti, eds. *Post-Colonial Question: Common Skies, Divided Horizons.* London: Routledge, 1996.

Chanady, Amaryll. "Latin American: Imagined Communities and the Postmodern Challenge." *Sociocriticism* 11–12 (1990): 33–48.

Chandra, Sudhir. *The Oppressive Present: Literature and Social Consciousness in Colonial India.* New Delhi: Oxford University Press, 1992.

Chatterjee, Partha. *Nationalist Thought and the Colonial World: A Derivative Discourse.* Minneapolis: University of Minnesota Press, 1993.

Chaturvedi, Vinayak, ed. *Mapping Subaltern Studies and the Postcolonial.* London: Verso, 2000.

Chaudhuri, Nupur, and Margaret Strobel, eds. *Western Women and Imperialism: Complicity and Resistance.* Bloomington: Indiana University Press, 1992.

Cheng, Vincent J. *Joyce, Race, and Empire.* Cambridge, UK: Cambridge University Press, 1995.

Cheung, King-Kok. *Articulate Silences: Hisaye Yamamoto, Maxine Hong Kingston, Joy Kogawa.* Ithaca, NY: Cornell University Press, 1993.

Childs, Peter, ed. *Postcolonial Theory and English Literature.* Edinburgh: Edinburgh University Press, 1999.

Ching-Liang Low, Gail. *White Skins/Black Masks: Representation and Colonialism.* London: Routledge, 1996.

Chomsky, Noam. *Year 501: The Conquest Continues.* Boston: South End Press, 1993.

Chow, Rey. "Race/Imperialism." *Feminism and psychoanalysis: A Critical Dictionary.* Ed. Elizabeth Wright. Cambridge, MA: Blackwell, 1992. 361–364.

---. *Writing Diaspora: Tactics of Intervention in Contemporary Cultural Studies.* Bloomington: Indiana University Press, 1993.

Chowdhury, Kanishka. "Theoretical Confrontations in the Study of Postcolonial Literatures." *Modern Fiction Studies* 37 (1991): 609–615.

Chraibi, Driss. *Le passé simple.* Paris: Denoël, 1986.

---. *L'inspecteur Ali et la C.I.A.* Paris: Denoël, 1997.

---. *Vu, lu, entendu.* Paris: Denoël, 1998.

Chrisman, Laura. "The Imperial Unconscious? Representation of Imperial Discourse." *Critical Quarterly* 32.3 (1990): 38–58.

Cisneros, Sandra. *Mango Street*. New York: Random House, 1997.

Clarke, Patricia. *The Governesses: Letters from the Colonies, 1862–1882*. London: Hutchinson, 1985.

Clark, Steve. *Travel Writing and Empire: Postcolonial Theory in Transit*. London and New York: Zed Books, 1999.

Clifford, James. *Routes: Travel and Translation in the Late Twentieth Century*. Cambridge, MA: Harvard University Press, 1997.

Coetzee, J. M. *Doubling the Point: Essays and Interviews*. Ed. David Atwell. Cambridge, MA: Harvard Univeristy Press, 1992.

Cofer, Judith Ortiz. *Silent Dancing: A Partial Remembrance of a Puerto Rican Childhood*. Houston: Arte Publico Press, 1990.

Cohen, Jeffrey Jerome, ed. *The Postcolonial Middle Ages*. London: Macmillan, 2000.

Cohen, Phil, ed. *New Ethnicities, Old Racisms?* London: Zed Books, 1999.

Cohen, Philip, and Harwant S. Bains, eds. *Multi-Racist Britain*. Basingstoke, UK: Macmillan, 1988.

Cohn, Bernard S. *Colonialism and Its Forms of Knowledge: The British in India*. Princeton, NJ: Princeton University Press, 1996.

Cohn, Norman. *Europe's Inner Demons*. St. Albans: Paladin, 1976.

Cole, John. *Development and Underdevelopment: A Profile of the Third World*. London: Methuen, 1987.

Collier, Gordon, ed. *Us/Them: Translation, Transcription and Identity in Post-Colonial Literary Cultures*. Amsterdam: Rodopi, 1992.

Comaroff, Jean, and John Comaroff. "Through the Looking-Glass: Colonial Encounters of the First Kind." *Journal of Historical Sociology* 1 (1988): 6–32.

Coombes, Annie E. *Reinventing Africa: Museums, Material Culture and Popular Imagination in Late Victorian and Edwardian England*. New Haven, CT: Yale University Press, 1994.

Coronil, Fernando. "Beyond Occidentalism: Toward Nonimperial Geohistorical Categories." *Cultural Anthropology* 11.1 (1996): 51–87.

---. "Can Postcoloniality Be Decolonised? Imperial Banality and Postcolonial Power." *Public Culture* 5 (1992): 89–108.

---. "Listening to the Subaltern: Postcolonial Studies and the Neocolonial Poetics of Subaltern States." *Essays and Studies 1999: Postcolonial Theory and Criticism.* Laura Chrisman and Benita Parry, eds. Cambridge: D. S. Brewer, 2000.

Chrisman, Laura, and Benita Parry, eds. *Postcolonial Theory and Criticism.* Cambridge, UK: D. S. Brewer, 2000. 37–55.

Cronin, Richard. *Imagining India.* London: Macmillan, 1990.

Cvetkovich, Ann, and Douglass Kellner. *Articulating the Global and the Local: Globalization and Cultural Studies.* Boulder, CO: Westview Press, 1997.

Davis, Geoffrey V. *Crisis and Creativity in the New Literatures in English.* Amsterdam: Rodopi, 1990.

---. *Southern African Writing: Voyages and Explorations.* Amsterdam: Rodopi, 1994.

Dayal, Samir. "Creating, Preserving, Destroying: Violence in Bharati Mukherjee's Jasmine." *Bharati Mukherjee: Critical Perspectives.* Ed. Emmanuel S. Nelson. New York: Garland, 1993. 65–88.

---. "Postcolonialism's Possibilities: Subcontinental Diaporic Intervention." *Cultural Critique* 33 (1996): 113–150.

de Certau, Michel. *The Practice of Everyday Life.* Berkeley: University of California Press, 1984.

---. *The Writing of History.* Trans. Tom Conley. New York: Columbia University Press, 1988.

Delanty, Gerard. *Inventing Europe: Idea, Identity, Reality.* Basingstoke, UK: Macmillan, 1995.

Deleuze, Giles, and Felix Guattari. *Mille Plateaux: capitalisme et schizophrénie.* Paris: Editions de Minuit, 1980.

Desai, Anita. *In Custody.* Harmondsworth, Middlesex, UK: Penguin Books, 1985.

"Desirable Daughters: A Novel." *Hyperion Books Review.* <http://www.hyperionbooks.com/theia/2002win/desirabledaughters.htm>.

Di Leonardo, Micaela. *Exotics at Home: Anthropologies, Others, American.* Chicago: Chicago University Press, 1998.

Dib, Mohammed. "Rencontres." *Enfances algériennes*. Ed. Leila Sebbar. Paris: Gallimard, 1999. 117–125.

Dirks, Nicholas B., ed. *Colonialism and Culture*. Ann Arbor: University of Michigan Press, 1992.

Dirlik, Arif. *The Postcolonial Aura: Third World Criticism in the Age of Global Capitalism*. Boulder, CO: Westview Press, 1998.

---. "Three Worlds, or One, or Many? The Reconfiguration of Global Divisions under Contemporary Capitalism." *Nature, Society, and Thought* 7.1 (1994): 19–42.

Divakaruni, Chitra Banerjee. *Arranged Marriages: Stories*. New York: Anchor Books, 1995.

---. *Mistress of Spices*. New York: Anchor Books, 1997.

Donaldson, Laura E. *Decolonizing Feminisms: Race, Gender, and Empire-Building*. Chapel Hill and London: The University of North Carolina Press, 1992.

---. "The Miranda Complex: Colonialism and the Question of Feminist Reading." *Diacritics* 18.3 (1988): 65–77.

Dostoevsky, Fyodor Mikhailovich. *Prestuplenie i nakazanie* (*Crime and Punishment*). Moscow: Prosveshchenie, 1982.

---. *Winter Notes on Summer Impressions*. Trans. David Patterson. Evanston, IL: Northwestern University Press, 1988.

Drakakis-Smith, David. *The North China Lover*. Trans. Leigh Hafrey. New York: The New Press, 1994.

---. *The Third World City*. London: Methuen, 1987.

Drinnon, Richard. *Facing West: The Metaphysics of Indian-Hating and Empire-Building*. New York: Schocken Books, 1990.

Dudley, Edward, and Maximillian E. Novak, eds. *The Wild Man Within: An Image in Western Thought from the Renaissance to Romanticism*. Pittsburgh: University of Pittsburgh Press, 1972.

Durand, Gilbert. *Les structures anthropologiques de l'imaginaire*. Paris: Bordas, 1984.

Duras, Marguerite. *The Lover*. Trans. Barbara Bray. New York: Harper Perennial Books, 1992.

Durham, Jimmie. *A Certain Lack of Coherence: Writings on Art and Cultural Politics*. Ed. Jean Fisher. London: Kala Press, 1993.

Dussel, Enrique. *The Invention of the Americas: Eclipse of "the Other" and the Myth of Modernity*. Trans. Michael D. Barber. New York: Continuum, 1995.

Dworkin, Dennis L., and Leslie G. Roman, eds. *Views beyond the Border Country: Raymond Williams and Cultural Politics*. New York and London, 1993.

Dyer, Richard. *White*. London: Routledge, 1997.

Eckstein, A. M. "Is There a 'Hobson-Lenin Thesis' on Late Nineteenth-Century Colonial Expansion?" *Economic History Review* 44.2 (1991): 297–318.

Errington, Shelley. *Anderson's Imagined Communities: Reflections on the Origin and Spread of Nationalism*. 1997. 1 Feb. 2002 <http://www.uniblab.com/collie/library/communities.html>.

Fabian, Johannes. "Presence and Representation: The Other and Anthropological Writing." *Critical Inquiry* 16 (1990): 753–772.

---. *Time and the Other: How Anthropology Makes Its Object*. New York: Columbia University Press, 1983.

Fanon, Frantz. *Peau noire, masques blancs*. Paris: Editions du Seuil, 1952. Rpt. in *Black Skin, White Masks*. Trans. Charles Lam Markmann. New York: Grove Press, 1967.

---. *A Dying Colonialism*. Trans. Haakon Chevalier. London: Routledge, 1980.

---. *Toward the African Revolution*. Trans. Haakon Chevalier. London: Writers and Readers, 1980.

Featherstone, Mike. *Undoing Culture: Globalization, Postmodernism and Identity*. London: Sage, 1995.

Ferguson, Moira. *Subject to Others: British Women Writers and Colonial Slavery, 1670–1834*. London: Routledge, 1992.

Fernández Retamar, Roberto. *Caliban and Other Essays*. Minneapolis: University of Minnesota Press, 1989.

Fiedler, Leslie. *The Return of the Vanishing American*. London: Paladin, 1972.

Firan, Florea, and Constantin M. Popa. *Literatura diasporei (Antologie comentata)*. Craiova, RO: Editura Poesis, 1994.

Flaubert, Gustave. *Flaubert in Egypt: A Sensibility on Tour*. 1850. Ed. and trans. Francis Steegmuller. London: Bodley Head, 1972.

Foster, Shirley. *Across New Worlds: Nineteenth-Century Women Travelers and Their Writings*. London: Harvester Wheatsheaf, 1990.

Frankenberg, Ruth. *White Women, Race Matters: The Social Construction of Whiteness*. Minneapolis: University of Minnesota Press, 1993.

Friedman, Jonathan. *Cultural Identity and Global Process*. London: Sage Publications, 1994.

Fredericksen, Brooke. "At Home in Words: Exile, Writing and Twentieth-Century Literature." Diss. University of Arizona, 1992.

Fukuyama, Francis. *The End of History and The Last Man*. London: Penguin, 1992.

Gandhi, Leela. *Postcolonial Theory: A Critical Introduction*. New York: Columbia University Press, 1998.

Garcia, Cristina. *Dreaming in Cuban*. London: Harper Collins, 1992.

Gee, Sue. "The Country of Writing." *Literary Expressions of Exile: A Collection of Essays*. Ed. Roger Whitehouse. Lewiston, NY: The Edwin Mellen Press, 2000. 9–31.

Gendelev, Mikhail. *Poslaniya lemuram* (*Messages to the Lemures*). Jerusalem: Lexicon, 1984.

Giddings, Robert, ed. *Literature and Imperialism*. Basingstoke, UK: Macmillan, 1991.

Gidley, Mick, ed. *Representing Others: White Views of Indigenous Peoples*. Exeter, UK: University of Exeter Press, 1992.

Gikandi, Simon. *Maps of Englishness: Writing Identity in the Culture of Colonialism*. New York: Columbia University Press, 1996.

Gilbert, Helen, and Joanne Tompkins. *Post-Colonial Drama: Theory, Practice, Politics*. London: Routledge, 1996.

Gillan, Maria Mazziotti, and Jennifer Gillan, eds. *Unsettling America: An Anthology of Contemporary Multicultural Poetry*. New York: Penguin Books, 1994.

Gilroy, Paul. *There Ain't No Black in the Union Jack*. London: Hutchinson, 1987.

---. *The Black Atlantic: Modernity and Double Consciousness*. Cambridge, MA: Harvard University Press, 1993.

---. *Small Acts: Thoughts on the Politics of Black Cultures*. London: Serpent's Tail, 1993.

Ginsburgh, Yitzchack. *The Alef-Beit: Jewish Thought Revealed through the Hebrew Letters*. Northvale, NJ: Jason Aronson, 1991.

Giroux, Henry, and Peter Mclaren. *Between Borders: Pedagogy and the Politics of Cultural Studies*. New York: Routledge, 1994.

Gish, Jen. *Who's Irish?* London: Granta, 1999.

Glad, John, ed. *Literature in Exile*. Durham, NC and London: Duke University Press, 1990.

Glissant, Edouard. *Caribbean Discourse*. Trans. J. Michael Dash. Charlottesville: University Press of Virginia, 1989.

Godlewska, Anne, and Neil Smith. eds. *Geography and Empire*. Oxford, UK: Blackwell, 1994.

Goldie, Terry. *Fear and Temptation: The Image of the Indigene in Canadian, Australian, and New Zealand Literature*. Kingston: Mcgill-Queen's University Press, 1989.

Gordimer, Nadine. "Afterword: The Prison-House of Colonialism." *An Olive Schreiner Reader: Writings on Women and South Africa*. Ed. Carol Barasch. London: Pandora, 1987. 221–227.

---. *The Essential Gesture: Writing, Politics, and Places*. Ed. Stephen Clingman. New York: Knopf, 1988.

---. *My Son's Story*. New York: Farrar, 1990.

---. *None to Accompany Me*. New York: Farrar, 1994.

Gordon, Lewis R., T. Denean Sharpley-Whiting, and Renée T. White, eds. *Fanon: A Critical Reader*. Oxford, UK: Blackwell, 1996.

Goslinga, Marian. *Caribbean Literature: A Bibliography*. London: Scarecrow Press, 1998.

Graburn, Nelson H. H., ed. *Ethnic and Tourist Arts: Cultural Expressions from The Fourth World*. Berkeley: University of California Press, 1976.

Griffiths, Gareth. "Imitation, Abrogation and Appropriation: The Production of the Post-Colonial Text." *Kunapipi* 9 (1987): 13–20.

---. *A Double Exile: African and West Indian Writing between Two Cultures*. London: Marion Boyars, 1978.

Grossberg, Lawrence, et al., eds. *Cultural Studies*. New York: Routledge, 1992.

Hall, Catherine. *White, Male and Middle Class: Explorations in Feminism and History*. Cambridge, UK: Polity Press, 1992.

Hall, Edward T. *Beyond Culture*. Garden City, NY: Anchor Books, 1977.

Hallam, Elizabeth, and Brian V. Street, eds. *Cultural Encounters: Representing 'Otherness.'* London: Routledge, 2000.

Hammond, Dorothy, and Alta Jablow. *The Myth of Africa*. New York: The Library of Social Science, 1977.

Hargreaves, Alec G., and Mark Mckinney, eds. *Post-Colonial Cultures in France*. London: Routledge, 1997.

Harlow, Barbara. *Resistance Literature*. New York: Methuen, 1987.

Hastings, W. K. "The Wakefield Colonization Plan and Constitutional Development in South Australia, Canada, and New Zealand." *Journal of Legal History* 11.2 (1990): 279–299.

Hawthorn, Jeremy. *A Glossary of Contemporary Literary Theory*. 4th ed. London: Arnold, 2000.

Head, Mike. "US Orchestrated Suharto's 1965–66 Slaughter in Indonesia." 19 July 1999. 17 Jan. 2002 <http://www.wsws.org/articles/1999/jul1999/indo1-j19_prn.shtml>.

Heald, Suzette, and Ariane Deluz, eds. *Anthropology and Psychoanalysis: An Encounter through Culture*. London: Routledge, 1994.

Herodotus. *The Histories*. Trans. Henry Cary from the text of Baehr. London: Folio Society, 1992.

Hicks, D. Emily. *Border Writing: The Multidimensional Text*. Minneapolis: University of Minnesota Press, 1991.

Hill, Tracey, and William Hughes, eds. *Contemporary Writing and National Identity*. Bath, UK: Sulis Press, 1995.

Hobsbawm, Eric. *Nations and Nationalism Since 1780: Programme, Myth, Reality*, Cambridge, UK: Cambridge University Press, 1991.

Hobsbawm, Eric, and Terence Ranger, eds. *The Invention of Tradition*. Cambridge: Cambridge, UK: Cambridge University Press, 1983.

Hoch, Paul. *White Hero, Black Beast: Racism, Sexism and the Mask of Masculinity*. London: Pluto Press, 1979.

Hodgson, Marshall G. S. *Rethinking World History: Essays on Europe, Islam, and World History*. Ed. Edmund Burke, III. Cambridge, UK: Cambridge University Press, 1993.

Hofmann, Eva. *Lost in Translation*. London: Heinemann, 1989.

## Selected Extensive Critical Bibliography 181

Hong, EE Tiang. *A Sense of Exile*. Ed. Bruce Bennett. Nedlands, Western Australia: Centre for Studies in Australian Literature at the University of Western Australia, 1988.

hooks, bell. *Feminist Theory: From Margin to Center*. Boston: South End Press, 1984.

---. "The Politics of Radical Black Subjectivity." *Talking Back*. Boston: South End Press, 1989.

Hoving, Isabel. *In Praise of New Travelers: Reading Caribbean Migrant Women Writers*. Stanford, CA: Stanford University Press, 2001.

Huggan, Graham. *The Post-Colonial Exotic: Marketing the Margins*. London: Routledge, 2001.

Hutcheon, Linda. *A Poetics of Postmodernism: History, Theory, Fiction*. New York: Routledge, 1988.

---. "The Post Always Rings Twice: The Postmodern and the Postcolonial." *Textual Practice* 8.2 (1994): 205–238.

Hyam, Ronald B. *Empire and Sexuality: The British Experience*. Manchester, UK: Manchester University Press, 1990.

Inden, Ronald. *Imagining India*. Oxford, UK: Blackwell, 1990.

Iyer, Pico. *Video Nights in Kathmandu, and Other Reports from the Not-So-Far-East*. London: Black Swan, 1988.

Jabes, Edmond. *From the Desert to the Book*. New York: Station Hill, 1990.

Jacobs, Jane M. *Edge of Empire: Postcolonialism and the City*. London: Routledge, 1996.

James, C. L. R. *Beyond a Boundary*. Durham, NC: Duke University Press, 1993.

Jameson, Fredric. *The Geopolitical Aesthetic: Cinema and Space in the World System*. Bloomington: Indiana University Press, 1992.

---. "Third-World Literature in the Era of Multinational Capitalism." *Social Text* 15 (1986): 65–88.

Janmohamed, Abdul R. "The Economy of Manichean Allegory: The Function of Racial Difference in Colonialist Literature." *Critical Inquiry* 12 (1985): 59–87.

Jaspers, Karl. *Truth and Symbol*. Trans. Jean T. Wilde, William Kluback, and William Kimmel. New Haven, CT: College and University Press, 1959.

Jauss, Hans Robert. *Pour une esthétique de la réception.* Paris: Gallimard, 1978.

Jayawardena, Kumari. *Feminism and Nationalism in the Third World.* London: Zed, 1986.

Jung, Carl. *Psychology and Religion.* New Haven, CT: Yale University Press, 1938.

Kabbani, Rana. *Europe's Myths of Orient: Devise and Rule.* Bloomington: Indiana University Press, 1986.

Kain, Geoffrey, ed. *Ideas of Home: Literature of Asian Migration.* East Lansing, MI: Michigan State University Press, 1997.

Kakutani, Michiko. "*The Ground Beneath Her Feet*: Turning Rock'N'Roll Into Quakes." *NY Times Books of the Times.* Jan 2006. <http://www.nytimes.com/books/99/04/11/daily/041399rushdie-book-review.html>.

Kaplan, Amy, and Donald E. Pease, eds. *Cultures of United States Imperialism.* Durham, NC: Duke University Press, 1993.

Kaplan, Caren. *Questions of Travel: Postmodern Discourses of Displacement.* Durham, NC: Duke University Press, 1996.

---, Norma Alarcon, and Minoo Moallem, eds. *Between Woman and Nation: Nationalism, Transnational Feminisms, and the State.* Durham, NC: Duke University Press, 1992.

Kaplan, E. Ann. *Looking for the Other: Feminism, Film, and the Imperial Gaze.* London: Routledge, 1997.

Kapur, Akash. "Between Father and Son: Family Letters by V. S. Naipaul." *Salon Reviews.* Jan 2006. <http://www.salon.com/books/review/2000/01/18/naipaul/print.html>.

Kazantzakis, Nikos. *Zorba the Greek.* Trans. Carl Wildman. New York: Ballantine, 1952.

Kiernan, Victor G. *Imperialism and Its Contradictions*, London: Routledge, 1995.

---. *The Lords of Human Kind: European Attitudes Towards the Outside World in the Imperial Age.* London: Weidenfeld & Nicolson, 1969.

Kincaid, Jamaica. *Lucy.* New York: Farrar Straus Giroux, 1990.

Kingston, Maxine Hong. *The Woman Warrior: Memoirs of a Girlhood among Ghosts.* London: Picador, 1975. London: Picador, 1981.

Knox, Bruce. "The Concept of Empire in the Mid-Nineteenth Century: Ideas in the Colonial Defense Inquiries of 1859–1861." *Journal of Imperial and Commonwealth History*, 15 (1987): 242–263.

Kogawa, Joy. *Itsuka*. New York: Anchor Books, 1994.

---. *Obasan*. New York: Doubleday, 1982.

Kuhiwczak, Piotr. "When the Exile Returns." *Literary Expressions of Exile: A Collection of Essays*. Ed. Roger Whitehouse. Lewiston, NY: The Edwin Mellen Press, 2000. 31–47.

Lagos-Pope, Maria-Ines, ed. *Exile in Literature*. Lewisburg: Bucknell University Press, 1988.

Lambropoulos, Vassilis. *The Rise of Eurocentrism: Anatomy of Interpretation*. Princeton, NJ: Princeton University Press, 1993.

Lamming, George. *The Emigrants*. London: Michael Joseph, 1954.

---. *The Pleasures of Exile*. London: Allison & Busby, 1984.

Langer, Jiri. *Nine Gates to the Chassidic Mysteries*. Trans. Stephen Jolly. New York: Behrman, 1976.

Leask, Nigel. *British Romantic Writers and the East: Anxieties of Empire*. Cambridge, UK: Cambridge University Press, 1993.

Lee, Ang. *Eat Drink Man Woman, the Wedding Banquet*. New York: Overlook Press, 1994.

Lee, A. Robert, ed. *Other Britain, Other British: Contemporary Multicultural Fiction*. London: Pluto Press, 1995.

Lee, Chang-Rae. *Native Speaker*. London: Granta Books, 1995.

Lee, Rachel C. *The Americas of Asian American Literature: Gendered Fictions of Nations and Transnations*. Princeton, NJ: Princeton University Press, 1999.

Lefevere, Andre. "Interface: Some Thoughts on the Historiography of African Literature Written in English." *The History and Historiography of Commonwealth Literature*. Ed. Dieter Riemenscheineider. Tubingen, Germany: Gunter Narr Verlag, 1983.

Levinas, Emmanuel. *Collected Philosophical Papers*. Trans. Alphonso Lingis. The Hague: Martinus Nijhoff, 1978.

---. *Nine Talmudic Readings*. Trans. Annette Aronowicz. Bloomington: Indiana University Press, 1990.

Li, David Leiwei. *Imagining the Nation: Asian American Literature and Cultural Consent*. Stanford, CA: Stanford University Press, 1998.

Lim, Shirley Goek-lin. *Among the White Moon Faces: An Asian-American Memoir of Homelands*. New York: Feminist Press at the City University of New York, 1996.

Lim, Shirley Goek-lin, and Amy Ling, eds. *Reading the Literatures of Asian America*. New York: Oxford University Press, 1998.

Linebaugh, Peter, and Marcus Rediker. *The Many-Headed Hydra: The Hidden History of The Revolutionary Atlantic*. London: Verso, 2000.

Linton, Joan Pong. *The Romance of the New World: Gender and the Literary Formations of English Colonialism*. Cambridge, UK: Cambridge University Press, 1998.

Loomba, Ania. *Colonialism/Postcolonialism*. London: Routledge, 1998.

Lowe, Lisa. *Critical Terrains: French and British Orientalisms*. Ithaca, NY: Cornell University Press, 1991.

Loxley, Diana. *Problematic Shores: The Literature of Islands*. London: Macmillan, 1990.

Lutz, Katherine A., and Jane L. Collins. *Reading National Geographic*. Chicago: University of Chicago Press, 1993.

Lyotard, Jean-Francois. *The Postmoderne explique aux enfants*. Paris: Galilee, 1986.

Maccannell, Dean. *The Tourist: A New Theory of the Leisure Class*. New York: Schocken Books, 1976.

Machiavelli, Niccolo. *The Prince*. Trans. Paul Sonnino. Atlantic Highlands: Humanities Press, 1996.

Mackenzie, John M. *Imperialism and Popular Culture*. Manchester, UK: Manchester University Press, 1986.

---. *Orientalism: History, Theory and the Arts*. Manchester, UK: Manchester University Press, 1995.

---. *Propaganda and Empire*. Manchester, UK: Manchester University Press, 1984.

Mahood, Molly Maureen, ed. *The Colonial Encounter: A Reading of Six Novels*. London: Rex Collings/Totowa, NJ: Rowman and Littlefield, 1977.

Mani, Lata, and Ruth Frankenberg. "The Challenge of Orientalism." *Economy and Society* 14 (1985): 174–192.

Mannoni, Octave. *Prospero and Caliban: The Psychology of Colonization.* Trans. Pamela Powesland. Ann Arbor: University of Michigan Press, 1990.

Marangoly George, Rosemary. *The Politics of Home: Postcolonial Relocations and Twentieth-Century Fiction.* Cambridge, UK: Cambridge University Press, 1996.

Mason, Peter. *Deconstructing America: Representations of the Other.* London: Routledge, 1990.

Mason, Peter. *Infelicities: Representations of the Exotic.* Baltimore: Johns Hopkins University Press, 1998.

Matar, Nabil. *Turks, Moors, and Englishmen in the Age of Discovery.* New York: Columbia University Press, 1999.

Mattelart, Armand. *Multinational Corporations and the Control of Culture.* Brighton, UK: Harvester Press, 1979.

McClintock, Anne. "The Angel of Progress: Pitfalls of the Term 'Post-Colonialism.'" *Social Text* 31/32.1 (1994): 84–98.

---. *Imperial Leather: Race, Gender, and Sexuality in the Colonial Context.* London: Routledge, 1995.

Mcgrane, Bernard. *Beyond Anthropology.* New York: Columbia University Press, 1989.

Meaudre, Yves. *France, terre d'exil.* Paris: Fayard, 1989.

Melman, Billie. *Women's Orients: English Women and the Middle East, 1718–1918.* London: Macmillan, 1992.

Memmi, Albert. *The Colonizer and the Colonized.* London: Souvenir Press, 1974.

---. *Portrait du colonisé, précédé du portrait du colonisateur.* Paris: Payot, 1973.

Meyer, Susan. *Imperialism at Home: Race and Victorian Women's Fiction,* Ithaca, NY: Cornell University Press, 1996.

Meyers, Jeffrey. *Fiction and the Colonial Experience.* Totowa, NJ: Rowman and Littlefield, 1973.

Michaels, Walter Benn. "Race Into Culture: A Critical Genealogy of Cultural Identity." *Critical Inquiry* 18 (1992): 655–685.

Midgley, Clare, ed. *Gender and Imperialism.* Manchester, UK: Manchester University Press, 1998.

Mignolo, Walter D. "Misunderstanding and Colonization: The Reconfiguration of Memory and Space." *South Atlantic Quarterly* 92 (1993): 209–260.

Miller, David P., and Peter Hanns Reill, eds. *Visions of Empire: Voyages, Botany, and Representations of Nature.* Cambridge, UK: Cambridge University Press, 1996.

Mills, Sara. *Discourses of Difference: An Analysis of Women's Travel Writing and Colonialism.* London: Routledge, 1991.

Minh-Ha, Trinh T. "Difference: 'A Special Third World Women Issue.'" *Discourse* 8 (1986): 11–37.

---. *Woman, Native, Other: Writing Postcoloniality and Feminism.* Bloomington: Indiana University Press, 1989.

Mitter, Partha. *Much Maligned Monsters: A History of European Reactions to Indian Art.* Oxford: Oxford University Press, 1977.

Moore-Gilbert, Bart. *Postcolonial Theory: Contexts, Practices, Politics.* London: Verso, 1997.

Moreiras, Alberto. "Hybridity and Double Consciousness." *Cultural Studies* 13.3 (1999): 373–407.

Morey, Peter. *Fictions of India: Narrative and Power.* Edinburgh: Edinburgh University Press, 2000.

Morley, David, and Kuan-Hsing Chen. *Stuart Hall: Critical Dialogues in Cultural Studies.* London: Routledge, 1996.

Mortimer, Edward. *Faith & Power: The Politics of Islam.* New York: Vintage Books, 1982.

Muller, Carl. *Yakada Yaka.* New Delhi: Penguin Books, 1994.

Muller, Gilbert H. *New Strangers in Paradise: The Immigrant Experience and Contemporary American Fiction.* Lexington, KY: University Press of Kentucky, 1999.

Nandy, Ashis. *The Intimate Enemy: Loss and Recovery of Self under Colonialism.* Delhi and Oxford, UK: Oxford University Press, 1991.

Narayan, R. K. *My Days: A Memoir.* London: Penguin, 1989.

Nelson, Emmanuel S., ed. *Writers of the Indian Diaspora: A Bio-Bibliographical Critical Sourcebook.* Westport, CT: Greenwood, 1993.

Newman, Judie. *The Ballistic Bard: Postcolonial Fiction.* London: Arnold, 1995.

Ngugi Wa Thiong'o. *Decolonizing the Mind: The Politics of Language in African Literature*. London: James Currey, 1986.

---. *Moving the Centre: The Struggle for Cultural Freedoms*. London: James Currey, 1993.

Nielsen, Niels Kayser. "Welfare-Nationalism? Comparative Aspects of the Relation between Sport and Nationalism in Scandinavia in the Inter-War Years." 1997. Jan 2006. http://www.umist.ac.uk/sport/6_art6.htm.

Niranjana, Tejaswine. *Sitting Translation: History, Post-Structuralism, and the Colonial Context*. Berkeley: University of California Press, 1990.

Nkosi, Lewis. *Home and Exile*. Harlow, UK: Longman, 1983.

Nkrumah, Kwame. *Neo-Colonialism: The Last Stage of Imperialism*. London: Nelson, 1965.

Obeyesekere, Gananath. *The Apotheosis of Captain Cook: European Mythmaking in the Pacific*. Princeton, NJ: Princeton University Press, 1992.

O'Brien, Susie. "The Place of America in an Era of Postcolonial Imperialism." *Ariel* 29.2 (1998): 159–183.

O'Hanlon, Rosalind. "Recovering the Subject: Subaltern Studies and Histories of Resistance in Colonial South Asia" *Modern Asian Studies* 22 (1998): 189–224.

---. David Washbrook. "After Orientalism: Culture, Criticism, and Politics in the Third World." *Comparative Studies in Society and History* 34 (1992): 141–167.

Ondaatje, Michael. *The English Patient*. London: Pan Books, 1993.

---. *Running in the Family*. London: Pan Books, 1984.

Ortiz, Fernando. *Cuban Counterpoint: Tobacco and Sugar*. Trans. Harriet De Onís. Durham, NC: Duke University Press, 1995.

Parker, Andrew, et al., eds. *Nationalisms and Sexualities*. New York: Routledge, 1992.

Parker, Michael, and Roger Starkey, eds. *Postcolonial Literatures: Achebe, Ngugi, Desai, Walcott*. London: Macmillan, 1995.

Parry, Benita. "Problems in Current Theories in Colonial Discourse." *Oxford Literary Review* 9 (1987): 27–58.

---. "Signs of Our Times: Discussion of Homi Bhabha's *The Location of Culture*." *Third Text* 28–29 (1994): 5–24.

Pascal, Blaise. *Pensees*. Paris: Club des Libraires de France, 1961.

Pathak, Zakia, et al. "The Prisonhouse of Orientalism." *Textual Practice* 5 (1991): 195–218.

Patterson, David. *Exile: The Sense of Alienation in Modern Russian Letters*. Lexington, KY: The University Press of Kentucky, 1995.

Pearce, Roy Harvey. *Savagism and Civilization*. Berkeley: University of California Press, 1988.

Percy, Walker. *The Message in the Bottle*. New York: Farrar, 1982.

Phillips, Richard. *Mapping Men and Empire*. London: Routledge, 1997.

Pietz, William. "The 'Postcolonialism' of Cold War Discourse." *Social Text* 19–20 (1988): 55–75.

Piper, Adrian. "Passing for White, Passing for Black." *Transition* 58 (1992): 4–32.

*Playwrights of Exile: An International Anthology*. Preface by Andrei Codrescu. NY: UBU Repertory Theater Publications, 1997.

Polukhina, Valentina. *Joseph Brodsky: A Poet for Our Time*. Cambridge, UK: Cambridge University Press, 1989.

Porter, Dennis. *Haunted Journeys: Desire and Transgression in European Travel Writing*. Princeton, NJ: Princeton University Press, 1991.

Pullen, J. M. "Malthus on Colonization and Economic Development: A Comparison with Adam Smith." *Utilitas* 6.2 (1994): 243–266.

Prakash, Gyan. "Subaltern Studies as Postcolonial Criticism." *American Historical Review* 99 (1994): 1475–1490.

---. "Writing Post-Orientalist Histories of the Third World: Perspectives from Indian Historiography." *Comparative Studies in Society and History* 32 (1990): 383–408.

Prakash, Gyan, ed. *After Colonialism: Imperial Histories and Postcolonial Displacements*. Princeton, NJ: Princeton University Press, 1995.

Pratt, Mary Louise. "Conventions of Representation: Where Discourse and Ideology Meet." *The Taming of the Text: Explorations in Language, Literature and Culture*. Ed. Willie Van Peer. London: Routledge, 1988. 15–34.

---. *Imperial Eyes: Travel Writing and Transculturation*. London: Routledge, 1992.

---. "Mapping Ideology: Gide, Camus, and Algeria." *College Literature* 8 (1981): 157–174.

Price, Sally. *Primitive Art in Civilized Places.* University of Chicago Press, 1989.

Punter, David. *Postcolonial Imaginings: Fictions of a New World Order.* Edinburgh: Edinburgh University Press, 2000.

Rahman, Tariq. *A History of Pakistani Literature in English.* Lahore: Vanguard, 1991.

Rajan, Rajeswari Sunder, ed. *The Lie of The Land: English Literary Studies in India.* Delhi: Oxford University Press, 1992.

---. *Real and Imagined Women: Gender, Culture and Postcolonialism.* London: Routledge, 1993.

Raskin, Jonah. *The Mythology of Imperialism.* New York: Delta, 1971.

Rattansi, Ali, and Sallie Westwood, eds. *Racism, Modernity and Identity: On the Western Front.* Cambridge, UK: Polity Press, 1994.

Ray, Sangeeta. *En-Gendering India: Woman and Nation in Colonial and Post-Colonial Narratives.* Durham, NC: Duke University Press, 2000.

---. "Shifting Subjects Shifting Ground: The Names and Spaces of the Post-Colonial." *Hypatia* 7 (1992): 188–201.

Reeves, Geoffrey. *Communications and the 'Third World.'* London: Routledge, 1993.

Rich, Paul B. *Race and Empire in British Politics.* Cambridge, UK: Cambridge University Press, 1986.

Richards, David. *Masks of Difference: Cultural Representations in Literature, Anthropology and Art.* Cambridge, UK: Cambridge University Press, 1994.

Richardson, Michael, ed. *Refusal of the Shadow: Surrealism and the Caribbean.* London: Verso, 1996.

Robbins, Bruce. "Colonial Discourse: A Paradigm and Its Discontents." *Victorian Studies* 35.2 (1992): 209–214.

---. "Secularism, Elitism, Progress, and Other Transgressions." *Social Text* 40 (1994): 25–37.

---, et al. "Edward Said's *Culture and Imperialism*: A Symposium." *Social Text* 40 (1994): 1–23.

Robertson, George, et al., eds. *Travelers' Tales: Narratives of Home and Displacement.* London: Routledge, 1994.

Robertson, Roland. "Globalization: Time-Space and Homogeneity-Heterogeneity." *Global Modernities*. Ed. Mike Featherstone, Scott Lash, and Roland Robertson. London: Sage, 1995. 25–44.

Robinson, Dave. *Nietzsche and Postmodernism*. New York: Totem, 1999.

Robinson, Douglas. *Translation and Empire: Postcolonial Theories Explained*. Manchester, UK: St. Jerome Publishing, 1997.

Rodney, Walter. *How Europe Underdeveloped Africa*. London: Bogle-l'Ouverture, 1972.

Rodríguez, Ileana. *House Garden Nation: Space, Gender, and Ethnicity in Post-Colonial Latin American Literatures by Women*. Trans. Robert Carr and Ileana Rodríguez. Durham, NC: Duke University Press, 1994.

Roediger, David R. *The Wages of Whiteness: Race and the Making of the American Working Class*. London: Verso, 1991.

Rorty, Richard. "On Ethnocentrism: A Reply to Clifford Geertz." *Michigan Review Quarterly* 31(1986): 525–534.

Ross, Kristin. *Fast Cars, Clean Bodies: Decolonization and the Reordering of French Culture*. Cambridge, MA: MIT Press, 1995.

Rosaldo, Renato. *Culture and Truth: The Remaking of Social Analysis*. Boston: Beacon Press, 1989.

Roughley, Alan. "Joyce's Writings of Exile." *Literary Expressions of Exile: A Collection of Essays*. Ed. Roger Whitehouse. Lewiston, NY: The Edwin Mellen Press, 2000. 159–181.

Rowlands, Michael. "Centre and Periphery: A Review of a Concept." *Centre and Periphery in the Ancient World*. Ed. Michael Rowlands, Mogens Trolle Larsen, and Kristian Kristiansen. Cambridge, UK: Cambridge University Press, 1987. 1–11.

Rutherford, Anna, ed. *From Commonwealth to Post-Colonial*. Sydney: Dangaroo Press, 1992.

Saady, Ouaffai. *Société et Islam dans l'ouvre de Driss Chraibi*. Doctorat De Iiie Cycle, Université De Nice, 1994.

Said, Edward W. *After the Last Sky: Palestinian Lives*. New York: Pantheon, 1986.

---. "American Intellectuals and Middle East Politics: An Interview with Edward W. Said by Bruce Robbins." *Social Text* (1988): 37–53.

## Selected Extensive Critical Bibliography

---. *Covering Islam: How the Media and the Experts Determine How We See the Rest of the World.* New York: Pantheon Books, 1981.

---. "An Ideology of Difference." *Critical Inquiry* 12 (1985): 38–58.

---. "Intellectuals in the Post-Colonial World." *Salmagundi* 70–71 (1986): 44–81.

---. *Musical Elaborations.* New York: Columbia University Press, 1991.

---. "Orientalism and After: An Interview with Edward Said by Anne Beezer and Peter Osborne." *Radical Philosophy* 63 (1993): 22–32.

---. "Permission to Narrate." *London Review of Books* 6.3 (1984): 13–17.

---. "The Problem of Textuality: Two Exemplary Positions." *Critical Inquiry* 4 (1978): 673–714.

---. *The Question of Palestine.* New York: Times Books, 1979.

---. "Representing the Colonized: Anthropology's Interlocutors." *Critical Inquiry* 15 (1989): 210–29.

---. "Third World Intellectuals and Metropolitan Culture." *Raritan* 1 (1990): 27–50.

---, and Christopher Hitchens, eds. *Blaming the Victims: Spurious Scholarship and the Palestinian Question,* London: Verso, 1988.

Saldívar, José David. *Border Matters: Remapping American Cultural Studies.* Berkeley: University of California Press, 1997.

---. *The Dialectics of Our America: Genealogy, Cultural Critique, and Literary History.* Durham, NC: Duke University Press, 1991.

Salgado, Minoli. "Tribal Stories, Scribal Worlds: Mahasweta Devi and the Unreliable Translator." *Journal of Commonwealth Studies* 35 (2000): 131–145.

Samuel, Raphael, ed. *Patriotism: The Making and Unmaking of British National Identities.* 3 vols. London: Routledge, 2000.

San Diego Bakhtin Circle, ed. *Bakhtin and the Nation.* Lewisburg, PA: Bucknell University Press, 2000

Sanga, Jaina. *Salman Rushdie's Postcolonial Metaphors: Migration, Translation, Hybridity, Blasphemy and Globalization.* London: Greenwood Press, 2001.

---, ed. *South Asian Novelists in English: An A-to-Z Guide.* Westport, CT: Greenwood, 2003.

Sangari, Kunkum. "The Politics of the Possible." *Cultural Critique* 7 (1987). Rpt. in abridged form in *The Post-Colonial Studies Reader*. Bill Ashcroft, Gareth Griffiths, and Helen Tiffin, eds. London: Routledge (1995): 143–147.

Santiago-Valles, Kelvin. *'Subject People' and Colonial Discourses*. Albany: SUNY Press, 1994.

Sardar, Zia, et al. *Barbaric Others*. London: Pluto, 1994.

Schwarz, Bill, ed. *The Expansion of England: Race, Ethnicity and Cultural History*. London: Routledge, 1996.

Schwarz, Henry, and Richard Dienst, eds. *Reading The Shape of the World: Towards an International Cultural Studies*. Boulder, CO: Westviewpress, 1996.

Serhane, Abdelhak. *Le deuil des chiens*. Paris: Seuil, 1998.

Seton-Watson, Hugh. *Nations & States: An Enquiry into the Origins of Nations and the Politics of Nationalism*. London: Methuen, 1997.

Shakury, Sabah A. "The Rise of Neo-Colonialism in Conrad's Nostromo." *Panjub University Research Bulletin* 18.2 (1987): 3–22.

Shapiro, Michael. *Violent Cartographies: Mapping Cultures of War*. Minneapolis: University of Minnesota Press, 1997.

Sharpe, Jenny. *Allegories of Empire: The Figure of Woman in the Colonial Text*. Minneapolis: University of Minnesota Press, 1993.

---. "Is the United States Postcolonial? Transnationalism, Immigration, and Race," *Diaspora*, 4:2: 1995: 181–199.

Sharpley-Whiting, T. Denean. *Black Venus: Sexualized Savages, Primal Fears, and Primitive Narratives in French*. Durham, NC: Duke University Press, 1995.

Sharrad, Paul. "Countering Encounter: Black Voyaging after Columbus in Australia and the Caribbean." *Kunapipi* 14.3 (1993): 58–72.

Shohat, Ella. "Imaging Terra Incognita: The Disciplinary Gaze of Empire." *Public Culture* 3 (1991): 41–70.

---. "Notes on the 'Post-Colonial.'" *Social Text* 31/32.1 (1994): 99–113.

---. Robert Stam. *Unthinking Eurocentrism: Multiculturism and the Media*. London: Routledge, 1994.

---. "The Struggle over Representation: Casting, Coalitions, and the Politics of Identification" Ed. Román De La Campa et al. *Late Imperial Culture*. London: Verso: 1995. 166–178.

Sibony, Danielle. "Remarks Sur L'Affect 'Ratial.'" *Elements Pur Une Analyse Du Fascisme*. Ed. Maria-Antonia Macciocchi et al. Vol. 2. Paris: 1976. 141–206.

Simone, Roberta. *The Immigrant Experience in American Fiction: An Annotated Bibliography*. Lanham, MD and London: Scarecrow Press, 1995.

Singh, Amritjit, and Peter Schmidt, eds. *Postcolonial Theory and the United States: Race, Ethnicity, and Literature*. Jackson: University Press of Mississippi, 2000.

Singh, Jyotsna G. *Colonial Narratives/Cultural Dialogues: "Discoveries" of India in the Language of Colonialism*. London: Routledge, 1996.

Sivan, Emmanuel. "Edward Said and His Arab Reviewers." *Interpretations of Islam: Past and Present*. Princeton, NJ: Princeton University Press, 1985. 133–154.

Sivanandan, A. *Communities of Resistance: Writings on Black Struggles for Socialism*. London: Verso. 1990.

Sjoberg, Katarina. *The Return of the Ainu: Cultural Mobilization and the Practice of Ethnicity in Japan*. Langhorne: Harwood Academic Publishers, 1993.

Slemon, Stephen. "Magic Realism as Post-Colonial Discourse." *Canadian Literature* 116 (1998): 9–24.

---. "Post-Colonial Allegory and the Transformation of History." *Journal of Commonwealth Literature* 23.1 (1998): 157–168.

---. "Modernism's Last Post." *Past the Last Post*. Eds. Ian Adam and Helen Tiffin. New York: Harvester Wheatsheaf, 1991.

Smith, Bernard. *European Vision and the South Pacific*. London: 1959.

---. *Imagining the Pacific: In the Wake of the Cook Voyages*. New Haven, CT: Yale University Press, 1992.

Smith, M.G. "Some Problems with Minority Concepts and a Solution." *Ethnic and Racial Studies* 10 (1987): 341–362.

Smorkaloff, Pamela Maria. "Shifting Borders, Free Trade, and Frontier Narratives: U.S., Canada, and Mexico." *American Literary History* 6 (1994): 88–102.

Soja, Edward W. *Postmodern Geographies: The Reassertion of Space in Critical Social Theory*. London: Verso, 1989.

Sollors, Werner. *Beyond Ethnicity: Consent and Descent in American Culture*. New York: Oxford University Press, 1986.

---. "Introduction: The Invention of Ethnicity." *The Invention of Ethnicity*. Ed. Werner Sollors. New York: Oxford University Press, 1989. ix–xx.

---. "National Identity and Ethnic Diversity: 'of Plymouth Rock and Jamestown and Ellis Island.'; or, Ethnic Literature and Some Redefinitions of 'America.'" Ed. Werner Sollors and Maria Diedrich. 1994: 92–121.

---, and Maria Diedrich, eds. *The Black Columbiad: Defining Moments in African American Literature and Culture.* Cambridge, MA: Harvard University Press, 1991.

Solzhenitsyn, Alexander. *The Gulag Archipelago.* Trans. Thomas P. Whitney. New York: Harper, 1973.

Sommer, Doris. *Foundational Fictions: The National Romances of Latin America.* Berkeley: University of California Press, 1991.

Spencer, Dorothy M. *Indian Fiction in English: An Annotated Bibliography.* Philadelphia: University of Pennsylvania Press, 1960.

Spivak, Gayatri Chakravorty. "Poststructuralism, Marginality, Postcoloniality and Value." *Literary Theory Today.* Ed. Peter Collier and Helga Geyer-Ryan. Cambridge, UK: Polity Press, 1990. 219–244.

Spivak, Gayatri Chakravorty. *In Other Worlds: Essays in Cultural Politics.* New York: Methuen, 1987.

---. "The Making of Americans, the Teaching of English, and the Future of Culture Studies." *New Literary History* 21 (1990): 781–798.

---. *The Post-Colonial Critic: Interviews, Strategies, Dialogues.* Ed. Sarah Harasym. New York: Routledge, 1990.

Sprinker, Michael, ed. *Edward Said: A Critical Reader.* Oxford, UK: Blackwell, 1992.

Spurr, David. *The Rhetoric of Empire: Colonial Discourse in Journalism, Travel Writing and Imperial Administration.* Durham, NC: Duke University Press, 1993.

Staub, Michael E. "(Re) Collecting the Past: Writing Native American Speech." *American Quarterly* 43 (1991): 425–456.

Stam, Robert. *Subversive Pleasures: Bakhtin, Cultural Criticism, and Film.* Baltimore: Johns Hopkins University Press, 1989.

Stewart, David H. "Kipling, Conrad and the Dark Heart." *Conradiana* 19.3 (1987): 195–205.

Stocking, George W., Jr., ed. *Colonial Situations: Essays on the Contextualization of Ethnographic Knowledge.* Madison: University of Wisconsin Press, 2000.

---. *Race, Culture, and Evolution: Essays in the History of Anthropology.* Chicago: Chicago University Press, 1982.

Stolcke, Verena. "Is Sex to Gender as Race Is to Ethnicity?" *Gendered Anthropology.* Ed. Teresa Del Valle. London: Routledge, 1993. 17–37.

---. "Talking Culture: New Boundaries, New Rhetorics of Exclusion in Europe." *Current Anthropology* 36 (1995): 1–24.

Stoler, Ann Laura. "Carnal Knowledge and Imperial Power: Gender, Race, and Morality in Colonial Asia." *Gender at the Crossroads of Knowledge: Feminist Anthropology in the Postmodern Era.* Ed. Micaela Di Leonardo. Berkeley: University of California Press, 1991. 51–101.

Storey, John. *An Introduction to Cultural Theory and Popular Culture.* 2nd ed. Athens, GA: The University of Georgia Press, 1998.

Strada, Vittorio, ed. *György Lukács, Michail Bakhtin e altri: problemi di teoria del romanzo.* Turin: Giulio Einaudi, 1976.

Sullivan, Zohreh T. "Memory and the Colonial Self in Kipling's Autobiography." *Prose Studies* 12.1 (1989): 72–89.

Taussig, Michael. *Shamanism, Colonialism, and the Wild Man: A Study in Terror and Healing.* Chicago: University of Chicago Press, 1987.

Taylor, Charles. "Understanding and Ethnocentricity." *Philosophy and the Human Sciences.* Cambridge, UK: Cambridge University Press, 1985. 116–133.

Taylor, Miles. "Imperium Et Libertas? Rethinking the Radical Critique of Imperialism during the Nineteenth Century." *Journal of Imperial and Commonwealth History* 19.1 (1999): 1–23.

Tedlock, Barbara. "From Participant Observation to the Observation of Participation: The Emergence of Narrative Ethnography." *Journal of Anthropological Research* 47 (1991): 69–94.

Teltscher, Kate. *India Inscribed: European and British Writing on India 1600–1800.* Delhi: New Delhi University Press, 1995.

Tennenhouse, Leonard. "The Case of the Resistant Captive." *South Atlantic Quarterly* 95.4 (1996): 919–146.

Thomas, Nicholas. *Colonialism's Culture: Anthropology, Travel & Government.* Cambridge, UK: Quality Press, 1994.

---. *Entangled Objects: Exchange, Material Culture, and Colonialism in the Pacific.* Cambridge, MA: Harvard University Press, 1991.

Thomas, Ronald R. "The Fingerprint of the Foreigner: Colonizing the Criminal Body in 1890s Detective Fiction and Criminal Anthropology." *Journal of English Literary History* 61.3 (1994): 655–683.

Thompson, Eva. *Imperial Knowledge: Russian Literature and Colonialism*. Westport, CT: Greenwood Press, 2000.

Tiffin, Chris, and Alan Lawson, eds. *De-Scribing Empire: Post-Colonialism and Textuality*. London: Routledge, 1994.

Tiffin, Helen. *The post-colonial studies reader*. Bill Ashcroft, Gareth Griffiths, and Helen Tiffin, eds. London: Routledge, 1995.

---. "Post-Colonialism, Post-Modernism and the Rehabilitation of Post-Colonial History." *Journal of Commonwealth Literature* 23.1 (1988): 169–181.

---. "Metaphor and Mortality: The 'Life Cycle(s)' of Malaria," *Meridian* 12.1 (1993): 46–58.

Tobin, Beth Fowkes. *Picturing Imperial Power: Colonial Subjects in Eighteenth-Century British Painting*. Durham, NC: Duke University Press, 1999.

Todd, Emmanuel. *Le destin de immigrés*. Paris: Seuil, 1994.

Todorov, Tzvetan. *On Human Diversity: Nationalism, Racism, and Exoticism in French Thought*. Trans. Catherine Porter. Cambridge, MA: Harvard University Press, 1993.

Tomlinson, John. *Cultural Imperialism: A Critical Introduction*. London: Pinter Publishers, 1991.

Torgovnick, Marianna. *Gone Primitive: Savage Intellects, Modern Lives*. Chicago: University of Chicago Press, 1990.

Trinh T. Minh-Ha. *Woman, Native, Other: Writing, Post-Coloniality, and Feminism*. Bloomington: Indiana University Press, 1989.

---. *When the Moon Waxes Red: Representation, Gender and Cultural Politics*. London: Routledge, 1991.

Trivedi, Harish. *Colonial Transactions: English Literature and India*. Manchester, UK: Manchester University Press, 1995.

Trotter, David. "Colonial Subjects," *Critical Quarterly* 32.3 (1990): 3–20.

---. "Modernism and Empire: Reading *The Waste Land*." *Critical Quarterly* 28 (1986): 143–153.

Trouillot, Michel-Rolph. "Good Day Columbus: Silences, Power and Public History (1492–1892)." *Public Culture* 3.1 (1990): 1–24.

Trumpener, Katie. *Bardic Nationalism: The Romantic Novel and the British Empire*. Princeton, NJ: Princeton University Press, 1997.

Tucker, Judith, ed. *Arab Women: Old Boundaries, New Frontiers*. Bloomington: Indiana University Press, 1993.

Tully, James. *Strange Multiplicity: Constitutionalism in an Age of Diversity*. Cambridge, UK: Cambridge University Press, 1995.

Turner, Bryan S. *Marx and the End of Orientalism*. London: George Allen & Unwin, 1978.

Unamuno, Miguel De. *Tragic Sense of Life*. Trans. J. E. Crawford Flitch. New York: Dover, 1954.

Van Den Abbeele, Georges. *Travel as Metaphor: From Montaigne to Rousseau*. Minneapolis: University of Minnesota Press, 1992.

Vergès, Françoise. *Monsters and Revolutionaries: Colonial Family Romance and Métissage*. Durham, NC: Duke University Press, 1999.

Vinsonneau, Genevieve. *Culture et Comportement*. Paris: Armand Colin, 1997.

Viswanathan, Gauri. *The Masks of Conquest: Literary Study and British Rule in India*. New York: Columbia University Press, 1989.

---, ed. *Power, Politics, and Culture: Interviews with Edward W. Said*. New York: Pantheon Books, 2001.

Vonnegut, Kurt. *Wampeters, Foma and Granfalloons*. 1965. New York: Dell Publishing Company, 1974.

Walker, Alice. *The Color Purple*. New York: Pocket Books, 1982.

Wallerstein, Immanuel. *The Modern World-System: Capitalist Agriculture and the Origins of the European World-Economy in the Sixteenth Century*. New York: Academic Press, 1973.

---. *The Modern World-System II: Mercantilism and the Consolidation of the European World-Economy*. New York: Academic Press, 1980.

Walsh, William. *Indian Literature in English*. New York: Longman, 1990.

Ward, Patrick. *Exile, Emigration, and Irish Writing*. Dublin and Portland, Oregon: Irish Academic Press, 2002.

Ware, Vron. *Beyond the Pale: White Women, Racism and History*. London: Verso, 1992.

Watson, Ian. "Victorian England: Colonialism and the Ideology of Tom Brown's Schooldays." *Zeitschrift Fur Anglistik Und Amerikanistik* 29.2 (1981). 116–129.

Watson, Tim. "Is the 'Post' in Postcolonial the US in American Studies? The US Beginnings of Commonwealth Studies." *Ariel* 31.1–2 (2000): 51–72.

Werbner, Pnina, and Tariq Modood, eds. *Debating Cultural Hybridity: Multi-Cultural Identities and the Politics of Anti-Racism*. London: Zed Books, 1997.

Weiss, Timothy F. *On the Margins: The Art of Exile in V. S. Naipaul*. Amherst: University of Massachusetts Press, 1992.

West, Cornel. *Beyond Eurocentrism and Multiculturalism*. 2 vols. Monroe, ME: Common Courage Press, 1992.

Westin, Charles. "Migration, Time, and Space." *Migrants and the Homeland: Images, Symbols, and Realities. Uppsala Multiethnic Papers 44*. Ed. Harold Runblom. Uppsala, Sweden: Centre for Multiethnic Research Uppsala University, 2000.

Wiesel, Elie. *From the Kingdom of Memory: Reminiscences*. New York: Summit, 1990.

---. *Paroles d'etranger*. Paris: Editions Du Seuil, 1982.

---. *Souls on Fire*. Trans. Marion Wiesel. New York: Vintage, 1973.

---, and Phillipe De Saint-Cheron. *Evil and Exile*. Trans. Jon Rothschild. Notre Dame, IN: Imoversotu of Notre Dame Press, 1990.

Wilson, Elizabeth. "'Le voyage et l'espace clos': Island and Journey as Metaphor: Aspects of Woman's Experience in the Works of Francophone Caribbean Women Novelists." *Out of the Kumbla*: Eds. Carole Boyce Davies and Elaine Savory Fido. Trenton, NJ: Africa World. 45–57.

Williams, Patrick, and Laura Chrisman, eds. *Colonial Discourse and Post-Colonial Theory: A Reader*. New York: Columbia University Press, 1994.

Willinsky, John. *Learning to Divide the World: Education at Empire's End*. Minneapolis: University of Minnesota Press, 1998.

Wilson, Ernest J., III. "Orientalism: A Black Perspective." *Journal of Palestine Studies* 10.2 (1981): 59–69.

Yelin, Louise. *From the Margins of Empire: Christine Stead, Doris Lessing, and Nadine Gordimer*. Ithaca, NY: Cornell University Press, 1998.

Young, Robert J. C. *White Mythologies: Writing History and the West*. London: Routledge, 1990.

Yuval-Davis, Nira, and Floya Anthias, eds. *Woman-Nation-State*. London: Macmillan, 1989.

# INDEX

*After Empire: Scott, Naipaul, Rushdie,* 63, 119, 152
*After the Revolution: Waking to Global Capitalism,* 153
Afzal-Khan, Fawzia, 153
agency, 4, 33, 73, 74, 118
    (and) choice, 97
    colonial [see all the other entries]
    dichotomous, 33
    double: [see dichotomous] (and) ethics of (the) exile, 74, 78
    free: [see choice and powerful], (and) landscape, 105
    outside, 72, 75
    (and) notion, 78
    powerful, 28
Ahmad, Aijaz, 26, 36, 59, 60, 64, 140–142, 144, 145, 152, 153
Akhtar, Mirza Saeed, 48
alien, 1, 2, 7, 67, 68, 71, 113
    sounds, 43
alienation, 98, 111, 113
allegory, 87
"Allegory of the Cave," 35
alterity, 13, 33, 37, 65, 66, 79
    (and) difference, 3
    (of the) Oriental, 130
    radical, 31, 37
    (of human) subjectivity, 31
ambiguous, 142
ambivalence, 70, 80, 83, 112, 134, 136, 149
America, 5, 18, 28, 66, 67, 74, 84, 143
American, 3

citizen, 3, 5, 73
context, 5
consciousness, 84
dream, 76
housewife, 9 [see wife, too]
husband, 67
Indian, 14, 85 [see also Native]
Midwest, 66
multiculturalism, 18
nationalism, 5
Native, 83 [see also Indian]
(and) policies, 18
popular culture, 70
Puritan, 14
slang, 3
Vietnamese, 75
wife, 78 [see housewife, too]
woman, 78
writer, 84
"American Dreamer," 91
Americanized, 5, 14
Anderson, Benedict, 16, 35
Anglo-Indian, 2
Appiah, Kwame Anthony, 18, 35
archaeology, 125, 126, 152
arrival, 21, 31, 101, 114, 115, 124, 143, 149 [see also enigma]
articulation, 42
    double, 42
Ashcroft, Bill, 24, 36, 63, 119, 152
assimilation, 33, 40, 42, 68, 72, 73, 76, 96, 147
    exile's, 72
authenticity, 17, 23, 35, 97, 110, 136
    and discussion, 110
    of self, 136

and subject, 17 [see also larger entry subject]
authorial, 9, 150
  choice, 9, 150
  suggestion, 150
Ayesha, 48

Baden, 68, 70
Bakhtin, Mikhail, 152
being, 9, 11, 13, 17–20, 42, 49, 51, 58, 59, 67, 72, 75–78, 84, 107, 108, 117, 120, 121, 125, 127, 132, 133, 135, 136, 141
  actual/actuality, 77, 89
  alien, 113
  of the Black man, 11, 68
  categories, 131–132 [see also reified]
  (and) citizen, 18
  colonial, 12, 17, 49 [see all the other entries]
  coming-into-being, 20
  conception, 120 [see also western being]
  crumbling, 20
  (and) disguise, 49
  (and) distance, 20
  essential, 9
  exile, 19, 41, 42, 121
  existentialist model, 17
  free, 127
  (and) gaps(s), 136
  human, 141
  hybrid, 9, 115 [see also larger category hybrid] [see also hyphenated] [see also exile] [see also colonial]
  hyphenated, 9 [see also larger category hybrid] [see also larger category hyphenated]
  [see also exile] [see also colonial]
  inner, 110
  narrator's, 68, 101
  ontologically ethical, 78
  the "Other," 42, 133
  partial, 77 [see also larger category hybrid] [see also larger category hyphenated] [see also exile] [see also colonial]
  past, 117
  performance of, 20
  political, 18
  real, 110, 121
  reified, 131, 132 [see also categories]
  (and) self, 41, 135
  shuttling, 78
  stable, 18 [see also larger entry subject]
  static, 18 [see also larger entry subject]
  (and) structural position, 19
  (of/and subject), 11, 19, 20
  (and) subjectivity, 141
  (and) trace, 125
  (and) victim, 141
  Western, 120 [see also being+conception]
Also: being:
  at home, 52, 85, 113, 138
  in England, 115
  in exile, 19, 20, 85, 121 [see also larger category hybrid] [see also larger category hyphenated] [see also exile] [see also colonial]
  open to the play of differences, 86 [see also larger category hybrid] [see also larger

category hyphenated] [see also exile] [see also colonial] outside of discourse, 143
part of ethics of exile, 20, 86, 108 [see also larger category hybrid] [see also larger category hyphenated] [see also exile] [see also colonial]
trapped, 52 [see also larger category hybrid] [see also larger category hyphenated] [see also exile] [see also colonial]
a writer, 13, 26, 108, 110, 131
Benjamin, Walter, 47, 63, 121, 152
between and in-between, 2, 9, 10, 13, 26, 28, 33, 34, 38, 42, 43, 50–52, 55–58, 67, 77, 78, 81, 84, 102, 106, 110, 111, 131, 133, 142, 143, 146
authors, 27 [see also writers]
binaries, 67, 74
binary opposites, 51
black and white, 50
colonizer and colonized, 50, 84
continents, 9 [see also West and the rest of the world] [see also East and West]
cultures and/or cultural differences, 13, 123
cultures and people, 13
diasporic objective and ethnic mandate, 33
discourses, 32, 78
East and West, 3, 79 [see also West and the rest of the world]
forces of assimilation and othering, 42
globalism, 33

history and self, 57
history (imaginary) and subjectivity (open), 58
homelands and/or initial homeland and newly/acquired one and/or homeland and host country, 33, 34, 67, 52, 67
identity and other, 43
identity and poles of identity, 34
Indian subcontinent and British Isles, 2
individuals, 77
land and landscape(s) and/or lands, 19, 20, 38, 55, 58, 102, 112, 113
locality, 33
(he who) looks (and which) looks at, 56
identities, 77, 78
imperialism, 77
man and reflection in the mirror, 146
man and writer, 110
notions, 33
Occident and Orient, 81
patriarchy, 77
roles and notions of feminity, 28
roles and/or role-players, 10, 28, 76, 150
subject and landscape, 19, 20, 57
West and the rest of the world and/or Western and Indian, 86, 146 [see also East and West]
Western cannon and mimickers, 106
Worlds, 9 [see also East and West] [see also West and the rest of the world] [see also continents]
writer [see also author], 27, 36

writer and/or novelist and Marxist, 26
writer and traveler, 110
inbetweenness, 56
Bhabha, Homi, 11–13, 35, 41, 59, 63, 69, 73, 82, 91, 92, 110, 119, 129, 130, 133, 152
Bhagmati, 86, 88, 139
Bibi, 14, 28, 78, 81–84, 142
    Black Bibi, 81–83
    and colonial discourse, 83
Bibi, Salem, 14, 28, 83
binary, 9, 43, 51, 62, 67, 74, 82
    oppositions and/or opposites, 9, 43, 51, 74
biography, 6, 30, 66, 94, 108, 123
    fictional, 6
    faux, 123
*Black Skin, White Masks,* 35, 63, 95, 119
Boehmer, Elleke, 114, 120
border, 57
    crossing, 57
    fluid, 57
    transitioning, 57
Brenda, 112
Brennan, Timothy, 32, 36, 74, 91
British, 2, 42, 93, 109, 123
    books, 109
    culture [see also literary tradition], 109
    establishment [see also tradition], 2, 5
    heritage [see also literary tradition], 109
    home, 93
    Isles, 3
    police, 42
    tradition, 110

    literary, 109
Bryden, Ronald, 119

Cabral, Amilcar, 73, 91
canon, 30, 32, 93, 106, 110, 137, 139
    Western, 32, 106, 139
    (and) writers, 30
canonical, 25
    novel, 25
Caribbean, 33, 99, 106, 119, 123
carnival, 23, 29
    transgressive, 29
carnivalesque, 23, 32
    atmosphere, 23
center, 10, 15, 19, 20, 30, 47–49, 55, 62, 65, 103, 105, 106, 114, 115, 139, 142, 146, 147
    de-center, 82, 135, 136 [see also dissolution], 138
    of dialectical movement, 10
    of discourse, 62, 146
    of subjectivity, 15
    of malaise (of exilic subjectivity), 105
centered, 109
Chakrabarty, Dipesh, 81, 91
Chambers, Iain, 153
Chamcha, Saladin, 9, 29, 38, 39, 41, 49, 132, 133
change, 4, 5, 14, 15, 27, 39, 40, 45–47, 54, 55, 57, 72, 76, 80, 89, 97, 98, 102, 111, 112, 116, 117, 124, 129, 132, 138, 139, 141, 145, 147, 148
    (and) assimilation, 147
    as betrayal, 147
    (and) collaboration, 147
    cultural, 14
    (and) discourse, 147
    genetic, 76 [see also genetic]

# Index

geographical, 124
(of) and/or (on) landscape, 139
political, 47
(of) regime, 27
revolutionary, 141
social, 15
of subject, 138
changeability, 3, 116
of the world, 116
Chatterjee, Partha, 127, 152
character, 4, 8–10, 14–16, 20–23, 26, 28–31, 33, 38, 45, 48, 52, 54, 55, 66, 67, 69, 70, 76, 79, 97–100, 110, 113, 114, 123, 124, 128, 131, 133–135, 137, 143, 146, 147, 149
   (and) binary, 67
   central, 7, 9, 14, 20, 28, 29, 38, 52, 55, 66, 67, 69, 70, 76, 79, 114, 123, 124, 128, 133–135, 137, 138, 146, 147
   creative aspect, 21
   displacement, 7
      geographical, 7, 124
      psychological, 7
   enhancement, 66
   exile, 123
   of extravagant colonial, 97
   (and) fate, 54
   female, 138
   fragmentary, 111
   genetic transformation, 76
   (and) history, 123
   hyphenated, 14
   imagined life, 100
   (and) journey, 124
   (and) land, 15, 100, 113
   (and) landscape, 15, 99
   location, 124
      geographical, 124
   main, 7, 9, 14, 20, 28, 29, 38, 52, 55, 66, 67, 69, 70, 76, 79, 114, 123, 124, 128, 133–135, 137, 138, 146, 147
   (and) marriage, 124
   migrant, 69
   multiple, 10
   performance, 20
   personae, 28
   (playing of) roles, 28, 29, 76
   remembering, 22
   remembrance(s), 22
   roles, 76
   (and) sense of self, 15
   single, 124
   story, 33
   (and) subjectivity, 14, 15, 67, 69, 128
   victimized, 4

Chen, Tina, 92
childhood, 14, 22, 108
   remembrance, 22
   second, 108
Clifford, James, 22, 36, 81, 91
colonial, 1, 5–7, 9, 11–18, 24, 25, 27–31, 34–36, 41–43, 63, 67, 76, 77, 79–82, 84–97, 99, 102, 103, 109, 110, 116–120, 128–130, 132, 133, 135–137, 141–146, 150–153
   17th century, 84
   being, 17
   dandy/dandified, 95, 97
   discourse, 9, 11–13, 24, 28, 35, 36, 63, 77, 79, 81, 82, 90, 91, 110, 128, 130, 150
   Western, 128
   change, 117
   character, 28

context, 34
country/countries, 76
culture, 24
desire, 35, 92, 152, 153
drama, 128
enterprise, 102
epistemology, 17
(and)/ (as) exile, 99, 118
exotic, 128
extravagant, 97
finance, 29
freedom, 29, 96
game, 9
gaze, 42
greed, 29
history, 94, 135
imagination, 80, 82
identity, 11, 12
individual, 31
instrument, 1
land, 80
life, 12
manifestation, 28
master, 24, 29, 41, 76, 103, 133
method/methods, 96
moment, 81, 151
nature, 118
need, 41
notion, 25, 34
objectification, 97
oppression, 11, 12, 41, 128, 141, 144, 146
oppressor, 132
outpost, 102
past, 136
peak, 15
period, 5
personae, 28
portrait, 82

power, 25, 41–43, 94, 102, 103, 117, 129, 130, 141, 151
pressure, 142
project, 145
question, 79, 88
rich, 97, 102
self, 7, 110
settlement, 117
scene, 87
situation, 6, 11, 41, 42, 79, 84, 85, 89, 118, 129, 130, 142, 143
stereotype, 12, 67, 97
subject, 6, 11, 16, 18, 24, 27, 29, 34, 41, 87, 94, 132
subjectivity, 12, 97
subjugation, 137
studies, 36
system, 41, 117, 142, 143
technique, 96
tension, 30
time/times, 103, 132
trade, 86
Trinidad, 116
upbringing, 93
violence, 29, 96, 144
white, 14, 99
World
   Old, 84
   New, 84
   (and)/ (as) writer, 118,
*Colonial Desire: Hybridity in Theory, Culture, and Race*, 35
*Colonial Discourse and Postcolonial Theory: A Reader*, 36, 63
*Colonial Encounters*, 109, 119
colonialism, 13, 18, 24, 27–29, 52, 68, 71, 76, 79, 84, 90, 95, 96, 99, 144, 146, 147, 153

colonialist, 12, 32, 79, 83, 127, 128, 146
colonist, 80, 81, 113
colonization, 7
   decolonization, 5, 7, 24
   economic, 7
colonized, 6, 11–13, 24, 26, 49, 50, 52, 60, 73, 79, 80, 82, 84, 85, 95, 128, 141
colonizer, 13, 18, 27, 50, 60, 84, 85, 103
colony, 79
   English, 79
condition, 2, 5, 24, 26, 27, 34, 38, 45, 46, 49, 51, 53, 61, 63, 75, 76, 136, 141
   character, 45, 61
   exilic, 2, 5, 34, 38, 75, 136
   material, 141
   migrant, 136
   ontological, 26
   postmodern, 51
   social, 46
Cone, Allie, 50
Conrad, Joseph, 25
constellation, 122
contact, 4, 46, 51, 85, 113, 138, 140, 141
   culture, 4
   zone, 84
country, 5, 7, 10, 11, 13–16, 26, 30, 33, 39, 41, 42, 45, 47, 50, 52, 53, 55, 57, 58, 61, 67, 73, 74, 76, 93, 100, 101, 103, 107, 111, 112, 117, 123 134, 137, 150
   colonized, 11
   dream, 53, 137
   foreign, 7
   home, 10, 15, 52, 93
   host, 13, 33, 42, 45

   house, 30
   imagined, 41
   metropolitan, 26
   native, 13
   new, 52, 57, 74, 112, 137
   old, 47, 111, 112
   real, 100, 101
*Course in General Linguistics*, 35
crossroad, 13
Cudjoe, Selwyn, 119
cultural, 2, 3, 6, 11, 14–16, 18, 19, 22, 36, 45, 53–57, 63, 64, 66–68, 70–72, 74–78, 80–82, 85–87, 102, 103, 114, 120, 123, 127, 129, 135, 136, 144, 147, 148, 152, 153
   ambivalence, 136
   background, 54
   binary, 57
   change, 14
   construction, 2, 19
   context, 56, 87
   discourse, 78, 82, 129
   edifice(s), 15, 16
   expatriation, 114
   expression, 86
   formation, 85, 86
   framework, 11, 86
   imperialism, 72
   identity, 22, 36, 55, 63, 64, 74, 75, 85, 86, 103
   influence(s), 66, 135
   interchange, 3
   intransigence, 86
   milieu(s), 15, 18, 68, 76, 77, 136
   mix, 3
   position, 6
   process, 54
   reference, 3

setting, 67
sum, 53
system, 11, 86
tag, 80
understanding, 14
value(s), 129
*Cultural Imperialism and the Indo-English Novel: Genre and Ideology in R. K. Narayan, Anita Desai, Kamala Markandaya, and Salman Rushdie,* 153
culture, 2–4, 6, 7, 9, 12, 13, 15–19, 24, 29, 32–36, 38, 41, 51, 63, 65, 66, 68–74, 76, 79, 81–84, 86, 90–92, 102, 112, 115, 119, 121, 122, 126, 129–131, 136, 141, 143, 145, 146, 152, 153
   Academic, 72
   adopted, 2
   African, 73
   American, 70
   circular, 33
   colonial, 24
   colonized, 12, 73
   contact, 4
   detritus (of), 74
   discourse, 69, 72, 121, 122
   dominant, 7, 69, 70, 76
   European, 126
   foreign, 7
   host, 13, 29, 68
   (and) imperialism, 33
   Islamic, 3
   (and) landscape, 15, 38
   liberal, 72
   location, 63, 91, 119, 129
   mixing, 146
   monolithic, 83
   multiplicity, 82
   national, 16, 19, 24, 73
   new, 81, 92, 102
   notion (of), 17
   popular, 70
   reified, 34
   religious, 84
   sexually liberal, 81
   Symbolic Order (of), 70
   textual, 141
   Western, 3, 71, 130
*Culture after Humanism: History, Culture, Subjectivity,* 153
*Culture and Imperialism,* 36

*Darkness,* 4
decolonization, 5, 7, 24
dependency, 108, 135
de Saussure, Ferdinand, 21, 35
Derrida, Jacques ix, 10, 21, 35
Dialogic, 83, 135, 149, 152
*The Dialogic Imagination: Four Essays,* 152
diaspora, 22, 36, 55, 63
différance, 10
difference, 4, 6, 10–13, 19, 21, 22, 25–27, 29, 31, 34, 35, 37, 39, 41–45, 47–51, 67, 68, 71, 72, 82–89, 91, 110, 112, 121, 123, 125, 129, 130, 131, 133, 135, 138, 139, 142, 144–147, 149, 150
Dirlik, Arif, 140–145, 153
discourse, 6, 7, 9, 11–13, 18, 19, 24, 25, 27, 28, 32–36, 41–43, 45, 47–49, 51, 57, 58, 62, 63, 69, 71–85, 87–91, 102, 105, 110, 118, 121, 122, 125–130, 132, 133, 135, 139, 141–143, 145–151
   agency, 75
   alien, 7

## Index

ambivalence, 83
analysis, 125, 127
authoritative/authoritarian, 48, 62, 76, 147
(of) binary/binaries, 85
(of) capitalism, 32
colonial/colonizing/colonialism, 6, 7, 9, 11–13, 18, 24, 27, 28, 35, 36, 63, 73, 77, 79, 81, 82, 84, 89–91, 105, 110, 128–130, 147, 150, 151 [see also colonial discourse]
construction, 125, 139 [see also creation such as page 126, 127]
contradictory/contradiction, 128
cultural/culture, 69, 72, 78, 82, 121, 122, 129
deconstructed, 89
deterministic, 89
disrupted, 89
dominant, 25, 28, 69, 76, 85, 89, 127, 128, 139, 146–148
double-voiced, 135
essentialist/essential, 130
ethics (of), 81
European, 87
exile/exiled, 81, 89, 145
(of) exotic, 147
foreign, 7, 47
fractured/fracturing, 133
fundamentalist, 32
hegemonic/hegemony, 71, 151
hybrid, 110
hyphenated, 76
historical/history, 121, 122
identity, 6
imperialist, 102
Indian, 147
(of) Islam, 32
literary, 105
materialist/materialism, 58, 79
matrice, 76
migrant, 147
monolithic, 90
nationalist, 58
object (of), 77, 78
ongoing, 126
oppressive, 13, 127
outside, 127, 146
overdetermined political, 126, 146, 148
post-colonial/post-colonialism, 87–89, 143, 151
postmodern, 141
power, 74, 118, 148, 151
rebellious, 57
resistance, 147
ruling, 27
secular/ (of) secularism, 48
(of) sublime, 87
shuttling, 77
singular, 76, 82
static, 130
subversion, 83
theoretical, 19, 87, 139
transformation, 47
travel, 79
unitary, 133
victim, 133
(of) violence, 33
Western, 32, 41–43, 45, 48, 72, 73, 126, 128, 129, 132, 133, 141
dislocation, 8, 16, 61, 108
displacement, 1, 6, 7, 33, 120, 129
  effects, 1
  geographical, 7
  notion, 6
  psychological, 7

double, 2, 3, 12, 23, 32, 34, 42, 47, 62, 68, 95, 135
Du, 10
dualism, 83

East, 2, 3, 25, 69, 79, 81, 82, 106, 119
Eastern, 42, 51, 84
"The East is Blue," 2
Easton, Hannah, 28, 78, 79, 83, 87, 142
Easton, Rebecca, 83
*Écrits,* 35
emigration, 1, 3
Emperor's Tear, 88
empire, 1, 63, 94, 102, 107, 117, 119, 144, 152, 153
England, 2, 5, 9, 11, 13, 14, 16, 22, 28–30, 39–41, 80, 81, 84, 93, 95, 97, 106, 109, 115, 118, 122, 124, 131, 132, 137, 148
Englishness, 39, 40
*The Enigma of Arrival,* 5, 13–16, 21, 29–31, 108, 110–115, 117, 118, 120, 123, 124, 131, 132, 134, 137, 138, 144, 148
*Essential Works of Foucault,* 119, 152
ethic, 4, 24, 27, 30, 51, 78, 108, 118, 147, 149
  (of) exile, 51, 149
  (of) inaction, 118
  (of) openness, 51
  (of) multiplicity, 51
  poles, 4
ethics, 27, 49, 73, 74, 76, 78, 81–83, 86, 89, 90, 119, 127, 147, 152
  (of) exile, 27, 73, 74, 76, 78, 81–83, 86, 90, 127
    (of) intervention, 89
ethnic, 3, 4, 33, 68
  identity, 68
  mandate, 33
  violence, 4
ethnicity, 6, 16–18, 21, 36, 68, 73, 131
ethnocentric, 127, 140, 146
European, 18, 25, 41, 42, 52, 87, 126
exile, 1–16, 19–47, 49, 56, 58, 61–70, 72–76, 78, 81–83, 85–87, 90, 92, 93, 95, 98, 99, 105, 111, 112, 114, 115, 118, 119, 121–123, 127, 128, 130, 131, 133, 134, 136, 139, 142, 146, 149–152
*Exile and the Narrative Imagination,* 35, 63

failure, 94, 104, 137
Fanon, Frantz IX, 35, 63, 73, 91, 95, 119
fantastical, 8, 38, 133
Farishta, Gibreel, 9, 38, 39, 47–50, 52, 61, 124
fatwa, 3, 19, 48, 145
"Feminist Fiction and the Uses of Memory," 22, 36
feminity, 86
  marginality, 86
Fischer, Michael M. J., 21, 36
foreign, 1, 7, 13, 67, 68, 83, 98, 101, 131
foreigner, 13, 75, 130
foreignness, 39, 47, 68, 70, 72, 134
Foucault, Michel, 25, 26, 46, 59, 74, 75, 77, 91, 101, 119, 125, 136, 152
"frontier dream," 84
fragmentation, 83, 111
  (of) characters, 83, 111
freedom, 6, 29, 59, 96, 103, 108, 131, 146, 148

*From Commonwealth to Postcolonial: Critical Essays,* 36
funambulistic, 38
Fuss, Diana, 110, 119

Gabriel, 15, 79
Gandhi, 54, 134, 147, 148
gender, 3, 4, 18, 67, 71, 81
  violence, 4
genetic, 3, 10, 28, 75–77
geneticist, 3
global, 33, 153
globalism, 33
globalization, 143, 153
Gordon, Lilian, 68
Gorra, Michael, 41, 63, 108, 119, 135, 152
*Of Grammatology,* 35
Greene, Gayle, 23, 36
Griffiths, Gareth, 24, 36, 63, 119, 152
*Grimus,* 2
Goudie, Sean X, 92
Gurnah, Abdulrazak, 120

Half-face, 69, 72
Hall, Stuart, 22, 36, 55, 61, 63, 64
Hannah, 28, 78, 79, 83, 87, 142
Hardt, Michael, 153
Harootunian, Harry D., 143, 153
Hasnapur, 66, 68, 70
  modesty, 68
*Heart of Darkness,* 25
hegemony, 151
Hester, 86, 139
history, 3, 5–8, 20, 22, 24, 26, 28, 29, 31, 36, 40, 47, 51–78, 87, 89, 91, 94, 95, 101, 104–107,
history, (*continued*) 113, 116–118, 121–125, 132–135,137, 139, 141, 143–146, 148, 150, 152, 153

*History after the Three Worlds: Post-Eurocentric Historiographies,* 153
Hodge, Ian Vere Robert, 91
*The Holder of the World,* 4, 7, 14, 17, 28, 29, 78–80, 82, 83, 87, 123, 124, 137–139, 142, 145
home, 1, 2, 3, 5, 10, 14–16, 18, 19, 21–23, 26, 30, 33, 34, 37, 39, 44, 52, 54, 57, 65, 67, 73, 76, 83, 93, 95, 98–102, 107, 111, 113–117, 124, 127, 136, 138, 149–151
  ancestral, 22
  Asian/Asiatic, 95
  arrive (home), 124
  "at home," 65, 67, 73, 93, 101, 113, 138,
  "away from home," 33
  British, 93
  construct/construction, 33
  dream (home), 19
  factual, 54
  hybridity (of), 149
  imaginary, 3, 33, 150
  (as) liminal space, 33
  native, 95
  return/returned (home), 22, 23, 34, 44, 113, 114, 124
  Trinidad, 116
homeland, 2, 3, 5, 9, 13, 15, 16, 19, 21, 22, 33, 34, 39, 44, 50, 52, 62, 63, 65, 67, 68, 79, 80–83, 85, 87, 92, 93, 100, 104, 105, 107, 111, 113, 137, 145, 146
  doubled, 2
  fictional, 146
  imaginary, 3, 16, 17, 24, 31, 33, 34, 41, 53, 57, 62, 63, 79–81, 85, 87, 99, 100, 111, 113, 137, 145

homesickness, 115
housewife, 9 [see also wife]
Hulme, Peter, 109, 119
hybrid, 9, 10, 13, 28, 33–35, 45, 50, 115, 131–133
hybridity, 33, 35, 92, 110, 149, 152, 153
   intrinsic, 33
hyphenated, 9, 10, 14, 75, 76, 133

Ideal-I, 53
Ideology, 26, 125, 143, 150, 153
identity, 2, 4, 6, 10, 11, 18, 19, 22, 24, 29, 30, 34–37, 40, 43, 45, 51–53, 55, 61, 63, 66, 68, 70–77, 83, 85, 86, 92, 94, 95, 97–99, 101–103, 107, 112, 115, 121, 133, 136, 138, 144
imaginary, 3, 16, 17, 24, 31, 33, 34, 41, 53, 57, 58, 62, 63, 67, 79–81, 85, 87, 99, 100, 102–107, 111, 113, 114, 118, 130, 137, 149–151
*Imaginary Homelands: Essays and Criticisms 1981–1991*, 63
"Imagined Communities: Reflections on the Origin and Spread of Nationalism," 16, 35, 45
immigrant, 4, 5, 9, 18, 32, 48, 55, 68, 84, 89, 109, 145, 147
   discontent, 48
   discourse, 89
   experience, 32
   female, 4
   figure, 4
   illegal, 147
immigration, 5, 46
imperialism, 33, 36, 72, 77, 109, 117, 144, 153
imperialistic, 109
   trap, 109

"In Good Faith" (part of *Imaginary Homelands: Essays and Criticisms 1981–1991*), 51, 145
*In Theory: Classes, Nations, Literatures*, 36, 64, 152
indeterminacy, 87
   (of) reading, 87
India, 2, 5, 7, 9, 14, 17, 28, 31, 38, 39, 43, 44, 52, 53, 56, 66–68, 78–81, 84, 89, 93, 116, 137, 139, 142, 145, 147
   17th century, 17
   notion (of), 53
   rural, 14
Indian, 2–7, 9, 11, 13, 14, 20, 22, 24, 28, 31, 40, 41, 43, 50, 52, 55, 58, 67–70, 72, 73, 79–81, 83, 85, 86, 89, 90, 96, 106, 110, 119, 123, 130, 131, 134, 137, 144, 147
Indianess, 45, 50
*An Introductory Guide to Post-Structuralism and Postmodernism* investigation, 4, 28
   ontological, 28
Iowa, 67
irony, 114
Isabella, 95, 96, 99–103, 106, 123
Islam, 3, 17, 32, 48, 50, 51, 84
Islamic, 3, 32, 50
   culture, 3
   religion, 50, 51
Islamist, 17, 48
   extremism, 17

Jahilia, 15, 17, 48, 124
*James Joyce: The Augmented Ninth*, 35

## Index

Jameson, Fredric, 137, 152
Jane, 70, 71, 75, 77, 78
Jase, 71
Jasme, 70, 77, 78
Jasmine, 4, 9, 13, 14, 21, 69–71, 77, 124
*Jasmine*, 4, 9, 13, 14, 21, 22, 28, 66, 70, 72, 74–76, 78, 79, 82, 83, 86, 89, 123, 124, 134, 144, 146, 147
Joshi, Jumpy, 46
journey, 6, 13, 14, 21, 24, 31, 67, 78, 84, 101, 114, 118, 124, 128, 131, 134
Jullundhar, 67
Jyoti, 70, 71, 75, 77

Kate, 72
*Key Concepts in Post-colonial Studies*, 63
Khomeini, Ayatollah Ruhollah, 3
King, Bruce, 106, 119
Kripalsingh, Ranjit (see also Singh, Ralph), 94, 95, 100, 102–106, 108, 124, 146
Kristeva, Julia, 63, 66, 91

Lacan, Jacques, 20, 35, 53, 63
landscape, 5, 9, 14–20, 22–24, 31, 33, 34, 38, 41, 44, 49, 55–58, 62, 66, 67, 80, 83, 84, 99, 100, 102, 104–106, 111–113, 115, 116, 118, 136–139, 143, 149–151
language, 2, 8, 15, 17, 21, 23, 38, 43–46, 59, 60, 64, 92, 102, 113, 122, 126, 129, 135, 143
Lawson, Alan, 119
*Letters of Transit: Reflections on Exile, Identity, Language, and Loss*, 92

liminal space, 33, 34
*The Location of Culture*, 35, 41, 63, 91, 119, 129, 152
London, 39, 47, 48, 95, 97, 98, 101, 102, 105, 115, 116, 128
*London Calling: V. S. Naipaul. Postcolonial Mandarin*, 36, 119, 152
loss, 23, 24, 33, 34, 44, 103, 104
love, 14, 39
Lyotard, Jean-François, 51, 59, 63

Macaulay, Thomas, 96, 119
magic(al) realism, 3, 38, 133
Mahound (the Prophet), 3, 15, 48
man, 5, 6, 8, 11, 13, 16, 25, 30, 32, 35, 39–43, 45, 49, 52, 58, 68, 71, 72, 80, 85, 98, 104, 107–111, 116, 128, 131, 132, 146, 149
  Black, 11, 13, 25, 41, 68
  Brown, 25
  Chinese, 11
  Indian, 11, 131
  Mimic, 107, 108, 111, 128
  Western, 42
  White, 25, 68
margin, 11, 27, 62, 65, 83
marginality, 62, 86
Márquez, Gabríel García, 3, 38
Marxism, 15, 32
Marxist, 26, 31, 32, 36, 59, 60, 73, 140, 146
  criticism, 32
  praxis, 32
Masters, Beigh, 29, 87, 124
memory, 21–23, 33, 36, 38, 44, 51, 54, 55, 58, 66, 76, 78, 83, 85, 100
metaphor, 46, 47, 56, 65, 114, 120

meta-text, 104, 149
*The Middle Passage*, 6
*The Middleman and Other Stories*, 66
*Midnight's Children*, 2, 7, 10, 15, 16, 20–23, 25, 31, 44, 51–57, 59–61, 123, 134, 137–139, 144, 145, 147
Midwestern, 9, 14
migrant, 4, 5, 9, 18, 26, 27, 29, 33, 33, 49, 57, 62, 69, 80, 112, 120, 131, 132, 136, 147
migration, 1, 3, 5, 21, 36, 46, 51, 114, 120
*The Mimic Men*, 5, 7–9, 13, 22, 23, 29, 30, 94–96, 99, 103, 105–108, 110, 112, 114, 115, 117, 118, 123, 124, 128, 134–137, 146, 148
mimicry, 9, 13, 14, 19, 29, 35, 41, 42, 68, 69, 73, 95, 102, 103, 129, 133, 149
"Of Mimicry and Man: The Ambivalence of Colonial Discourse," 35
mirror, 14, 20, 40, 42, 56, 84, 130, 146
   cracked, 42
   image, 84
Mirror Stage, 20, 130
*The Missionary Martyr of Isabella*, 100
Mishra, Vijay, 91
mode, 8, 28, 59, 122, 129
   realist, 8
Mohammed (the Prophet), 3
Mohanty, Chandra Talpade, 91
Mughal, 84
Mukherjee, Bharati, 1, 3–9, 12, 14–18, 21, 27–31, 34, 35, 65–67, 69, 71, 73–75, 77–80, 84, 86, 87, 89–92, 121–128, 133, 134, 138, 141, 143–147, 151
Mukta, 86, 139
multiculturalism, 18, 35, 68
*Multiculturalism: Examining the Politics of Recognition*, 35
Muslim Emperor, 84
Mustafa, Fawzia, 119
myth, 9, 22, 31, 32, 36, 38, 49, 51, 54, 55, 91

Naipaul, V. S.
naming, 53, 71, 86, 95, 138
narrator, 4, 5, 9, 10, 13–17, 22, 23, 28–31, 39, 49, 51, 52, 54, 58, 60, 66–78, 82, 83, 87, 89, 94–108, 111, 112–118, 123, 124, 128, 131, 132, 134–138, 142, 146, 148, 149
   Unreliable, 23
narrative, 7, 8, 10, 13, 22, 23, 28, 29, 33, 35, 45, 47, 49, 51, 52, 54, 55, 63, 78, 87, 88, 106, 133, 134, 144
   authoritative, 148
   grand, 51
   linear, 33, 77
nation, 5, 11, 15, 16, 19, 36, 53, 55, 84, 91, 122, 123, 129, 137, 152, 153
*The Nation and Its Fragments*, 152
nationalism, 5, 6, 16, 18, 35, 58, 74, 103, 127, 145
nationhood, 24, 33
native, 3, 13, 16, 28, 44, 65, 67, 71, 82, 83, 85, 93, 95, 109–111, 113, 119, 124, 131
negotiation, 33, 57, 129, 139

## Index

Negri, Antonio, 36, 153
Negritude, 73
Negro, 12, 24, 95
New York, 22, 116
Nixon, Rob, 29, 30, 36, 98, 119, 152
nostalgia, 22, 33, 44, 45, 149

Occident, 81, 125
Orient, 74, 79–81, 125–128, 140, 141
Orientalism, 74, 75, 127, 130, 132
*Orientalism*, 63, 73, 74, 75, 91, 125, 127–129, 139, 132, 140, 152,
"The Other Question... ," 35, 36

Pakistan, 2, 36, 53, 57, 58
patriarchy, 72, 77
periphery, 65
pharmakon, 10
pilgrimage, 13, 48
politics, 4, 6, 17–19, 24, 26, 35, 36, 45, 49, 59, 68, 103–105, 108, 117–122, 139, 140, 144–150
post-colonial, 1, 2, 4, 7, 11, 12, 17, 18, 20, 24, 26, 27, 32, 33, 36, 41, 43, 46, 49, 51, 53, 63, 67, 72, 74, 77, 87–90, 93, 94, 102, 103, 108, 110, 113–115, 117–119, 122, 125–129, 136, 139–143, 145, 146, 148–152
post-colonialism, 11, 33, 89, 102, 108, 118, 120, 126, 140, 141, 143, 146, 147, 150
"Postcoloniality's Unconscious/ Area Studies' Desire," 153
postmodern, 21, 23, 24, 36, 59, 88, 89, 137, 139, 140–142
nihilism, 24
thinkers, 24, 141

*The Postmodern Condition*, 51, 63
*Postmodernism, or The Cultural Logic of Late Capitalism*, 152
post-structuralism, 36
power, 6, 19, 24–29, 34, 38, 41–43, 46–50, 53, 56, 58–62, 69, 74, 80, 82, 84–86, 94, 102, 103, 109, 112, 117, 118, 122, 126, 128–132, 138, 139, 141, 142, 144, 145, 148, 149, 151
apparatus/apparati, 74, 142
colonial, 25, 29, 42, 43, 94, 102, 103, 117, 126, 129, 130, 139, 141, 145, 151 [see also colonial power] discourse [see discourse power] feminity, 86
(and)/(of) history [see also history] masculinity, 86
subversive, 69
Western, 42, 132, 145
Prakash, 67, 70, 71, 77
*The Predicament of Culture: Twentieth-Century Ethnography, Literature, and Art*, 91
Professorji, 67
projection, 19, 20, 147
protagonist, 17, 37, 94, 96, 101, 103, 106, 107, 109, 113, 118
dual, 37
*Provincializing Europe: Postcolonial Thought and Historical Difference*, 91
Puritan, 14, 28, 78, 83, 84, 137, 139

Qur'an, 3
exegesis, 3
reference, 3

race (n), 17, 18, 35, 48–50, 71, 73, 92, 110, 131, 152, 153
Raja, 84, 86
rape, 4, 77
real, 7–10, 12, 15, 29, 40, 46, 47, 49, 54, 56, 57, 88, 96, 98–104, 110, 112, 117, 128, 133, 136, 137, 139–142, 146
realism, 3, 38, 46, 49, 109, 133
  magical, 3, 38, 133
  social, 46
reality, 8–10, 12, 13, 16, 17, 19, 20, 25, 27, 29, 31, 34, 38, 40, 42, 46, 47, 49, 55–58, 69, 79, 80, 82, 100, 101, 110, 111, 115, 124–126, 129, 130, 133, 136–139, 144, 145
  in-between, 13, 110, 133
  linguistic, 126
  reified, 130
  textual, 126
remembrance, 22, 23
representation, 3, 5, 7, 8, 12–14, 21, 24, 25, 27, 41, 59, 81, 82, 87, 127, 130, 131, 143, 144, 148
  allegorical, 13, 21, 87, 143
  biographical, 148
  disguised, 3
  factual, 24
  false, 82, 130
  fictional, 7, 8, 41
  fixed, 12, 82, 130
  metaphorical, 8
  reified, 41
  stereotypical, 12, 27
  veiled, 14
  Western, 127
resistance, 32, 57, 59, 76, 83–85, 122, 127, 128, 129, 131, 139, 141, 143–145, 147, 150, 151

return(n), 22, 23, 34, 43, 44, 46, 47, 76, 79, 91, 108, 110, 113, 114, 124, 138, 146, 149
  actualized, 114
  (to) England, 124
  glorious, 47
  home, 22, 23, 34, 44, 76, 113, 124
  (to) India, 43
  (to) innocence, 146
  ironical, 114
  metaphorical, 114
  trope, 114
  (to) Vietnam/Vietnamese (roots), 76
rim, 13, 110, 133, 146
Ripplemeyer, Bud, 67, 69–71, 75, 77, 78, 134
Rodríguez, María Cristina, 33
*Routes: Travel and Translation in the Late Twentieth Century*, 36
Rushdie, Salman, 1–3, 5–9, 12, 14, 15, 17, 18, 23, 26, 27, 31, 32, 34, 36–66, 69, 74, 91, 119, 121, 122, 124, 125, 127, 128, 132, 133, 136, 137, 139, 141–145, 147, 151–153

Said, Edward, 21, 36, 42, 43, 63, 73–75, 77, 79, 80, 91, 125–131, 133, 140, 141, 152
Saleem, 20–23, 52–59, 61, 123, 134, 135, 137, 138, 145, 147, 148
Salisbury, 109, 111–113, 116
Sarup, Madan, 25, 36
*The Satanic Verses*, 3, 9, 13, 17, 29, 32, 37–39, 43, 45–47, 49, 51–57, 120, 123, 124, 132, 145

Seidel, Michael, 19, 35, 47, 63
self, 2, 7–15, 17, 21–23, 25, 28, 30, 33, 39–45, 52, 53, 55–58, 62, 67, 68, 72, 74–85, 93–96, 101, 102, 104, 108–110, 113, 122, 126, 129, 130, 134–136, 138, 140, 150
  American, 75
  authentic, 104, 136
  closed-off, 42, 43
  colonial, 7, 13, 110
  construction, 53
  crumbled, 95
  cultural, 102
  definition, 102
  deformed, 25
  dissolution, 13, 122
  divided, 83
  earlier, 109
  English, 40, 43
    centered, 43
  essential, 130
  exile, 44
  exiled, 82
  formation, 81
  former, 28, 68, 109
  fragile, 102
  Hindu, 84
  historical, 102
  Imaginary, 17, 102, 130
  Imago, 130
  Indian, 9, 43, 110
  linguistic, 102
  meaningful, 134
  metaphysical, 102
  migrant, 33
  multiple, 45
  Muslim
  "Other," 13
  own, 76
  reinvention, 21
  reflexivity, 22, 93
  single/singular, 10, 11, 39, 41, 82, 135, 150
  social, 102
  stable, 8, 10, 11, 17, 39, 82, 150
  transformation, 13, 74, 78, 79, 82–85
  Trinidadian, 110
  underground, 43, 126
  unified/unity, 95, 140, 150
  unsure, 102
  younger, 30
Senghar, Sédor Léopold, 91, 103
sexual, 11, 18, 81
*Shalimar the Clown*, 2
Shaheed, 53
Shiva, 53, 54, 59, 60, 114
*Shaping Discourses: Reading for University Writers*, 35
shuttling, 10, 22, 23, 34, 56, 58, 65, 71, 73, 77, 78, 86, 138, 143
Sinai, Saleem, 20, 52
Singh, Jadev, 85
Singh, Ralph (see also Kripalsingh, Ranjit), 94, 95, 100, 102–106, 108, 124, 146
snow, 101, 109, 111, 112
Socialist, 46, 95, 110
space liminal, 33, 34
Spivak, Gayatri Chakravorty, 34–36, 77, 87, 89, 91, 92, 135, 152
*Step Across the Line: Collected Nonfiction 1992–2002*, 2
stranger, 47
stance, 2, 18, 51, 76, 97, 118, 145, 147–149
  transcendental, 2
stereotype, 11–14, 42, 67–70, 76, 82, 84, 97, 102, 130–132

subaltern, 77, 87
subject, 1, 2, 6, 7, 10–20, 22–29,
    31, 33, 34, 41–43, 49, 53–58,
    60, 61, 71, 74, 75, 77–79, 82,
    83, 87–89, 94–96, 98, 99,
    101, 109, 110, 118, 125, 130,
    132–136, 138, 139, 141–143,
    146, 147, 149, 150
  colonial, 6, 11, 16, 18, 19, 24,
      27, 29, 34, 41, 83, 87, 94, 97,
      132, 145
  construction, 19, 54
  constructor, 19
  dissolution, 135
  fictional, 41
  hybrid, 34
  resolution
  stable, 26, 78
  static, 21, 82, 138, 141
subjectivity, 3, 8, 10, 12–16,
    19, 20, 24–29, 31, 33, 39,
    40, 42–44, 49, 50, 52, 54,
    58, 67, 69, 70, 74–76, 82,
    88, 96–99, 100, 102, 105,
    115, 123, 127–129, 136,
    138, 139, 141, 147, 149, 150,
    153
  ambivalent, 67
  authentic/authenticity, 127
  colonial, 97
  drifting, 138
  fissured, 29, 115
  free, 97
  full, 16, 128
  malaise, 105
  notion, 12, 25, 74, 75, 99, 128,
      129
  open, 28, 58, 149
  static, 82
Sufyan, Hind, 43

Taylor, 71, 72, 78
theory, 11, 15–18, 35, 36, 45, 59, 63,
    64, 67, 71–74, 89, 92, 122, 124,
    125, 127, 140, 142, 152, 153
Thieme, John, 96, 119
Third, 3, 33, 36, 59, 71, 74, 91,
    125, 149
  space, 33
  world, 71, 91
    women, 71
Tiffin, Helen, 24, 26, 36, 63, 119, 152
trace, 10, 37, 87, 125
  textual, 125
transcendental, 2, 72, 126, 128,
    129, 143
transformation, 10, 13, 14, 28, 32,
    37, 40, 42, 47, 70, 74–76, 78,
    79, 82, 83, 120, 132
  genetic, 10, 76
  hybrid, 10
  hyphenated, 10
transhistorical, 140, 141
translation, 36
translated, 51, 53
travel (n), 1, 2, 10, 13, 79, 108,
    111, 124
  discourse, 79
  metaphor [see journey]
  writing, 2
travel (v), 1, 5, 10, 13–15, 22, 28, 39,
    40, 66, 78, 79, 86, 109, 124, 137
Trinidad, 5, 7, 15, 16, 22, 30, 93,
    99, 109, 110, 111, 113, 115,
    116, 124, 131
trope, 114
  (of) return, 114
truth, 3, 7–9, 21, 25, 29, 31, 39, 54,
    57, 58, 68, 89, 107, 109, 111,
    112, 130, 131, 135, 142
  (and) history, 3, 58

## Index

memory, 54
  (of) world, 7, 8

"Ulysses' Gramophone: *Hear SayYes in Joyce,*" 35
urban, 110, 113

Venn, 87, 88
victim, 1, 4, 26, 54, 60, 94, 95, 127, 130, 135, 141, 142, 147, 149
victimhood, 147
victimized, 4, 90
violence, 1, 4, 12, 27, 29, 30, 33, 41, 45, 47, 48, 51, 58, 72, 85, 86, 96, 117, 127, 130, 131, 144, 149, 151
  colonial, 29, 96, 117, 144
  discourse (of), 33, 48, 51, 127
  ethnic, 4
  gender, 4
  historical, 1
  (of) nationalism, 58
  victim, 149

war, 17, 86
Webb, Mary, 69
West, 3, 6, 25, 54, 67, 68, 73, 74, 79, 80, 82, 125, 126, 128–130, 132, 133, 140, 143, 146
  ethnocentric, 146
Western, 3, 5, 24, 32, 41–43, 45, 48, 50, 51, 67, 68, 72, 73, 79, 80, 84, 86, 91, 95, 106, 110, 121, 125–128, 130, 132, 133, 139, 141, 145
  Age of Enlightenment, 125
  behavior, 68
  being, 120
  canon, 32, 106, 139
  capitalism, 32

civilization, 51, 79
colonial, 24
colonialist, 128
couple, 67
culture, 3, 24, 72, 130
debates
dichotomy, 67, 68
discourse, 41–43, 45, 72, 73, 126, 128, 132, 133, 141
dominance, 127
elite, 32
European, 41
eye, 80
gaze, 95
imagination, 42, 43
Imago, 133
language, 126
machine, 5
man, 42
"Other," 73
representation, 127
  of the Orient, 127
perspective, 132
power, 42, 145
secularism, 48, 51
socialist, 110
subject, 79
tradition, 127
woman, 72
world, 50, 133
*What Women Lose: Exile and the Construction of Imaginary Homelands in Novels by Caribbean Writers*, 33
white, 14, 25, 35, 41, 50, 63, 68, 77, 79, 82, 95, 99, 100, 102, 119, 131, 148
  colonial, 14, 79, 99
  European, 41
  man, 25, 68

woman, 82
writer, 131
White, Paul, 113, 120
Whitetown, 15, 82, 86
whole, 16, 20, 22, 27, 29, 31, 33, 40, 50, 52, 56, 98, 71, 82, 95, 96, 98, 104, 117, 126, 130, 134, 137, 147, 148, 150
wholeness, 16, 33, 65, 76, 96, 98, 107, 133
   certainty, 16
   illusion, 76
*Wife*, 4
wife [see also housewife], 4, 9, 14, 40, 78, 81, 124
Wiltshire, 117
woman, 8, 11, 14, 67, 70–72, 77, 79, 82, 83, 86, 89, 108, 117, 147
   American, 78
   Black, 11, 81
   Chinese, 11
   city, 70
   Indian, 11, 14, 70, 89
   Native, 67, 83
   Puritan, 78
   Third-World, 71
   Western, 72
   White, 82
world, 2–4, 6–9, 14, 15, 17, 18, 21, 24–31, 35, 36, 38–41, 44, 46, 48–51, 53, 55, 56, 58–63, 70–74, 78–80, 82–85, 87–89, 91, 96, 98–102, 106, 108–113, 115–118, 120, 123–126, 128, 130, 131, 133, 134, 136–140, 142–145, 147, 150, 153
   (and) acting, 73
   (of)/(and) action, 29, 73, 108
   (in)-between, 133

binary, 51
certainty, 61
(and)/(of) change, 89
(of)/(and) city, 98, 99
colonial, 24, 25, 102, 128
   oppression, 128
   power, 25
colonized, 24
concept (of), 89
(of)/(and) culture(s), 9, 80, 115
decolonized, 6
(and) discourse/discursive practices, 17, 24
dream/(of) dreamers, 59, 60, 137
(and)/(of) ethics, 49
exile, 51, 56, 70
(and) fiction/(as) fiction, 9
(and)/(of) history, 24, 56, 58
imagined, 16, 22, 41
(and) intervention, 28
(and) individual, 15, 123, 130, 131
(and) landscape, 99
lost, 21
material, 26
migration/migrant, 51
modern/of modern life, 9
multiple, 25, 26
(of)/and myth/mythical, 9, 51
nature/nature (of), 3, 115
new, 9, 39, 71, 72, 96, 113, 128
   of fauna, 113
   of flora, 113
New, 80, 84, 85, 106
niche in, 38
(of)/(and) nostalgia, 21
notion (of), 25, 27
old, 44, 84, 112
Old, 84, 85

# Index

original, 14
outside, 17, 46, 145, 146
outsider, 110, 111
perfect, 115
post-colonial, 51, 74, 117, 118, 139, 140, 145, 146, 150
Puritan, 139
real, 7, 49, 88, 101, 136, 137, 140, 142, 101, 136, 137, 140, 142
realistic, 109
(and) reality, 27, 58
(and) relationship, 82
(of)/(and) religion(s), 9
(and) representation (of), 41, 46
(and) role, 27
(and) self, 82
single, 27 [see unitary] [see unified]
stable, 26, 27
(and) subject, 14, 15, 17, 56, 61, 118, 139
(and) subjectivity, 98
truth, 7, 8
understanding (of), 24
unified, 3, 27
unitary, 27 [see single]
version, 24, 60, 82
violence/violent, 4, 27, 30
West, 147
Western, 50, 133
whole, 39[see unitary] [see unified] [see stable]
*The Wretched of the Earth,* 35, 91
writer, xiii, 1–8, 12, 14–16, 18, 20, 22, 24, 26–28, 30–36, 38, 40, 42, 44, 46, 48, 50, 52, 54, 56, 58, 60, 62, 64, 66, 68, 70, 72–128, 130–132,

writer *(continued)* 134, 136–140, 142–146, 148–152
homeland, 93, 95 [see all chapter 4, "V. S. Naipaul and the Search for the Writer's Homeland"]
writing, 2–4, 6, 23, 27, 29–32, 34–36, 38, 41, 46, 59, 63, 66, 69, 73, 90, 93–95, 104–115, 118, 120, 122, 125, 134, 148
ability, 112
act (of), 104, 115
career, 2, 3
death, 114
deferral (of), 115
diasporic, 33
diary, 110
discourse, 148
ethical/and ethics, 118
exile, 6, 8, 66, 93, 105
(of) history, 59, 94, 105
(and) identity, 94
importance (of), 23
journey, 118
(and) landscape, 113
(of) life, 106
memory and/or, 106
narrator/narrator's/narrative, 115, 134, 148
nature (of), 94
past, 111
post-colonial, 125
power, 148
process, 94, 106, 107, 113, 114
project, 94
reality (of), 38
rewriting, 106
role, 107
satirical, 69
(the) self, 41, 108

    story, 109
    subject/subject of, 95, 110
    world (of), 118
*Writing and Difference*, 35
Wylie, 68, 72

young, 5, 6, 9, 11, 13, 30, 45, 48, 110, 111, 113, 115, 116
Young, Robert, 11, 35, 85, 92, 127, 128, 149, 152, 153

# About the Author

Cristina Emanuela Dascălu holds a PhD in English from the University of Tulsa where she was the recipient of Teaching and Research Assistantships, a Publication Fellowship, and the Chapman Award. She also holds international Masters of Arts degrees in Communication (where she won the NAFSA Grant and PSU International Scholarship) and English (where she was awarded a Teaching Assistantship and the PSU International Scholarship) from Pittsburg State University. Dr. Dascălu's other accomplishments include being on the Dean's National List, the Award for Excellence of Research, Scholarship, and Teaching in the Department of Communication and Department of English, the Department of Foreign Languages' Meritory Award (French), and the Wilson Scholarship.

Dr. Dascălu also holds bachelor's and master's degrees, as well as a Diploma de Licență de Merit (*Summa cum Laude*), All A+/Best Student, National Meritory Scholarship, from Al. I. Cuza University of Iași, Romania, in addition to a baccalaureate degree from Colegiul Național Ștefan cel Mare of Tg. Neamț, Romania.

Printed in the United States
200374BV00003BA/6/A